FOREVER LOVE
God's Plan for Happiness

by Nicholas Maestrini, PIME

PIME WORLD PRESS
17330 Quincy Avenue
Detroit, MI 48221-2765

Copies of this book can also be ordered from the publisher:

PIME WORLD PRESS
17330 Quincy Avenue
Detroit, MI 48221-2765 USA

If you wish an autographed copy by the author,
please write to:

Fr. Nicholas Maestrini, PIME
1550 Beach Road
Tequesta, FL 33469-2815 USA

Revised Edition

Library of Congress Catalog Card Number 97-068069

Cover design by Brian Coughter
19305 Caribbean Ct., Tequesta, FL 33469

Printed in the USA
ISBN 0-9642010-5-4

DEDICATION

TO ALL MY FRIENDS

In humble homage to the Holy Trinity, the Virgin Mary, my Guardian Angel and Heavenly Helpers, and in acknowledgement of the countless blessings I have received,

I DEDICATE THIS BOOK TO YOU, MY FRIENDS

-- my relatives, members of PIME, fellow priests, Sisters, and lay people scattered over the five continents, -- as a token of my boundless gratitude. I owe you all this tribute of love because it is you, who through my long life in Europe, Asia, and the Americas have constantly given me the inspiration, courage, and strength I needed to carry on my work in the Lord's vineyard. You are all part of my spiritual family, and I assure you all, and all my readers, a constant remembrance in prayer in time and after.

With love and prayers,
Fondly
Nicholas Maestrini.

Fr. Nicholas Maestrini, PIME

TABLE OF CONTENTS

The Meaning of Suffering and Evil; God Did Not Abandon
Us After the Fall; The Death of Jesus on the Cross:
A Scene of Death and Life; The Cross in the Center;
The Cross of the Bad Thief; The Cross of the Good Thief;
The Meaning of the Three Crosses

From Darkness to Light; Jesus' Physical Sufferings; Mental
and Spiritual Sufferings; Why Did Jesus Have to Suffer?;
Nature and History Confirm Jesus' Teachings on Suffering;
Jesus is the Answer to Our Problem of Suffering

His Gifts to Us from the Cross; *First Gift*: Forgiveness of
Sin through a Ritual Sacrifice; *Second Gift*: The New and
Everlasting Covenant: An Alliance of Love; *Third Gift*:
Restoration of God's Life To Our Soul and Forgiveness of Sins;
Human and Divine Adoption

His Gifts to Us from the Cross, continued. *Fourth Gift*:
Jesus' Death Helps Us to Atone for Our Sins; The Meaning
in Suffering? Suffering as an Atonement for Sin;
Fifth Gift: A New Dimension of Suffering: Helping Others;
Sixth Gift: Jesus -- A Perfect Example of Endurance

The Human Need to Offer Sacrifices; The Perfect Sacrifice
of Love; Our Participation in Jesus' Sacrifice; Jesus' Role
at Mass; Our Role at Mass; The Offertory of the Mass;
Consecration and Communion

Happiness; Christianity is a Religion of Joy; The Way to
the Cross; Our Quest for True Happiness; God's Love for Us;
Suffering Is An Instrument of Love; From the "*Imitation of Christ*"

Mary is Unique; The Role of Mary in the World; Mary
the Mother of God; Mary Our Mother; Mary Is the
First Disciple of Jesus and a Perfect Model of Christian Life

Natural Love; Christian Love; A NEW COMMANDMENT:
Jesus Links Love of God and Neighbor...; A NEW
COMMANDMENT: The Meaning of the Word
Neighbor is extended...; A NEW COMMANDMENT:
Jesus changed the term of comparison...

Jesus: A Model of Love of Neighbor; Jesus is All Goodness:
The Ingredients of Christian Love; Characteristics of
Christian Love; Christian Love and the Will of God

Jesus' Patience; Patience in the Bible; The Practice of
Patience; Patience and the Will of God; The Practice of Patience

Cana of Galilee; the Samaritan Woman; The Woman Caught
in Adultery; On the Road to Naim; Jesus' Kindness to Peter;
Mary Magdalene: the Woman Who Loved Much; Learning
How to Love Others

The Beauty of Kindness; Why Are We Not Kinder?
Causes of Lack of Kindness; Positive Suggestions:
Kind Thoughts, Words, and Deeds

Envy and Jealousy; Envy and Jealousy in the Bible;
The Evil Effects of Envy and Jealousy; The Insanity of
Envy and Jealousy; Controlling Envy and Jealousy

The Humility of Jesus; The Parable of the Pharisee
and the Tax Collector; What is Humility? Humility:

A Basic Necessity; Practicing Humility

ACKNOWLEDGEMENTS

This book would have never seen the light of day if it were not for the collaboration, the help, the kindness, the assistance, and above all, the inspiration I have received from hundreds of friends, near and far, through the almost four years of work on it. I can publish only but a few names here, but I want to assure all those dear friends not listed here that their names are engraved in my heart and memory as I remember them prayerfully each day. **I dedicate this book to all those who have helped me in one way or another** as a token of my great love and deepest gratitude.

I wish to mention first my faithful and dedicated collaborator, assistant and secretary, Mrs. Helen Coughter. To describe her help in detail would take pages. Be sufficient to say that she devoted over fifteen hundred working hours to the preparation of the manuscript wearing many different hats, such as that of steno/typist, proof-reader, computer-operator, consulting editor, researcher and layout artist. Each chapter of the book was written, rewritten, revised, and retyped, on average, twelve times. Her patience and dedication have been beyond the call of duty.

My associate and confrere, Fr. Pasquale Persico deserves a special mention, because he took over most of the administration work of the house, allowing me to devote more time to writing this book.

I also have to thank in a special way the authors and publishers who have kindly given me permission to quote from their books. They are mentioned in the footnotes, but I wish to mention a few of them in a special way: Professor Peter Kreeft from Boston College; Monsignor G. Ravasi, Director of the Ambrosiana Library in Milan, Italy; The Westminster Press for their permission to quote from the books of William Barclay; and The Peter Pauper Press, publisher of Henry Drummond's little gem, *The Greatest Thing In The World;* the Newman Secretariat of the Oratory for permission to quote some of the beautiful prayers of the saintly Cardinal from *A Newman Prayer Book;* my old and dear friend Bill Deneen of New York for suggesting, after a long search, the final title of the book; Fr. John Devany, C.P., Fr. Edward C. Vacek, S.J., (and *America* magazine) for permission to quote them; Fr. John B. Boracco, PIME, for reading the draft of the book and his invaluable suggestions regarding theological matters; Robert C. Bayer, former editor of PIME mission books and magazine, for the final editing of the entire book; Mariellen Howell at St. Joseph's Adoration Monastery in Portsmouth, Ohio, for an extensive revision of the earliest draft of the manuscript.

In addition, I want to also mention, in alphabetical order, those who have worked very closely with me on this project: Mrs. Florence Barnes of Detroit for her valuable suggestions; Mr. and Mrs. Carl Benson for financial assistance; Fr. Antimo Boerio, PIME, of Rome for sending me valuable information; Sr. Carmela Biolchini for her kind advice; Mrs. Eileen Burns for reading and commenting on the manuscript; Mrs. Barabar Cheng for her insightful comments; Mr. and Mrs. Walter Foran for their generous financial assistance; Mr. John Giba for invaluable comments and suggestions; Ms. Sally Henshaw for advice and review; Mr. and Mrs. Frank Heinrich for their helpful advice; Fr. Bernard Hwang, O.S.B. of Oregon City, Oregon, theological consultant; Mr. Denis Killane for financial assistance; Donald Larson of Jupiter for proofreading; Dr. Mike Longo and his wife, Ginnie, for much financial assistance; Sr. Madonna Murphy for revision and comments on the manuscript; Mr. and Mrs. Christopher Mannino for advice and financial support; Mr. and Mrs. Armand (Buzz) Moens, Jr., for their

valuable suggestions and generous financial help; Mr. and
Mrs. Tom O'Brien for advice; Mrs. Laura Oller for revision
work; Mr. and Mrs. John Roland for suggestions and
editorial revision of the final draft; Mr. and Mrs. John F.
(Bud) Rooney for financial assistance; Mrs. Anne Saldich of
Palo Alto, California, for revisions and suggestions; Mrs.
Pamela Shreck, West Palm Beach, our most valuable com-
puter consultant; Dr. and Mrs. William Schofield of Minneapolis, Minnesota, for consultation, comments and editing of
several chapters; Mr. and Mrs. William Shannon for their
valuable comments; Mrs. Constance Swenson for her
insightful comments; Ms. Mary Louise Tully for proofreading
and comments; Dr. James Vollmer, PhD. Physics, and his
wife, Avi, for much advice and financial assistance. To all,
my heartiest "Thank you" and a prayerful remembrance in
time.... and after.

KEY TO ABBREVIATIONS AND AUTHORS

1. BARCLAY -- Rev. William Barclay, lecturer at the University of Glasgow. Author of a commentary on each Gospel and Letters of the Apostles. Part of the *Daily Study Bible Series*. Revised Version. Published by Westminster Press ⊙ 1975, William Barclay.

2. CCC -- Excerpts from the English translation of the *Catechism of the Catholic Church* for use in the United States of America ⊙ 1994, United Catholic Conference, Inc.-- Libreria Editrice Vaticana.

3. DRUMMOND -- Rev. Henry Drummond, author of *The Greatest Thing in the World*. Published by Peter Pauper Press, Inc. Mount Vernon, NY. (Public domain).

4. KREEFT -- Peter Kreeft, Professor at Boston College, Boston, MA. Author of *Making Sense Out of Suffering,* and *Knowing the Truth About God's Love,* (Servant Books, Ann Arbor, MI), and *Everything You Ever Wanted to Know About Heaven* (Ignatius Press, San Francisco, CA). He is also the author of other books on religion and psychology.

5. NCC -- *New Catholic Encyclopedia.* 18 Volumes. Copyright 1967.

6. RAVASI -- Mons. Gianfranco Ravasi, PhD. President of Ambrosiana Librar, Milan, Italy. A well-known Italian author, many of whose books have been translated into several foreign languages. *Mattutino* is a collection of daily Christian thoughts and reflections.

7. WU -- Dr. John Ching Hsiung Wu (John C. H. Wu). Chinese scholar and convert to the Catholic faith; in 1947-48, the first Ambassador of the Republic of China to the Vatican. Author of *Beyond East and West*, Sheed and Ward, NY. 1951; *The Science of Love, A Study in the Teachings of St. Therese of Lisieux*, 1st edition Catholic Truth Society of Hong Kong, 1941; PIME USA edition, PIME (Pontifical Institute for Foreign Missions) Detroit, MI. 1953.

INTRODUCTION

The Way to Happiness

We all want to be happy. Our desire for happiness, or at least contentment, is one of the basic instincts all humans have in common. Along with the basic instinct for the preservation of life, the search for happiness is one of the most universal motivating forces that we all possess. From the most sophisticated executives in their high-rise office buildings in New York to the most primitive of people in the jungles of Papua New Guinea, we all want one thing more than anything else: **to be happy**.

When we ask what happiness really is, though, we get as many different answers as there are men and women in the world. Happiness means different things to different people, and since everyone wants to be happy in his or her own particular way, there are bound to have conflicts. It is these conflicts, the bumping into each other as we pursue our individual happiness, that are the cause of most of the evils, sufferings and quarreling in the world.

It is difficult to come up with a definition for happiness that would satisfy everyone, but generally speaking, we can say that we are happy, or content, when we possess what we love and do what satisfies us. Consequently, happiness depends **on possessing the object of our love.** We love whatever is presented to our mind (intellect) as enjoyable and worth having. Unfortunately, too many times what seems to us to be worth having, in the end, becomes a source of misery. We have only to look at the world around us to see how much unhappiness there is and to realize that even those few who claim to be happy, in reality, live under constant fear of losing what they possess.

Why is there so much unhappiness in the world? Because we fail to look beyond the material glitter of life.

We waste our time pursuing the superficial with neither energy nor interest left to dig deeper into life to discover what is of true value and what is truly good for us. The end result is misery, not happiness.

Where can we turn to find true, lasting happiness?
For us Christians who accept and believe in one, eternal, all-powerful and loving God, the answer is clear: *God.* As our Maker and Father who created each one of us as individual, immortal beings to be eternally happy with him, he shows us what true happiness really is and how to attain it.[1]

Our search for happiness would be so much easier and clearer if we were merely spirits, but we are not. We are a complex *combination* of matter and spirit, body and soul, with contradictory desires and inclinations. In our lifelong quest for happiness we experience within us a perpetual conflict between good and bad, right and wrong. Hence, the necessity of making the right decisions. God is always ready to give us the help we need, if we ask for it.

****

Religion, love for God, friendship with Jesus, life of the soul, spiritual maturity, and many other such expressions mean much the same thing, and they all have one characteristic in common: they are all part of the life of the spirit -- that elusive, indefinable thing we call our *soul.* Body and soul have their respective lives, and while we are ever so careful (and rightly so) in protecting, nourishing, and caring for the life of the body, we too often neglect the life of our immortal soul. This book is about love and happiness -- more specifically, about **helping you to find happiness in the**

---

[1] The *Creed* or The Profession of Faith. CCC #26.

love for God and neighbor. I have written it with you in mind and for the purpose of helping you in your lifelong quest for a more meaningful and fulfilling way of life.

****

The Christian religion is not a set of rules, laws, and a long list of don'ts. Nor is it a passport to heaven. On the contrary, Christianity is a very positive religion, a religion dedicated to promoting all-out love, total love, burning, self-sacrificing love for God and neighbor according to Jesus' example and his tremendous love for us. Jesus described a relationship with God as a *"a living and life-giving spring of water*[2] *that cleanses us"*[3] and that *"can quench our thirst for the living God."*[4] This is religion, and Christianity truly is **God's Circle of Love** linking him to us and us to him.

Let us explore together the various segments of this Circle of love:

First, we reflect on God's immense love for us from all eternity, our divine origin, the coming of Jesus among us as a brother, friend, and savior and how he gives meaning and purpose to life. (Chapters 1-4).

The *second* segment presents the problem of the ever-present evils and sufferings in life and how Jesus' passion and death give meaning and purpose to the sufferings we all have to endure. (Chapters 5-8).

The *third* segment reviews Jesus' gifts to us from the cross, culminating in the institution of the Sacrifice of the Mass as the Mystery of Faith. (Chapters 9-12).

---

[2] John 4:10.
[3] Zechariah 14:5
[4] Psalm 44:3

Chapter 13 is totally dedicated to describing the role of Mary as mother of Jesus and as our own spiritual mother, according to the teachings of the Bible.

The *fourth* segment examines in detail our love response to God through love for our neighbor and the practice of Christian virtues as described in Chapter 13 of the first letter of St. Paul to the Corinthians, the "Magna Carta" of Christian love. (Chapters 14 to 25)

Chapter 26, the final segment explains how to fit all that has been learned in the preceding chapters into daily life, so each can live a true Christian life in deep union with God according to each person's personality, individuality, and station in life.

In brief, this book explores the world of the spirit, in particular, *God's Circle of Love* as Jesus has revealed it to us, and suggests ways and means of how our life fits into this exchange which goes on between God and us in time and eternity. It is intended for all Christian people -- from teenagers to adults -- who have some background in Christianity but cannot find happiness in the materialism of our present-day society. Above all it is intended for recent converts and people who are searching for a spiritual vision of life and a meaningful existence. It is also meant for Christians who live marginally spiritual lives and who relegate God to last place on their list of priorities. Last but not least, it is intended for devout Christians who are seeking to grow to spiritual maturity.

****

Why did I write this book? Throughout my 66 years of priestly life as a missionary in Hong Kong and China and as a priest among Christians in Europe and the United States, I have been baffled by two questions: Why do people, in general, have so little interest in God? And why do they live self-centered, spiritually stagnant lives when they should be afire with love for God and their fellow man?

In my role as priest, I have come to realize that too many so-called Christians think they know all about Christianity when, in reality, they know very little. Their knowledge of religion is, to say the least, nebulous, confused, and self-centered; it is based more on self-interest (fear of hell) than true love for God. The cause of this disastrous situation is the attraction and desire for material possessions with their glitter and offer of instant pleasure that are far more alluring than the mysterious, abstract, spiritual truths of religion. Even though almighty God became one of us and took on a human face and form in the person of Jesus, people continue to ignore him. Some are oblivious to their own divine origin and eternal destiny. Many more pray and worship God as a social habit, never even thinking of love. They fail to see in God the lover, the "desired one of all ages."

The life of every priest, like that of the prophets of old, is dedicated to bringing people to God and God to people, to assist them in discovering the dimension of the spirit, and to fill their lives with love and hope. I feel that offering spiritual enlightenment is the greatest contribution we priests can make to the lives of our fellow men and women. This is why I have written this book: to fulfill my calling by bringing spiritual vision, knowledge, and love for God to all those who are seeking him and looking for the meaning and purpose of life in both the mission lands and those countries to which the Gospel has already reached.

Books of a religious nature cannot be read in a hurry, like a novel, and this book is no exception. It must be digested slowly through personal reflection and meditation in order to let the spiritual truths it teaches sink into the soul and move the will to a greater love for Jesus. Religion is a matter of the mind and heart, of will and feelings; we need time for spiritual reflection of the spirit to grasp the truths that concern God and our souls. The chapters are short, the text is divided by subtitles, and there is an outline for personal reflection and prayer at the end of every chapter. This structure is intended to help the reader to reflect on the subject matter and move the will to think more about God, to pray to him at greater length and, thus, *fall in love with Jesus.*

You will find in this book several points of doctrine that are often repeated. These repetitions are necessary in a book of meditation, and I trust you will indulge me.

****

This is a book about your personal relationship and love for God, not a theology textbook. Theology requires a vast background of philosophical and historical sciences that are not normally a part of a layman's cultural background. Nor is this a scholarly book steeped in philosophy. I have endeavored to avoid even conventional theological terms using everyday language with the hope of being understood by all who read it.[5]

There is a great need for spiritual reading. Every day, all day long, our senses are bombarded with pictures, noise, and the sight of worldly and sensually-attractive images that clutter our minds and stifle our love for God, leaving us little or no time to pursue what really matters most: *the life of the spirit.* I pray that this book will uplift

---

[5] In the matter of gender I have generally used inclusive language, except for direct quotations and, in some special cases, in the interest of simplicity.

your soul into the world of the spirit and eternity. May it be for you a breath of fresh air from heaven, giving you a glimpse of what life can be like when it is dedicated to love... true, self-sacrificing love for God and neighbor.

This book is very much the result of my long, working experience as God's priest and missionary and of my close association with so many people of different races, nations and religions. I owe a debt of gratitude to them all, and also to all those who will read these pages. I promise that I will keep all of you in my daily prayers in this life and, God willing, ever after.

I have written this *Introduction* today, August 15, 1996, as we celebrate the feast of the Assumption of Mary, and the 51st anniversary of the end of World War II in the Pacific. I call this day my second birthday because after four-and-one-half years of war and looking death in the face under the Japanese military occupation in Hong Kong, freedom returned on August 15, 1945, when Japan surrendered to the Allies, and the war in the Pacific ended. That day was the beginning of a new period of my life in the service of the Lord.

I believe that I survived the war because of the help and protection of the Blessed Virgin Mary, and today, her feast day and the 51st anniversary of the end of World War II in the Pacific, I am happy to sign this FOREWORD and to offer this little work to Mary as a token of my undying gratitude, as well as to all my friends who have graced me with their friendship and helped me throughout my life.

August 15, 1996

Fr. Nicholas Maestrini, PIME
1550 Beach Road
Tequesta, FL 33469 USA

1

THE SPLENDOR OF GOD

"There are three things that remain -- faith, hope and love -- and the greatest of these is Love." [1]

"God of Abraham, God of Isaac, God of Jacob, not god of philosophers and scholars. Certitude, certitude. Feelings. Joy. Peace. God of Jesus Christ. My God and your God. Your God will be my God. Oblivion of the world, and of everything else, except of God. He cannot be found except along the ways and byways indicated by the Gospel." [2]

Here, the genius of Pascal contrasts the cold, rigid, unfriendly god of human reason -- of philosophers and scholars -- to the Gospel's warm, living, loving God who can give humans what they crave most in life: Love. Certitude. Joy. Peace. Love. [3]

What Is the Most Important Thing in Life?

Since the beginning of humanity, humans have asked: *"What is the all-important GOOD that is worth*

---

[1] 1 Corinthians 13:13

[2] Blaise Pascal (1623-1662), famous French philosopher and mathematician, wrote this personal memorial entitled, *FIRE,* in 1654 after a very deep spiritual experience. A personal profession of faith that witnesses to the strong belief and spiritual maturity of the writer, he carried this memorial, sown in his clothes, to his death eight years later.

[3] Free translation from Gianfranco Ravasi. *Mattutino.* p. 431.

*pursuing above all else in order to give meaning to our lives
and achieve happiness?"*

Like the rest of the world you, too, are craving for a
contented, meaningful life. You have only one life to live.
What do you think you need most to make it worth living,
to make it purposeful and successful? To become rich and
famous? To be a millionaire? Success in politics? Beauty?
Popularity? Power? Fame?

All these things are certainly good, and they can
bring us a certain amount of joy and consolation, but do
they really make a person happy? Should we look for what
is most pleasurable or for what is the best for us? All the
things mentioned above are very attractive, but they are also
fleeting, unstable, and perishable. All of them will pass
away. They cannot make a person truly happy for they
bring with them endless worries that destroy peace of mind.
After all, very few specially gifted people will attain them.
And will these earthly goods really satisfy the deepest needs
of the human soul? We are immortal beings, we are made
for eternity. Our souls crave something more satisfying than
fleeting pleasures and perishable possessions.

What then is the supreme, the highest good that is
worth pursuing throughout life at whatever cost? *Where can
we find the right answer?* Certainly not in the ancient nor
modern theories of philosophers who can only create imaginary gods, the fruits of their limited, human minds. Certainly not in the writings of those scientists who proudly
proclaim that the universe is a cold, unknown mystery, that
we humans are but an unplanned accident of evolution and
that after death our consciousness will disappear and there
will be nothing left but oblivion. Certainly not in one of the
many home-made, historically unfounded religions which,
like the mythologies of old, simply deify human passions and
wickedness. And certainly not in the post-Christian, neo-

paganism of today which has lost all sense of spiritual values and is totally dedicated to the pursuit of material goods and enjoyment. Where then *can* we find an authoritative answer to our question? In the Bible, of course.

Love Is the Answer

The Bible is God's personal letter to each of us, and it is in this "letter" that he reveals our divine origin and our ultimate goal. In it, he tells us of his eternal love for us and gives us the guidelines to achieve spiritual growth. God, alone, can answer our questions because he made us and he knows us better than we can ever know ourselves.

Long before Jesus appeared on earth God, himself, answered our all-important question about the supreme GOOD to be pursued in life as he solemnly proclaimed through Moses[4]: *"You shall love the Lord your God with all your heart, and with all your soul, and with all your strength."* [5]

LOVE is the answer because love is the beginning and the end of our very existence. In order to stress God's request, Moses added: *"Hear, O Israel! The LORD is our God, the LORD alone. Take to heart these words which I enjoin on you today. Drill them into your children. Speak of them at home and abroad, whether you are busy or at rest. Bind them at your wrists as a sign and let them be as a pendant on your forehead. Write them on the doorsteps of your houses and on your gates."* [6]

This command as written in the Book of Hebrews sounds like an arbitrary, authoritarian imposition from above. On the contrary, it is a loving request made by a

---

[4] About 1200 B.C.
[5] Leviticus 19:18
[6] Deuteronomy 6:5

father to his children to guide them through the temptations and dangers of life. The Decalogue, even though worded as a series of commands, in reality is an explicit request for love. Love cannot be commanded, and it is worthless unless freely given. This is a law of nature established by God, himself, and God cannot contradict it.

In order to better understand the Ten Commandments, we must examine them within the framework of the covenant of love that God made with the Hebrew people. We will find that they are not arbitrary commands but straightforward guidelines intended to help people to live a righteous life and to secure the Lord's help, protection, and friendship. The Commandments proclaim that *love* is the all-important thing, the very essence of the relationship between God and us humans. This is the very basis of the Judeo-Christian tradition. The complete Bible, both Old and New Testaments, answers all our questions about life. It tells us that God exists and that we are his children. We come out of God's hands because of his love for us. All he asks us to do is to love him in return throughout our lives, and our proud destiny will be enjoying his love throughout eternity. Only love for God can fulfill the needs of our souls and lead us to true happiness.

For centuries after God gave Moses the Commandment of love, God repeatedly stressed that love is the only goal worth pursuing in life. The Books of Wisdom, especially the *Song of Songs,* the Psalms, and the prophets give witness to this. The Old Testament is the story of God's tender love for his chosen people and of his untiring efforts to help them to live lives of righteousness inspired by love and dedication.

A superficial reading of the Old Testament may give the impression that the Jewish people were more inclined to fear God than to love him, but there is no doubt that love is the foundation of the relationship between God and his people, and it is this relationship of love that Jesus came to fulfill, not destroy.[7] Psalm 139 sums up this beautiful love story between God and his people:

> *"Truly you have formed my inmost being,*
> *you knit me in my mother's womb.*
> *I give you thanks that I am wonderfully made,*
> *wonderful are your works.*
> *My soul you also knew full well;*
> *nor was my frame unknown to you.*
> *When I was made in secret,*
> *when I was fashioned in the depths of the earth.*
> *Your eyes have seen my actions,*
> *in your book they are written,*
> *my days were limited before one of them existed.*
> *How weighty are your designs, O God;*
> *how vast the sum of them."* [8]

Jesus' Proclamation of Love

When the time came for God to be "made flesh" and live in our midst as Jesus of Nazareth, he confirmed, enlarged, and stressed what he had already told us throughout the previous ages in the books of the Old Testament. When a lawyer asked Jesus: "Which commandment of the Law is the greatest?," Jesus repeated word for word the commandment God had given to Moses: *"You shall love the Lord your God with all your heart, with all your soul, and*

---

[7] Matthew 5:17
[8] Psalm 139:15-19

with all your mind. This is the greatest and the first commandment." Then Jesus added: *"The second is like it. You shall love your neighbor as yourself. The whole Law and the Prophets depend on these two commandments."* [9]

Later, at the very end of his life on earth, after he had washed the feet of his apostles at the Last Supper, Jesus solemnly unveiled to the world the highest goal of human love ever heard: to love others as he loved his apostles. *"This is my commandment, love one another as I have loved you."* [10]

The Teaching of St. Paul

St. Paul, the greatest of all theologians, divinely inspired by the Holy Spirit, briefly summarized all God has revealed to us about life and love in these words: *"There are in the end three things that last, faith, hope and love. The greatest of these is love."* [11]

Do you realize what this means? God is love. He has created us out of love. Love is our very beginning and it is our ultimate end, because through the mercy of Jesus, we all are called to spend eternity in the happiness of God's love. Love is the supreme good, the only important thing on earth worth pursuing. It is love forever -- it will never perish. It is the only good that truly gives meaning to our lives.

St. Paul further clarifies God's revelation of the supremacy of love in the same letter to the Corinthians by contrasting love with all major gifts of God to man. In order to understand this passage, however, we must remember

---

[9] Matthew 22:37-40
[10] John 15:12
[11] 1 Corinthians 13:13

that St. Paul was writing to a community of newly converted and fervent Christians who believed that the spiritual gifts of languages, understanding, and faith were the ultimate and most desirable gifts on earth. But St. Paul warns them that the greatest gift is LOVE:

"Now I will show you the way which surpasses all the others. If I speak with human tongues and angelic as well, but do not have love, I am a noisy gong, a clanging cymbal. If I have the gift of prophecy and, with full knowledge, comprehend all mysteries, if I have faith great enough to move mountains, but have not love, I am nothing. If I give away everything I have to feed the poor and hand over my body to be burned, but have not love, I gain nothing." [12]

His conclusion is emphatic: *"If I do all these things ....but I do not have love, I am nothing!"* Think of it! The greatest thing in life -- the only thing that can make our life meaningful and worth living -- is neither gold nor any other worldly possession, but pure and simple love. Love is God's gift to us, his children and his human family; and without love, life itself is meaningless and the world makes no sense. This is the first segment of God's circle of love.

Social Science and Religion Agree

Do you not feel deep within your heart that what you have read so far truly makes sense? Do not your heart and mind tell you that you need to love and to be loved as much as your body needs food and water to survive? To recognize our need for love is not only a matter of religion, but a

---

[12] 1 Corinthians 13:1-3

scientifically recognized human need.   The majority of psychologists, psychiatrists, philosophers, theologians, poets and writers of all faiths agree that in the realm of the spirit love is an essential need of human beings. Without love we are just part of brute creation; but with true love, we become the masterpiece of creation. We all need to love and to be loved because love is the life and soul of the universe. Dante wrote: "Love moves the sun and the stars." [13]

St. Augustine summed it all up when he wrote: "You have made us for yourself, Lord, and our hearts find no rest until they rest in you." [14] This is why we need love forever.

Personal Reflection

Is love of God the most important thing in my life? Do I share with St. Augustine and so many other great souls the desire to find God and love him with all my heart? Or am I squandering my life and my love on fleeting, perishable, worthless things? I have only one life to live! What am I making of it? I shall not pass this way again. I shall not have a second chance. If I fail now, what will happen to me?

The "*Imitation of Christ*" teaches that "to seek myself is to find myself -- but to my own destruction. If I do not seek the love of my Lord, I do more harm to myself than all the worldly temptations and all my enemies can do to me." [15]

---

[13]   Dante Alighieri, *The Divine Comedy*, Paradise, Canto 33.
[14]   St. Augustine, Bishop. "*Confessions.*"
[15]   Chapter 7.

GOD'S GRANDEUR
(by Gerald Manley Hopkins)
The world is charged with the grandeur of God.
  It will flame out, like shining from shook soil;
  It gathers to a greatness, like the ooze of oil
Crushed. Why do men then now not wreck his rod?
Generations have trod, have trod, have trod;
  And all is seared with trade; bleared, smeared with toil;
  And wears man's smudge and shares man's smell: the soil
  is bare now, nor can foot feel, being shod.

And for all this, nature is never spent;
  There lives the dearest freshness deep down things;
And though the last lights off the black West went
  Oh, morning, at the brown brink eastward, springs -
Because the Holy Ghost over the bent
  World broods with warm breast and with ah! bright wings.

P R A Y E R
(Adapted from John Henry Cardinal Newman)

O everlasting Light, surpassing all created light, send down your spiritual light from above to penetrate and enlighten the darkness of my heart and mind. Enliven my spirit and all its powers, cleanse it, gladden it, and enlighten it that it may cling to you and learn how to love you and serve you in my neighbor.[16]

Short Prayer
Jesus, teach me to seek you always first.

---

[16] *A Newman Prayer Book*, Publr. Vincent Ferrer Blehl, S.J., The Oratory, Birmingham, England. p.6

2

LOVE: THE WAY TO SPIRITUAL GROWTH

A Bridge Between Heaven and Earth.

St. Catherine of Siena,[1] a peasant woman of the
Middle Ages who went on to become a saint and a doctor of
the Church,[2] in her "Book of Divine Doctrine" compared Jesus
to a bridge between heaven and earth. She wrote: "As the
road to heaven broke down and was closed to traffic because
of the disobedience of Adam, God made a bridge of his Divine
Son. This blessed bridge has three levels that symbolize the
three stages of growth of the soul. Even though this bridge
leads to great heights, it is still joined to earth. The bridge is
made entirely of large, cut stones that symbolize true Christian
virtues. On the bridge there is a food stand to feed the
travelers. Those who walk on the bridge reach God and
eternal life; those who walk under the bridge, walk to perdi-
tion and death." [3]

God's Love for Us

Christ is the bridge which links heaven and earth,
and leads us to happiness. The three levels represent
different phases of our growth in love. The food stand

---

[1] Born in 1347, St. Catherine was the 23rd child from the same
mother in a very poor family living in Siena, an important city not
far from Florence, Italy. She died in 1380, at the age of 33.

[2] She was declared a Doctor of the Church by Pope Paul VI in
1970.

[3] Translated from Ravasi. p.147.

serving meals to travelers symbolizes the strength and help that Jesus offers us on the way to eternity, especially by means of the Holy Eucharist, as he proclaimed to the crowds.[4]

We already know this doctrine. We know that God, alone, is the ultimate goal of our lives. We have heard this thousands of times. We believe it, we cherish it; but has it ever brought about a decisive growth in our spiritual lives? If not, why not? Because we are neither profoundly convinced of God's love for us, nor do we know the depth and magnitude of his love.

"Love begets love." If we really want to offer God a better love response than what we have offered so far, if we are not satisfied with ourselves and our spiritual life is stagnant, if we want to climb to a higher level of spiritual growth, then we must strive to acquire a greater knowledge and a better understanding of God's love for us. We must develop a more active and intensive spiritual life in order to reach spiritual maturity.

Father John Devany, C.P., beautifully describes our spiritual relationship with God as follows:

"I would like to reflect with you on spiritual growth. What does it mean and what does it demand of us? Father Bernard Haring, in his fine book, *Free and Faithful in Christ,* tells us that the essential meaning of growth is a new relationship with God -- a 'Being at Home' with Him Who is Immanuel -- God Always With Us. And he goes on to say that the focal point of Christian growth is always Christ -- a burning desire to know Him in an ever deeper discovery and to follow Him Who is Our Lord. He speaks of spiritual

---

[4] John 6:27

growth as a developing relationship in love with the Person of Jesus Christ.

"The focal point is always Christ. It strikes me that there is a single word which lifts the spiritual growth process out of the realm of theological abstraction and brings it to life -- our life...a word which goes to the ardent heart of the matter. That word is *friendship*. In its basic simplicity, to achieve spiritual growth is to respond to a divine invitation, an invitation to friendship with Jesus Christ...a vivid, vital, joyful, hopeful relationship with Our Lord. It is to this that we are called, and of this we are God's messengers to others.

"Looking first to the Old Testament, we find it surprisingly rich in its revelation of the friendliness of God. In the Garden of Eden, before their sad fall from grace, God welcomes our first parents to a friendly companionship, walking with them in the garden, enjoying together the cool of the evening...Abraham, our father in faith, is spoken of in Genesis as '*the friend of God*' and to Moses, God speaks '*as to a friend.*' David walks fearlessly into the dark valley because the Shepherd Lord is at his side, '*with me, to give me courage.*' Again and again, God speaks his words of companionship, consoling his people: '*Fear not...I have called you by name and you are mine...precious in my eyes...and I love you.*' [5] And in the Gospel from first to last, Jesus shows Himself the Incarnate Word of God.

"Scripture scholars tell us that Matthew's gospel can be summarized in a single word, a word speaking divine companionship: '*Immanuel -- God is with us.*' Mark's first word on Jesus' lips is an invitation: '*Come and see...and they were with him.*' Always and everywhere He is available by day and by night. We think of Nicodemus coming out of the

---

[5] Isaiah 43.

night and the way Our Lord made room for him beside Him. And how Jesus forgot His own weariness to reassure that troubled lady at Jacob's well. His most characteristic gesture is a wide-armed welcome: *'Come to me, all you who labor and find life a heavy burden...here, with Me, close by my side...you will find rest for your souls...'* We remember the upper room and the gentle urgency of Jesus' words: *'Abide in Me...Live in my love...'* Especially, *'Now I call you friends.'* And His final pledge of faithful friendship, there on the mountaintop: *'Remember, I am with you always, even to the end of time.'* Jesus Christ makes visible and believable the friendliness of God.

"What He was then, He is now and always. He comes to us as He came to Martha and Mary and Lazarus...as He came to Andrew and Peter, busy with their nets, and to Matthew bending over his counting table. He calls us as He called Zebadee's sons to leave their boat and their business just to be with Him.

"With the same intrusion of love with which He invaded Saul of Tarsus, He wants to invade us. In his prayer for his parish at Ephesus, St. Paul expresses for us God's loving purpose in sending His Son: *'May Christ find a home in your heart.'* For the Apostle, Jesus is just that -- his divine guest, his dependable friend -- never at a distance, but within, as close to him as he is to himself, *'at home in his heart,'* lending strength to his weakness, always <u>there</u>, reassuring him: *'Don't be afraid. I am with you.'*

"When we understand spiritual growth in this way, we find ourselves in the very best of company. St. Thomas Aquinas tells us that friendship is the highest form of love. It expresses the ideal relationship that unites us with God. And St. Teresa of Avila, in her teaching on prayer, defines it very simply: *'Tratar de Amistad -- The Practice of Friendship,'* that same Teresa who habitually spoke of Our Lord as familiarly as "my true friend." Pope John Paul II, speaking to 20,000 students during his first American visit, told them: 'This is the meaning of life -- to know Jesus Christ as friend.' This is the dynamic relationship which defines us as Christians." [6]

Dr. John C. H. Wu briefly summarizes these thoughts in his inspiring booklet, *The Science of Love*, about *St. Therese of Lisieux* (also known as the "Little Flower"). He writes: "The whole trouble about modern civilization seems to me to be just in this: *'There is too much love of science, and too little science of love.'*

" 'The science of love!' exclaimed little Therese. 'Ah! sweet is the echo of that word to the ear of my soul! I desire no other science than that. For the sake of love *having given all my riches* like the spouse in the Canticles[7], *I feel as though I had given nothing.* There is nothing except love which could render us agreeable to the good God. This is so plain to me that the love has become the sole treasure upon which I set my heart.' To give all and to reckon it as nothing -- that is the acme of love!" [8]

Different Kinds of Love

Before we proceed further, we must review briefly the meaning of the word *love*. Do we really know what *love* is? Love is very complex. It is like a priceless diamond with many beautiful sparkling facets. It is the task of psychologists

---

[6] *"The Meaning of Conversion,"* an address given to the P.I.M.E. Fathers of Detroit, April 24-25, 1995, by Fr. John Devany, C.P., a Passionist father at St. Paul of the Cross, Detroit, Michigan.

[7] Also called *The Song of Songs.*

[8] Wu, *The Science of Love - A Study...*, p. 18.

and philosophers to analyze the roots and nature of love, but here we have to clarify the different kinds of human love.

Fr. Edward C. Vacek, S.J.,[9] writes: "I want to describe briefly three forms of love for God. We can have an *agapic* love, an *eros* love or a *philia*[10] love for God. Normally, we will have all three mixed together. *Agape*, as I use the term, means love of something for its own sake. So, with an *agapic* love for God, we are not concerned for ourselves but are devoted to God for God's sake... Second, *eros*[11] means loving someone for our own sake. In the traditional act of contrition, Christians have prayed that they are heartily sorry for their sins because they dread the loss of heaven and the pains of hell, but most of all because these sins offend God. Their sorrow over offending God expresses agape. Their dread about losing God and going to hell expresses eros. An eros love for God is a genuine love. It is a biblical love, and it is quite Catholic. We love God for the good we gain in being close to God.

---

[9] Rev. Edward Collins Vacek, S.J., is associate professor of moral theology at Western Jesuit School of Theology and the author of several books. This quotation is from an article published in the Jesuit magazine *America* on March 9, 1996.

[10] These three words are from the Greek language and are frequently used by Western writers to designate the different kinds of love, because English, like many other languages, including Latin, have only the word "love".

[11] The word *eros* is mostly used to signify romantic, passionate, sexual love between the two sexes. Many writers object to using *eros* when speaking of love for God. However, Fr. Vacek is correct, because erotic love is basically *self-love*. Christian tradition has always taught that loving and serving God out of fear to go to hell (self-love) is legitimate love for God.

"Third, we have *philia* love when we love God for the sake of the 'friendship' we have with God. Our Jewish ancestors formed covenants with God, and through baptism we Christians form a new covenant with God. We are God's people, and God is 'our God.' We live out of this relationship. We do religious things like pray and sing in church, but we also relax at the seashore and work hard in the soup kitchen. The difference between us and unbelievers is that we want to do these things as part of our relationship with God. Growing in that desire is what it means to become a saint."

The Nature of Christian Love[12]

The response that God wants from us in return for his love cannot be mere human love; it must be some kind of **human-divine love.** God is pure spirit, and he loves us in a spiritual way. We, on the other hand, are body *and* spirit. We need God's help to love him with all our heart, soul, mind, and strength, in a spiritual way acceptable to him. For the sake of simplicity, I call this kind of love **Christian love,** a love for God and neighbor which is inspired by God and has God as its object. It is supported, strengthened and made possible by that special help from God called **grace.** In other words, it is not an ordinary, human kind of *agape;* it is a spiritual *agape.* It is a love that loses nothing of the human beauty and characteristics of love but is motivated by God and directed toward him. Its correct name in theological jargon is **charity.**

---

[12] What follows is a simplified summary of theories about love and how the word love is used in the Old and New Testaments as it appears in the American Catholic Encyclopedia.

The *Catechism* defines it this way: "Charity is the theological virtue[13] by which we love God above all things for his own sake, and our neighbor as ourselves for the love of God." [14]

The word charity (Latin *caritas*) was introduced in the original Latin translation of the Bible by St. Jerome.[15] The Latin translation of *agape, philia, eros,* is *amor,* (a generic name like *love* in English), but St. Jerome did not want to use it because it had a strong sexual connotation in the pagan culture of Rome. He also avoided using other Latin words such as *dilectio* (affection), and *amicitia* (friendship) because they were too secular and worldly. Thus "*charity*" entered the language of theology, and it came to be understood as a form of Christian *agape, philia and eros* put together.

In present day society the meaning of *charity* has changed; it is generally applied to some kind of benevolence toward those in need or even a patronizing for people at the bottom level of our society. This is why modern English translators of the Bible, both Catholic and Protestant, today use the word *love* instead of charity.

In this book, I often use *Christian love* as synonymous with "*charity*" in the theological sense, because these two words point out the inner drive of our humanity and the need of God's help and inspiration.

It is important to emphasize the difference between Christian love and *philanthropy*. Philanthropy is pure human benevolence and beneficence at the natural level, but

---

[13] "Theological virtue" is a virtue that has God as its very object, and one that cannot be acquired by human effort alone. We need God's help to acquire and practice it.

[14] CCC #1822.

[15] It is usually referred to as *the Vulgate,*

Christian love flows from God and regards God as the ultimate end. When St. Francis on his way to Assisi saw a leper begging for alms, he could not help feeling a tremendous physical repugnance; but in spite of it, he stopped to embrace and kiss him. In so doing, he performed a true act of Christian *charity*. But when we donate money to charities out of our surplus because it makes us feel good, that is *philanthropy,* not love of God.

Sexual love as such is not agape, but one particular and specific aspect of human love proper to our earthly condition; this is why it is mostly self-centered and possessive. When sanctified by the Sacrament of Matrimony, it becomes the supreme expression of human love and the symbol of the union of God with our soul.

Personal Reflection

Am I really convinced of the depth of Jesus' love for me? If I think that I am, how come I relegate him to the periphery of my life? I should be ashamed of thinking of Jesus so little and doing even less for him. Is it because I love myself, my ways, my plans, the people and things which please me more than I love him? Often, I love others for selfish reasons, thinking of what I can get out of them, not because they are my brothers and sisters in Christ. I often dislike unpleasant people, but do I remember that God "*makes the sun rise on the bad and good and causes rain to fall on the just and unjust?*" [16]

---

[16] Matthew 5:45.

PRAYER
(by John Henry Cardinal Newman)

My God, you are my life; if I leave you,I cannot but thirst. Lost spirits thirst in hell, because they have not God. I wish to be clad in that new (spiritual) nature, which so longs for you from loving you, as to overcome in me the fear of coming to you. I come to you, Lord, not only because I am unhappy without you, not only because I feel I need you, but because your grace draws me on to seek you. As the years pass away, and the heart shuts up, and all things are a burden, let me never lose this youthful, eager love of you...[17]

Short Prayer

Jesus, help me to love you.

---

[17] *A Newman Prayer Book*, p.3

3

DOES GOD LOVE ME?
SHOULD I LOVE HIM?

PART I: JESUS' LOVE FOR US

"I call you friends, you are my friends. It is not you who chose me. It was I who chose you."[1]

As we read in the Bible, all through the Old Testament, God often compared his love for his people to the love of a mother for her child, and to the love of a shepherd for his sheep. In the book of Isaiah, God tells his erring people, "Can a mother forget her infant? Be without tenderness for the child of her womb? Even should she forget, I will never forget you." [2] *It is the belief of all major religions that God in his mercy and love will forgive our sins. This is the "hidden golden thread which binds together all those who seek God with a sincere heart."* [3]

Jesus and the Father Are One

The main purpose of this book is to convince readers that Jesus loves each one of us with a deep and personal love and that we must love him in return with all our hearts, souls, minds, and strength and give him first place in our

---

[1] John, 15:14,16.
[2] Isaiah 49:15.
[3] Ravasi, pg. 205.

lives. If we doubt Jesus' love for us, how can we grow to spiritual maturity and make our lives meaningful?

Notice that I am using the name "Jesus" rather than "God." Is there a difference? Actually, no. Jesus is God, the *Incarnation of the Second Person, the WORD* of God, and HE is God as the Father and the Holy Spirit are God. This is the mystery of the Holy Trinity, three persons -- Father, Son, and Holy Spirit -- but ONE God. We cannot separate them in our love; and when we pray to one, we pray to all three Divine Persons.

However, we also believe that the Son assumed our human nature and became a human being like us in order to teach us about God and to suffer for our eternal salvation. As a human being, like us in everything except sin, he made it easier for us to relate to him as a human rather than to a pure spirit, like God.

Jesus said emphatically, *"I and the Father are one."*[4] With this simple statement he solemnly proclaims that *he is God and man at the same time.* This is the real meaning of the Incarnation and of the presence of God in our midst as one of us. St. John puts it briefly: *"The Word was made flesh and dwelt among us."*[5] Jesus is truly the human face of God.

Does Jesus Love Me?

Are you really convinced that Jesus loves you personally? Did you ever doubt Jesus' love for you, especially under pressure of suffering and adversity? A strong, firm belief in the personal love of Jesus for each of us is the very

---

[4]   John 10:30.
[5]   John 1:14.

foundation, the cornerstone of the growth of our spiritual life. We know that religion is love, but love must be reciprocal. **Love is a two-way street.**

How deeply convinced are you that Jesus really cares for you, that you are not just one out of billions of individuals born by chance and thrown into this world at the mercy of physical and genetic laws? Or do you think that your sins are too many and too serious for God to forgive you? Are you one of those who wonder: "How can Jesus love me with all my sins and all the wrongs I have done? I never felt a great love for him, so how can he love me so much as to forgive my sins?"

Let me assure you that even if you didn't care much about him in the past, he loves you still and wants you to love him in return. His love is forever.

Think. Hasn't he continued pouring his gifts on you, giving you life and blessings in spite of your sins and lack of love for him? He still wants to give you another chance. He wants you to realize what you are missing by neglecting him, and he is now offering you his help to find a better and more meaningful way of life. Even if you are a great sinner and have wronged many people, cheer up, you are in good company! Not only are we all poor mortals and sinners, but all the saints in heaven, even such great apostles as St. Peter and St. Paul were sinners, too. St. Paul made a public confession when, from his prison in Rome shortly before suffering martyrdom, he wrote: *"Christ came into this world to save sinners. Of these I am myself the worst."*[6] He had already written to the Romans: *"What proves that God loves us is the fact that Christ died for us who were still sinners."*[7]

And if all this still does not convince you, listen to

---

[6] 1 Timothy 1:15.

[7] Romans 1:8.

Jesus himself: *"I have not come to call the righteous, but sinners to repentance."*[8] So, the fact that Jesus has come into the world to help sinners out of their spiritual misery is the best guarantee you have that he loves you and me and all of us individually, especially because we are sinners. Doesn't a doctor care for his sickest patients in a more special manner? Can Jesus do less than a human physician? Rest assured that your belief in Jesus' personal love for you is solidly rooted in Sacred Scripture.

Will Jesus Forgive My Sins?

The fact that God wants the conversion of sinners brings up the broader question of his forgiveness. This is a fascinating truth that has its roots both in common sense and in the whole Judeo-Christian tradition. There are only two conditions necessary to receive God's forgiveness: to repent and to forgive.

REPENTANCE. Once we repent and are sorry for our sins, God will never refuse to forgive us. God will never force us to love him because love is worthless unless it is freely given; and when we tell Jesus sincerely, *"Lord, I am sorry!,"* we open the floodgates of his mercy -- we are as safe in his arms as an infant in its mother's arms. However, as long as we choose sin over God, and fail to repent, how can we expect God's forgiveness? Repentance is the indispensable condition to receiving God's forgiveness.

FORGIVING OTHERS. This is the second indispensable condition for receiving Jesus's forgiveness of our sins. The Gospel of St. Matthew relates that one day Peter came up to Jesus and asked him a simple, straightforward

---

[8] Luke 5:32.

question: *"Lord, when my brother wrongs me, how often must I forgive him? Seven times?"* "No," Jesus replied, *"not seven times; I say seventy times seven."*[9] (a Jewish expression meaning "always.") And if Jesus commands us to forgive our brother every time, can he do anything less and limit the number of times he is willing to forgive us? All through the Gospel Jesus repeats again and again that, besides repentance, the only condition for being forgiven is forgiving others.

We have another striking example of this truth in the parable of the unjust servant. After he obtained from his master the complete remission of his debt, he refused to forgive the small debt of his fellow servant and handed him *"over to the torturers until he paid back all he owed."* Jesus concluded the parable: *"My heavenly Father will treat you in exactly the same way unless each of you forgives his brother from the heart."* [10]

In the Sermon on the Mount Jesus also proclaimed: *"If you forgive others their transgressions, your heavenly Father will forgive you."* [11] When Jesus taught his apostles and us that most basic prayer which we call the *Our Father,* he directed us to pray, *"...forgive us our trespasses as we forgive those who trespass against us..."* That means: "Lord forgive me my offenses against you **in the same proportion** as I forgive those who offend me."

In his immense love for us, Jesus looks at the depth of our repentant love for him, *not* the number of times we offend him. Recall to mind how Jesus praised St. Mary Magdalene, the former street-walker. When she anointed his feet, he told the critical audience: *"She has been forgiven*

---

[9] Matthew 18:21-22.

[10] Matthew 18:34-35.

[11] Matthew 6:14.

much because she has loved much!" [12]   And on the morning
of the Resurrection he appeared first to Mary Magdalene and
only later to the other women and the apostles.

St. Therese of Lisieux used to say that she hoped to
go to heaven not because of the good deeds she had performed, but only because of the infinite mercy of the Lord.
She believed that for Jesus to forgive fifty, or fifty thousand
sins was the same, since his mercy is boundless. This belief
is theologically correct because no matter how great or how
numerous our sins may be, they can never be greater than
the infinite mercy of the Lord.

Dr. John C. H. Wu in *The Science of Love* writes:

"Love opened the eyes of little Therese to new truths and
new reasons for loving Jesus. She was not such a great
sinner as Magdalene and, logically speaking, she did not
need as much forgiveness from God as Magdalene, but does
it follow that she loved him less? No, on the contrary, she
loved him all the more. Love has its own logic that mathe-
maticians have no notion of. 'I love him,' she reasons,
'because he has forgiven me not much, but all. He has
forgiven me *beforehand* the sins which I could have committed.'

"She seems to know by intuition what very few
theologians have arrived at by their long-winded reasoning.
St. Thomas Aquinas had, indeed, pointed out that it is 'also
a divine benefit that God should keep a man from sin, just
as he forgives his past sins.' St. Augustine had also confessed: 'I put it down to your grace and mercy that you
melted the ice of my sins; I put it down to your grace all the
sins that I did not, that I could not commit.' But little
Therese went a step further than these great lights of the

---

[12]   Luke 7:47.

Church! She spoke, not in terms of 'also' but in terms of 'all the more...' " [13]

Jesus proved his love for us beyond any possible doubt: he died for us. For us he rose from the dead, and for us he ascended into heaven to prepare our dwelling place there: *"In my Father's house there are many dwelling places. If there were not, would I have told you that I am going to prepare a place for you?"* [14] He is the *one and only* person in the whole world who has loved each of us to the point of death. Nobody else died for love of us. Can he, then, refuse to forgive us if we turn to him for help?

PART II: DO WE LOVE GOD?

Now the big question is: How much do we love God in return for all his love for us?

Once a friend told me: "Father, I am a good Christian, I do some good for others, and I would never do anything to hurt anyone. But I don't go to Church. My religion is to love my neighbor, but God and churches are not for me." Does this sound familiar? This attitude is shared by a large number of Christians in all walks of life, from executives at the highest levels of industry and the media to ordinary workers. Father Vacek writes: "Almost all Christians talk approvingly about love for others; some talk confidently about God's love for us; but few are willing to talk about their love for God." [15]

---

[13] *The Science of Love*, Pp. 56-57. (PIME edition)   Note: Quotation from St. Thomas, *Selected Writings, Everyman's Library*, p. 3.

[14] John 14:12.

[15] *America* magazine, March, 1996.

It is true that different aspects of Christianity were emphasized differently during different periods in time. Up to the 19th century it was such truths as communing with God, or faith, or obedience to the Church that were emphasized most; today the emphasis is more on helping others in need. This is good, but it is not enough. Helping others without loving God does not make much sense in the light of eternity. If there is one idea which stand out above everything else in the Bible, it is the truth that God loves his people, wants us to love him, and wants us to love one another and forgive each other *for his sake.*

Father Vacek continues: "They (people) judge that it is wrong not to love people, but they have no such thoughts about neglecting God. In short, many contemporary Christians subscribe to Jesus' second great commandment, *(love one another,)* but not to his first, *(love of God above everything else.)*

"There is a great difference between seeking the truth and being in a personal relationship with God. Those who love God live differently.

"In short, it is not enough just to love our fellow human beings. Sincere conscience and anonymous theism are not enough... Giving water to a stranger is quite different from desiring to serve Christ. **Our explicit intentions make a great difference in our moral life.**

"At times, we can and must also direct our love immediately and directly to God. Of course, one way of expressing love for God is to care for God's creation. But much as taking the garbage out for sick neighbors is no substitute for directly developing an interpersonal relationship with them, so, too, doing good works to show love for God presupposes other activities devoted to directly loving God.

"A question that will challenge all of us today is this: 'Do you love God?' That question evokes the endlessness of our heart's quest as well as the incomprehensibility of God, and it gives us an absorbing center for our lives.

"I imagine that when Jesus went off to pray he was not just gathering up energy to love his fellow human beings, nor was he simply purifying and developing his inner life. Rather, he chose to spend time with his Abba. He wanted and needed that time. He prayed, and in that prayer he united his mind and heart with God. Our love for God requires something similar.

"How might such a relationship develop? The first step is one that, generally speaking, women seem to understand more quickly than men. That step is to accept God's love for us. In other words, our first response is *not* to return love to God, but rather to let God's love affect or change us. We deny God's transforming influence if we rush to return love to God or to spread love to our neighbor. Sitting with eyes closed and hands open, we let God's love touch and move us; there begins our salvation.

"Thereafter, we can and should love God in return. **Love means we effectively affirm God's goodness.** We want to be close to God, and we rejoice when we are close. At the same time, our love for God will not long let us rest but moves us to penetrate ever more appreciatively into God's goodness. Correlatively, we are disconsolate when we are alienated from God. We miss God when God no longer seems near.

"Our love for God also makes us want to cooperate with God in doing what God wants to do. That leads us to be involved in creation. Hence, love for God at one level moves us into the incomprehensibility of God and, at another level, moves us both to cherish the world and to want to overcome its ills and injustices." [16]

Jesus Loves Each of Us Individually

Jesus died out of love for each of us individually. As we look at a crucifix, each one of us can sincerely say: "I share responsibility for his death because he died to atone the sins of all of us, and that includes the large bundle of my own personal sins. How much do I appreciate his personal love for me?"

We must be convinced that we are not the product of "an assembly line." God creates each one of us individually, and as a loving Creator and Father, he cares for us individually throughout our entire lives. How could he be an infinitely perfect God if he did not care for the work of his own hands?

"*Behold, I stand at the door and knock. If anyone hears my voice and opens the door, (then) I will enter his house and dine with him, and he with me.*" [17] He is now knocking at the door of your heart, inviting you to open it for him.

This is the language of love. These are the words of Jesus. He has spoken them for each of us; they are ours. Let us carve them in our hearts. Let us think of them often, for they are a great source of courage and perseverance.

Personal Reflection

Do I seriously believe that Jesus loves me personally? Do I truly believe Jesus walked this earth, that he

---

[16] *America* magazine, March 9, 1996.
[17] Revelations 3:20.

suffered and died for love of me? Perhaps I am not very sincere with myself. I know that if I admit that Jesus loves me, then I have to admit my guilt in neglecting him and there are many things in my life I should change. Is this what holds me back from loving him? One thing is certain, I must learn more about Jesus and his love for me. Even though I do good to others, I must still love Jesus first. This is his will.

P R A Y E R
(From Psalm 51)

Have mercy on me, O God, in your goodness;
    in the greatness of your compassion
      wipe out my offence.
Thoroughly wash me from my guilt
    and of my sins cleanse me.
For I acknowledge my offence,
    and my sin is before me always:
Against you only have I sinned,
    and done what is evil in your sight...

Wash me and I shall be whiter than snow.
Let me hear the sounds of joy and gladness;
    the bones you have crushed shall rejoice.
Turn away your face from my sins,
    and blot out all my guilt...
My sacrifice, O God, is a contrite spirit;
    a heart contrite and humbled, O
    God, you will not spurn.

Short Prayer

Jesus, help me to believe in your love.

4

FALLING IN LOVE WITH JESUS

"As my Father has loved you, so I have loved you. Abide in my love."[1]

In his book, <u>The Science of Love....</u>, Dr. John C. H. Wu writes: *"But what exactly is God to us? Is He our Father? Yes, He is our Father, but He is more than that. Is He then our Mother? Yes, He is also our Mother, but he is more than that. He is, besides, our Friend, our Brother, our Sister, our Spouse, our Lord, our Minister, our All! His relation with us is so all-embracing that it includes all the five relations[2] of men and something more. We may call Him this or that; but all these names are used analogically, for human language has its limits, beyond it can no longer denote anything definite and can at best only hint. So long as we use them only as hints, all names of human relations can be applied to God, and with equal appropriateness... 'For Whosoever shall do the will of My Father that is in heaven, he is My brother, and sister, and mother.' "* [3]

Jesus and Me

We have seen in the previous chapter that we cannot reasonably doubt Jesus' love for us and that if we repent, God will never refuse to forgive us. We have seen that love for God is indispensable to make our lives meaningful. Now

---

[1] John 15:9

[2] According to Chinese beliefs all human relationships are divided into five categories.

[3] *The Science of Love..*, pp.19-20. Biblical quote, Matt. 12:49-50.

let us endeavor to better understand who Jesus really is, what he has done for each of us, and what our love response should be.

By its very nature love is an attraction to someone or something, and it requires knowledge of the beloved. The greater such knowledge, the greater the love. Unfortunately, this basic rule of love is seldom applied to our relationship with God. As already stated, there is a large number of Christians who could not care less about acquiring a greater knowledge and love for God, and Jesus is the least important person in their lives. They go through life with very little knowledge of God, of Jesus, or of religion. Their spiritual life is a perpetual winter; and their love for God, if there is any, is only superficial. Many of them regard religious practices as laws and obligations to be fulfilled (like paying taxes) and they fulfill them more out of fear (avoiding hell) and self-interest (to get help) rather than out of love. Ignorance of God is the real tragedy of mankind. It makes humanity a wintry wasteland.

G. K. Chesterton was right when he wrote: "The Christian ideal, it is said, has not been tried and found wanting; it has been found difficult and left untried."[4] It is vitally important, therefore, to dedicate more time learning from the Gospel who Jesus really is, and how we can *fall in love with him.*

Who Is Jesus?

He said of himself: *"The words I speak are not spoken of myself; it is the Father who lives in me accomplishing his*

---

[4] Bartlett, John. *Bartlett's Familiar Quotations.* 15th ed. p.742.

works. Believe me that I am in the Father and the Father is in me." [5]

He died as a criminal on a cross about 2,000 years ago. Yet, no other human being has ever influenced so many civilizations, nations, countries, so many people, cultures, societies, laws and social customs as he did. The essay, *"One Solitary Life,"* summarizes beautifully how Jesus influenced the world:

> *ONE SOLITARY LIFE. He was born in an obscure village...*
> *He worked in a carpenter shop until he was thirty... He then*
> *became an itinerant preacher. He never held an office. He never*
> *had a family or owned a house. He didn't go to college. He had no*
> *credentials but himself...*
> *   Nineteen centuries have come and gone, and today He is the*
> *central figure of the human race. All the armies that ever marched,*
> *and all the navies that ever sailed, all the parliaments that ever sat,*
> *and all the kings that ever reigned put together, have not affected*
> *the life of man on this earth as much as that...ONE SOLITARY LIFE."*

As a follow-up to this beautiful essay, I wish to quote a magnificent page from William Barclay's "The Gospel of St. John," describing the effects of the presence of Jesus in the world.

"God, (in the person of Jesus) entered into an ordinary home and into an ordinary family. God was not ashamed to do a man's work. It was as a working man that he entered into the world; Jesus was the carpenter of Nazareth. We can never sufficiently realize the wonder of the fact that God understands our day's work, the difficulty of making ends meet...and every problem which besets us in the work of every day.

---

[5] John 14:10

"God knows what it is to be tempted. The life of Jesus shows us not the serenity but the struggle of God. Anyone might conceive of a God who lived in a serenity and peace which were beyond the tensions of this world, but Jesus shows us a God who goes through the struggle that we must undergo.

"In Jesus we see God loving. God caring intensely, yearning over men, feeling poignantly for them and with them, loving them until he bore the wounds of love upon his heart.

"In Jesus we see God upon a cross. There is nothing so incredible as this in all the world. It is easy to imagine a God who condemns men; it is still easier to imagine a God who, if men oppose him, wipes them out. No one would ever have dreamed of a God who chose the Cross to obtain our salvation. Truly, *'He who has seen me, has seen the Father,'* [6] Jesus said to Philip. Jesus is the revelation of God and that revelation leaves the mind of man staggered and amazed."[7]

What Has Jesus Done for Me?
(A Personal Meditation)

And now, as the echo of these great lines lingers in your mind and soul, it will be good for you to reflect on what Jesus has specifically done for you. For a moment, forget everything and everyone around you and read the following passages in the first person. They apply to you, personally. Think only of yourself and Jesus.

---

[6] John 14:9

[7] Reproduced from *the Gospel of John*. Vol 2. in the <u>Daily Bible Series</u> by William Barclay. pp.160-161. Used by permission of Westminster John Knox Press.

As the second person of the Holy Trinity, Jesus was active with the Father and the Holy Spirit in creating me; out of nothingness he made me a human being unto his image to be eternally happy with him. I was not created in a haphazard way or by chance. From all eternity I have been in the mind and heart of Jesus (as the second person of the Holy Trinity) because he chose me out of countless billions of potential souls to receive his gifts of love and life. He created planet earth as my temporary dwelling place.

Through the genes of generations of my ancestors and the particular environment in which I was born he has given me the physical and spiritual gifts needed to become the kind of creature he wants me to be and to fulfill the role he has assigned to me in this world. He made himself known to me in my childhood and adulthood that I might know how much he loves and cares for me.

He has given me the privilege of knowing and embracing the Christian faith. He has nourished me with his body and blood; he has enlightened my mind; he has enkindled my heart and has again and again forgiven my sins. He has given me all I have in life -- my body, my mind, health, intelligence, education, family -- all the good qualities, all the blessings I have; they are all his free gifts to me.

Is there anything in my life which is strictly mine? Yes, my sins. The wrong I have done to others -- my selfishness, my pride, my arrogance, my lack of love and gratitude for all he has done for me -- yes, these are all mine. And yet, in spite of my indifference and coldness to him, and even in spite of my positive refusals to love him generously, he has continued to help me, to love me, to give me gifts, to protect me, to haunt me with his love, to let me know how much he loves me. Even the sufferings and trials that, like every mortal, I have to endure are gentle reminders inviting me to turn to him.

*In spite of all his generosity and love, how much have
I loved him? What have I done for him? Most of the time it
seems I freely choose to pursue what pleases me, slapping him
in the face when I deliberately choose to do wrong over his
love.*

My Love Answer:
Falling in Love with Jesus[8]

It is now time we begin to think about what we can
do for Jesus to show him our gratitude. The only thing he
asks of us in return for all he has done for us is **our love.**

Love must be proportional to the gift received. In
view of all the blessings we have received from Jesus, our
love for him cannot be just an ordinary love, an occasional
thinking of him, or a superficial thank you, or even a
superficial reading of prayer formulas. As we have seen in
Chapter Two, our love must be an intense, intimate love, a
real *"falling in love"* with him. Fr. John Devany, C.P.[9]
describes what our love should be like.

"The first test of authentic friendship is 'intimacy.'
There is no such thing as an abstract, impersonal friendship
any more than one can love another impersonally. As Saint
Albert the Great beautifully expressed it: 'Love draws the
lover out of himself and makes him dwell in the beloved and

---

[8] Is it correct to use this expression in relation to Jesus? Yes
it surely is, because *falling in love* means the highest form of
dedicated love of which we humans are capable. Referring to the
words of Jesus quoted at the beginning of this chapter (Mt.12:50)
about who is his brother and who is his sister, Dr. Wu comments:
"So, Peter, the rugged fisherman, was to Him (Jesus) not only
brother, but sister and mother as well!" This is the totally dedicated kind of love that we describe with the words *falling in love.*

[9] See Chapter 2, Note 5.

settles him intimately there. Thus, the soul is more truly where it loves than where it lives.' [10]

"Is this not precisely the way Our Lord, himself, expressed his mind on the matter? At the Last Supper, he told his friends: 'As the Father loves me, so have I loved you.' [11] And just a moment earlier, Jesus used that vivid metaphor of the vine and the branches to show how intimate should be our union with him -- a life-sharing intimacy. He is, Jesus tells us, the source of our vitality and our growth. 'Without me, you can do nothing.' [12]

"If we were to ask the apostle John what it all really comes down to, what it means to live in Christ and he in us, to "live in his love," to call him friend and to deserve the name in return, I think he would tell us: 'It means that his love must come first. Nothing and no one can be allowed to take precedence, to dispute his place in our hearts.'

"Surely anyone who is consciously and constantly setting his or her life course as a companionship with Our Lord cannot do so by thinking of him on alternative Tuesdays. Friendship demands more than an occasional passing thought or a half-distracted glance in his direction. In the letter to the Hebrews we read: 'Let us keep our eyes fixed on Jesus, who inspires our faith and brings it to perfection.' [13]

"For St. Paul, you must remember, faith is never just a sterile abstraction; for him it is a total surrender and a passionate response, a power and a presence which has invaded the very depth of his being. 'For me, life means Christ.' [14] 'I live, no longer I, but Christ lives in me.' [15] 'I

---

[10] *De Adhaerendo Deo.* (About Attachment to God.)
[11] John 15:9
[12] John 15:5
[13] Hebrews 12:29
[14] Philippians 1:21

live in the faith of the Son of God Who loved me and gave himself for me.' [16] Our Lord has so taken possession of him that He is literally *all that matters.* And so, too, it should be with us. Jesus is, indeed, all that matters.

"Such a preoccupation with Christ does not mean that we all are called to be Trappists. It means that we are *mind-full,* our minds are full of Our Lord, so that, somehow, he enters into every aspect of our lives and defines us.

"J. B. Phillips, in his translation of the letter to the Colossians, has St. Paul speaking of *'Jesus Christ -- the Secret Center of our lives.'* [17] The Secret Center... These words should capture our minds and hearts.

"This should lead to our spiritual growth, to a progressive transformation. Fr. Edward Leen, in his classic work, *In The Likeness of Christ,* tells us that our whole task as Christians consists in establishing a vital contact between the two life experiences -- the life experience of Jesus as we come to know Him in the gospel brought to life in prayer, and our own life experience -- a kind of inter-penetration by which the life of Our Lord molds and forms our own according to his spirit.

"Such an evident Christ-likeness is not something which happens in a day's attention or a week's retreat. It involves a life-long process, a *'putting on Christ'* [18] in a daily learning and living. It means reflecting on our attitudes and actions all that we are, continually discovering the mind and heart of Our Lord. He told his friends that night in the upper room: *'I give you a new commandment: love one another. As I have loved you, so you also should love one*

---

[15] Galatians 2:28
[16] Galatians 2:20
[17] Colossians 3:11
[18] Romans 13:14

another. *This is how all will know that you are my disciples,
if you have love for one another.'* [19] This is not just a suggestion; it is the charter of our growth in the life of the
spirit. *'You are my friends,'* Jesus tells us, *'if you do what I
command you.'* [20]

"The great master of spiritual theology, Abbot Colum-
ba Marmion, commenting on the Pauline expression *'to put
on Christ,'* tells us that for some, the life of Jesus is but one
subject among many. This is not enough. Christ is not just
one means of the spiritual life. He **is** our spiritual life. He
is the Source; he **is** the Model; he **is** the Mirror; he **is** the
object of our constant search. In his reflection, we test our
own spiritual progress toward the full stature to which we
are called, with him -- in him."

Expressing Our Love

Another important quality of spiritual growth is that
mutual love should be expressed and re-enforced by the exchange of gifts. We cannot say that we love a person unless
we convey our feelings to that person. Without communica-
tion our feelings of love remain just that, feelings. Looks,
words, touching, gifts are what makes our love real. In the
case of gifts, it is the sentimental or economic value of the
gift itself that is the language of love. This is what must
have been in the mind of the apostle when he wrote: *"I live
in the faith of the Son of God Who loved me and gave Himself
for me."*[21] Note the use of the singular. St. Paul understood that the divine friendship is always a personal relationship. He gave himself for me and he continues to give

---

[19] John 13:34-35
[20] John 15:14
[21] Galatians 2:20

himself to each of us, in his church, in his sacraments, and especially in the Eucharist. Such total, all-encompassing love demands an equally total love on our part. This is what it means to *fall in love* with Jesus.

Personal Reflection[22]

How much do I love Jesus? His generosity demands a return in kind. But can I say that Jesus is the "secret center" of my life, that I really am in love with him? To match in some little way the reality of my life to that of his generous love demands that I keep loving and giving through a lifetime of daily growth, turning to my Divine Friend in whole-hearted response, turning away from anything or anyone that would interfere with the gift of myself to him.

P R A Y E R
(Prayer of St. Ignatius Loyola)

"Take, O Lord, and receive my liberty, my memory, my understanding and my entire will -- all that I am and all that I possess. You have given it all to me. To you, Lord, I return it. Everything is yours. Give me only your love and your grace. That is enough for me."

Short Prayer
Teach me, O Lord, to grow daily in my gratitude and love for you.

---

[22] Adapted from Fr. Devany's writing. See Chapter 2, Note 5.

5

LOVE FOR GOD
AND HUMAN SUFFERING

"How long, O Lord, will you utterly forget me?
How long will you hide your face from me?
How long shall I harbor sorrow in my soul,
Grief in my heart day after day?
How long will my enemy (adversities) triumph
over me?
Look, answer me, O Lord, my God." [1]

Suffering in the World

King David wrote the above lines when he was suffering cruel adversities. His words reflect the heart of all humans when overwhelmed by pain and sorrow. In such moments even a strong faith is wounded, torn apart, shaken as the soul struggles to survive in the dark night on the brink of despair. These words are the desperate cry of human beings, limited and finite, turning to the Infinite that seems so cold and distant, and forever asking: *"Why should I suffer? If there is a God, why does he treat me like this? Why does ne hot alleviate my sufferings?"* The tragedy is that God has already answered our questions, but we refuse to accept the fact that suffering is an integral part of our life on earth.

---

[1]Psalm 13:2-4

The Reality of Suffering

We have seen that only true love for God can fulfill our basic need for happiness and that Jesus' love for us demands in return an all-out, dedicated love for him. Now we have to go one step further and come to grips with another basic reality of life: *suffering,* and how to reconcile this reality with our belief in a loving and caring Jesus. In contrast to the thoughts of love we have been reflecting on so far, we now have to face the harsh reality of a world full of pain. *This is the **Second Segment** of God's Circle of Love.*

The world in which we live often seems very far, indeed, from the one promised in the Bible. Our experiences of suffering, evil, great injustice, and death seem to contradict the Good News of the Gospel; they can all shake our faith, becoming a temptation against God.[2]

Some of our readers may doubt that suffering can shake our faith and become a temptation to turn against God... to the point of even hating him. There are in the world some mature people who have led sheltered lives, are very patient by nature, and for them ordinary sufferings do not create a problem affecting their faith. But such people are rare; they are the exception.

The majority of people, at one time or another, have experienced either mental anguish or intense spiritual or physical suffering. They have shared in the tragedy of millions killed by wars; they have suffered starvation, been afflicted with disease, or have experienced the trials of millions of victims of social injustices. As mentioned before, perhaps under the pressure of suffering you have asked: "If Jesus loves us so much, why does he make us go through

---

[2] Cf. CCC #164.

such horrible tragedies? Where is justice? If he has the power to solve all human problems, why doesn't he wipe away pain and suffering from the world?"

We have to recognize the fact that the goodness of God and the presence of evil in the world is one of the most profound mysteries of human life. Pope John Paul II, in his Apostolic Letter on Human Suffering, wrote that suffering "is a universal theme that accompanies man at every point on earth, in a certain sense it coexists with him in the world, and thus demands to be constantly reconsidered. *Suffering* seems to be particularly *essential to the nature of man.* It is as deep as man himself... It seems to be, and is, almost inseparable from man's earthly existence." [3] Someone once defined life as the span of time that elapses between two tears -- our first tear at the moment of birth and our last tear on our death-bed.

Of course, there is an answer to our question. According to Professor Kreeft it would be absurd to believe that God would abandon us and leave us lost in the depths of darkness and despair. However, the answer God has given us is not a classroom type of theoretical answer, it is his own solution to this deep mystery. In order to understand and accept it, we must first understand the problem of evil in the world and look at it in the light of God's love of expiation of sin, of eternal reward.

The Universality of Joy and Suffering

Suffering in different forms and degrees accompanies all of us through life. It truly is the *inseparable companion* of all human beings and it is *universally* present all over the

---

[3] Human Suffering I, 2-3.

world, at all times, among all peoples, regardless of age, sex, race, religion, education, social position.   It is truly and literally universal. However, on the other side of universal suffering there are in the world universal joys, beauty, pleasure, and spiritual greatness. Every human being is a micro-world unto himself, reflecting the grandeur, the beauty, the power of the physical world, as well as its conflicts, its tragedies, its destructive power and built-in obsolescence. It is this contrast between the physical and spiritual world that creates the harmony of the universe -- the *yin* and *yang*. Laughter and tears, heaven and earth, gentle breezes and furious storms, light and darkness, life and death are all realities that belong to both the physical and spiritual world. Their alternating creates the enchanting symphony of the universe which opens our minds and souls to God and strengthens our beliefs and our love.[4]

Right now, we have to *concentrate on the dark side of suffering and evil* in order to understand, as best we can, God's plan for the universe and his circle of love. For a better evaluation of the depth and widespread effects of suffering, we must bear in mind that suffering is not merely limited to *physical suffering* (the hurting or illness of the body) or *mental* and *emotional suffering*, but it also includes *moral suffering* (the pain of the soul). As the Holy Father stated: "The vastness and the many forms of moral suffering are certainly no less in number than the forms of physical suffering." [5]

Let us now take an imaginary trip around the world and discover the height and depth and width of this mystery

---

[4] Summarized from *Making Sense Out of Suffering,* ℗ 1986 by Peter Kreeft. Publ'd by Servant Publications, Box 8617, Ann Arbor, MI 48107. Used with permission.

[5]*Human Suffering, 1-4.*

of suffering. Imagine that we can fly around our planet, as NASA's astronauts do, and by some magic power see and understand what goes on in the hearts, minds, and souls of every man, woman, and child in every part of the world.

What would we see on our imaginary trip? We would be sickened, shocked and appalled by the amount of suffering going on in the whole world, every moment of the day and night, in every nation, among all classes of people. Earth would seem like an immense, boundless ocean of misery, where sickness, evil, and moral suffering reign supreme -- far outweighing joy and pleasure because they are often tinged with some hidden sorrow.

We would see hidden sorrows in the palaces of the rich. We would see tragedy and despair in the slums of the big cities and in hospitals and prisons. From the cities to the jungles on every continent on earth, we would see the most heart-rending spectacle of suffering... victims of either human malice or of blind natural forces. We would see suffering of all kinds -- spiritual, physical, and emotional. It would be spiritually imprisoning and paralyzing, affecting everyone, rich and poor, young and old, without hope of escape. Some would be longing for death, others hating to leave this "valley of tears," but all marching toward that inevitable end, death... until it arrives as a messenger of mercy to end all suffering.

This is not wild imagination. This is the reality of life. Pope John Paul II reminds us that "suffering is an *objective reality* which must be dealt with, meditated upon, and regarded as an explicit problem that needs answers." [6]

Is this an exaggerated, pessimistic view of the world? After all, there are also great joys and pleasures in life. The

---

[6]Human Suffering #5

fact that all people want to live as long as possible -- and the frantic research by medicine and science to prolong life would seem to prove this -- must mean this world is not such a bad place to live in after all. And we owe it to God's bounty to be able to enjoy life. But this is not the problem we are looking at here. Our problem is to reconcile suffering with the idea of an all-loving and caring God.

Why Suffering?

Very often sufferings strike us in a thousand different ways when we least expect them. This is why we must be prepared to cope with suffering at all times, under all circumstances. Professor Peter Kreeft in his book *Making Sense Out of Suffering*,[7] analyzes in depth the problem of suffering. With his kind permission, I am going to give some excerpts from his book, as they are very pertinent to the subject of this chapter.

Human suffering "seems to disprove God, a God who supposedly knows and loves and provides for each one of his children. An omnipotent God could have stopped that auto accident and saved four lives...[8] He didn't. Therefore, either he doesn't care, and then he is not all good; or he doesn't know, and then he is not all wise; or he isn't able to, and then he is not all powerful. In any case, the God of Christianity, the God of the Bible, the God millions believe in, is a myth. The facts of life prove that. Don't they?...

---

[7]This book was written as a commentary on the book *Why Bad Things Happen to Good People*, by Rabbi Kushner.

[8]This is a reference to a particularly tragic case mentioned in his book, but it also applies to all kinds of accidents.

"...But the strongest case against God comes not from them but from the billions of normal lives that are full of apparently pointless suffering ...it seems random and point-less, distributed according to no rhyme or reason but mere chance, and working no good, no end. For every one who becomes a hero and a saint through suffering, there are ten who seem to become dehumanized, depressed, or despair-ing....

"People hurt less physically in this century, especially this generation, than ever before, largely due to the progress of medicine... There are cures for more and more diseases. Industrial society gives most people a comfortable life, a life only the wealthy few used to have... A hundred years ago you were lucky to get through a single year without pain that we would today call terrible. Think of a world without anesthetics. Think. When was the last time you felt the equivalent of a sword through your arm?

"Yet people are hurting far more psychologically and spiritually today than ever before. Suicides are up. Depres-sion is up. Mindless violence is up. Boredom is up. (In fact, the very word boredom does not exist in any pre-modern language!) Loneliness is up. Drug escapism is up.

"But the barbarians are no longer at the gates. The Huns and the Norsemen have long gone. What are we escaping from? Why can't we stand to be alone with our-selves? Solitude, the thing which ancient sages longed for as the greatest gift, is the very thing we give to our most desperate criminals as the greatest punishment we can imagine. Why have we destroyed silence in our lives?

"We are escaping from ourselves (or trying to, since yourself is the one thing other than God that you can never escape from) because we all hurt, deep down. Usually it is not an unusual, spectacular, tragic kind of hurt but a general greyness that settles like dust over our lives, a drabness, a

dullness, a dreariness, an ugliness, an ordinariness of everything...

"This is more tragic, not less, than past sufferings.
Deep, passionate sufferings are at least deep and passionate;
and if there are very low valleys, there are also very high
mountains.

"So either you feel great tragedy and ask why, or you
don't, and then you are living an even greater tragedy and
have even more need to ask why.

"Modern man does not have an answer to the question why. Our society is the first one that simply does not
give us any answer to the problem of suffering except a
thousand means of avoiding it." [9]

This is why we must endeavor to discover how the
reality of human suffering can be reconciled with the idea of
God's love and care for us. In other words we must look at
suffering in the light of God's everlasting love for us.

Personal Reflection

What is my attitude toward suffering? Does suffering draw me closer to God or does it turn me against him?
When misfortunes and trials come into my life, do I regard
them as an unjust punishment from God and complain to
him: *"Why me, Lord, why me? I have done so much good
for the poor and the Church... why do you treat me like
this?"* Do I look at suffering, both mine and others', from

---

[9] From *Making Sense Out of Suffering*, © 1986 by Peter Kreeft.
Publ'd by Servant Publications, Box 8617, Ann Arbor, MI 48107.
pp. 8-12. Used with permission.

the Christian point of view or, rather, do I follow the thinking of the world, seeing no point to it, resenting it, considering it useless and meaningless? When I go through a period of more intense suffering than usual, do I ever think of the sufferings of Jesus, of his passion and death? Do I blame God for human sufferings or do I believe they have a providential role in life?

P R A Y E R
(Adapted from various Psalms)

O Lord, you are my rock and my fortress, I trust you will
lead me and guide me.
You are my refuge,
you will redeem me, O Lord, O faithful God.
You are my refuge and my strength,
and you are ever
present in my distress.
With you, I will not be afraid,
and I am confident that you will preserve me in time of
distress!

Short Prayer

Jesus help me to accept suffering
with love and resignation.

6

HOW SUFFERING ENTERED THE WORLD

Kabir Das, a medieval Indian poet,[1] in his efforts to elaborate on a new religious synthesis of Indian religions, has left us some precious moral gems: "A drop of rain remained pure and unsoiled until it fell and came into contact with earth. At that very moment, it became a speck of mud. Man also is pure in his beginnings, but the company of evil people contaminates him."[2] This simile reminds us of the beauty and purity of the first souls, Adam and Eve, when they came from the hands of God, and of their tragic change when they turned against God yielding to temptation. That was the moment when paradise was lost and suffering entered the world.

The Happy State of Adam and Eve

*"God looked at everything he had made,
and he found it very good."* [3]

It was not God but Adam and Eve who through their sin caused suffering to enter the world. To understand the meaning of this event, it is necessary to recall how it all happened.

The story of the "fall of man," that is, original sin, is clearly told in Chapter Three of the Book of Genesis. The *Catechism* says that in this narrative, the Bible "uses figura-

---

[1] Born in Benares, India, c.1398. He lived to be 119 years old. His life was dedicated to the search of spiritual truths.

[2] Ravasi, p. 196

[3] Genesis 1:31

tive language, but affirms a primeval event, a deed that took place *at the beginning of the history of man.*" [4] The Bible gives us the basic elements of man's rejection of God and the tragic consequences that followed. The details mentioned in the Bible (such as the tree and the snake) are symbolic.[5] What is clear is that at the suggestion of the devil our first parents *chose* to do what they wanted and consciously acted in full disregard for God's will. They did exactly what he had told them *not* to do. Fascinated by the promises of the devil they forgot God's love for them and disobeyed him. Thus, humanity is forever marked by this original act of disobedience committed by our first parents of their own free will.[6]

The fall of man and the redemption of mankind by Jesus are the *cornerstones on which Christianity is built.* The Bible tells us of God's love in creating Adam and Eve, the blessings he bestowed on them, their ingratitude, their pride and their disobedience which brought suffering into the world. Along with man's sin, however, the Bible also tells us how God took the initiative in forgiving us by promising a future Savior.[7]

Anatomy of Original Sin

The sequence of events that destroyed Adam and Eve's happiness and brought suffering into the world is relatively simple. God, being love, itself, and acting out of love, created mankind out of nothingness in the persons of

---

[4] CCC #390 Cf. *GS* 13 § 1.

[5] Many people believe that original sin was a sexual act. This is totally incorrect.

[6] Cf. CCC #390.

[7] Genesis 3:15

Adam and Eve in order *to share his eternal happiness with them*[8] and all future people on earth. For this reason, he gave them (and their children and all their descendants) an immortal soul made to his own image, and thus created them as spiritual and intelligent creatures. He bestowed on Adam and Eve the spiritual privilege of sharing in his own divine life and thus made them his own children. Furthermore, he added countless gifts that made their lives in the garden of Eden a most pleasant time. After a period of such life, they would pass from earth to heaven to enjoy eternal happiness with him in an endless circle of love.

However, because love cannot be commanded and it cannot exist unless it is freely given, God did not program his creatures like mechanical robots. Rather, he gave them a free will, the option to accept or reject his love. He warned them of the consequences of a wrong choice and told them: *"You are free to eat from any of the trees of the garden, except the tree of knowledge of good and bad. From that tree you shall not eat.. The moment you eat from it, you are surely doomed to die."* [9] In three short paragraphs, the *Catechism* explains the Biblical story of creation and the fall of man:

"God created man in his image and established him in his friendship. A spiritual creature, man can live this friendship only in free submission to God. The prohibition against eating 'of the tree of the knowledge of good and evil' spells out this: 'for in the day that you eat of it, you shall die.' The tree of knowledge of good and evil symbolically evokes the insurmountable limits that man, being a creature,

---

[8] Theologians say, "Amor est diffusivum sui," a Latin expression that beautifully and concisely defines that specific quality of love to reach out and to share with others.

[9] Genesis 2:15-17

must freely recognize and respect with trust. Man is dependent on the Creator and subject to the laws of creation and to the moral norms that govern the use of freedom.

Man's first sin was the result of the devil's temptation. He let his love for God die in his heart, and abusing his freedom, he disobeyed God. Thus, all human sins consist of a disobedience toward God and lack of trust in his goodness.

Through that sin, man preferred himself to God and scorned him by that very act. Man chose himself over God and, therefore, against his own good. Created in a state of friendship, man was destined to be like God. "Seduced by the devil, he wanted to 'be like God' but 'without God, before God, and not in accordance with God.' (St. Maximus the Confessor, *Ambigua*: PG 91, 1156; cf. *Gen* 3:5)" [10]

The traditional language of the Bible, of theologians, and of the *Catechism* uses the words "submission," "trust," "creaturely state," "command," "disobedience," and so on. But the core of the story of creation, of the Fall, and of our relationship with God is basically a matter of *love*. Adam and Eve liked the suggestion of the devil, and attracted by its glamour, they forgot God's love for them and the blessings he had bestowed on them. In plain language, *love for self* prevailed *over love for God*. They thought only of satisfying their impulse and 'doing their own thing.' By rejecting God they rejected heaven and chose death over life. Their sin, like our sins and the sins of all mankind, are a *"failure in genuine love."* [11]

---

[10] CCC #398.
[11] CCC #1849

The Consequences of the Fall: Suffering and Death

To better appreciate the tragic consequences of original sin, we must first be aware of the magnitude of the blessings and privileges God had bestowed on Adam and Eve in the garden of Eden. The *Catechism* describes their situation beautifully under the title, *Man in Paradise,* which I paraphrase here in simpler language.

The first man and woman were directly created by God. They enjoyed a special kind of friendship with him, and possessed a perfect harmony within themselves and with all the other creatures around them. This traditional doctrine is based on the interpretation of the true meaning of the symbolic language used in the Bible as we understand it in the light of Jesus' revelation and of the writings of St. Paul.

Our first parents were created in an original state of holiness, that is, as spiritual and intelligent creatures, and they shared in the divine and spiritual nature of their Creator. They truly were his *children.* This special gift of friendship and of sharing in God's life, (that is, *grace,)* gave them happiness, peace, and harmony. As long as they remained in this divine intimacy they would not know suffering or death.

The inner harmony within their human person, the harmony between the sexes, and finally the harmony between them and creation, comprised what we call the state of original *holiness.* They were free from any interior struggle in the mastery of self because they were free from *'carnal allurements, enticements for the eye, and the life of empty show.'* [12] This means they were free from craving the

---

[12] 1 John 2:16

illicit pleasures of the flesh, from the covetousness for earthly goods, and from human pride. They enjoyed familiarity with God and knew nothing of the misery, the despair, the inner struggle to resist temptation which is now our daily fare.[13]

This beautiful plan of God, this paradise that God had so lovingly and tenderly prepared for Adam and Eve, and *for us,* was lost forever by their catastrophic rebellion. As a result, they suffered the tragic consequences of rejecting God. His forewarning was to no avail.

While re-reading and reflecting on God's words of condemnation of Adam and Eve, we must remember that it was they who rejected the benefits he had bestowed on them. *"To the woman he said: 'In pain you will bring forth children.' To the man he said: 'By the sweat of your brow you will get bread to eat until you return to the ground from which you were taken for you are dust and to dust you shall return.' "*[14]

This judicial sentence meant that even though they had been created to fully share in the glory and happiness of God, now having preferred themselves to him and having believed the devil's lies, they had lost God's fatherhood, his friendship, and his gifts. As a result, they began to experience fear of God and their minds were confused. They conceived a distorted idea of him -- that of a God vengeful and jealous of his rights. With original sin, "death makes its entrance into human history." [15] So did suffering.

Peter Kreeft explains the tragic consequences of original sin by way of a similitude. Imagine "a chain of three iron rings suspended from a magnet. The magnet

---

[13] Cf. CCC #374-379.
[14] Genesis 3:16,18
[15] CCC #400 (Cf. *Rom* 5:12).

represents God, the source of all life. Magnetism represents life. The three rings represent the soul, the body and the world, or nature. When the first ring is attached to the magnet (when man's soul is in a state of friendship with God), the whole chain is magnetized together (there is harmony). But once Adam declares his independence from God (sin), the whole chain falls apart -- death (the alienation between soul and body), and suffering (the alienation between body and world), necessarily follow, and the end result is the alienation between soul and God.

"All three evils, sin and death and suffering, are originated by us, not by God, from our misuse of our free will, from our disobedience. We started it!" [16]

Original Sin and Us

"*Why should we be punished for the sin of Adam and Eve?*" This question, often asked, needs an answer and an explanation. In order to better understand how original sin affects us personally, I will paraphrase here the *Catechism's* description of the effects of original sin on the human race:

How does the sin of Adam become the sin of the whole human race? Because of Adam's privileged position as the *father of all mankind*, the whole human race was in him *as in one body*. So, in a certain sense, we were all implicated in his sin. Of course, the transmission of original sin is a mystery, and we cannot understand it completely. By Divine Revelation, however, we do know that the state of

---

[16] From *Making Sense Out of Suffering* © 1986 by Peter Kreeft. Publ'd by Servant Publications, Box 8617, Ann Arbor, MI 48107, pp.106-107. Used with permission.

special holiness in which Adam had been created was not meant for himself, alone, but for all mankind. By yielding to the temptation of the devil, Adam and Eve committed a *personal* sin that deprived them of the special state of holiness in which they had been created. Therefore, they could no longer hand down to their children the original good nature they had received from God in its integrity, only the *fallen* one -- a nature deprived of the special gifts of holiness and *grace* they had received. Thus, original sin is a *sin* that is transmitted to all mankind as it propagates all over the world. But please note: it is called a *sin* only in an analogical sense (because of its similarity to a personal sin). It is a sin *contracted*, not *committed* -- that is, a *state*, not an *act*, or much less, a *personal fault*.

In simpler terms, *original sin* is a deprivation of the original state of holiness and of the other gifts given to our first parents. Such deprivation did not corrupt our human nature entirely, but it *wounded* its natural powers and, therefore, subjected us "to ignorance, suffering, and the dominion of death, and...an inclination to evil..." [17]

It is because of the defective human nature we inherit that we are called to spiritual battle to overcome the effects of original sin. Our first parents gambled away the family's fortune. So it is through no fault on our part, we are born spiritually poor with a weak body open to sickness and a soul which is no longer in a state of friendship with God.

Why did the Lord allow this to happen? Because he respected the free will of his creatures and refused to force them to love him. However, in his divine mercy, he created a plan of salvation that in the end would turn this disaster

---

[17] CCC #405

to our good. Why didn't God prevent Adam and Eve from sinning? St. Leo the Great replies: "Christ's inexpressible grace gave us blessings better than those the demon's envy had taken away." (Cf. St. Leo the Great, *Sermo* 73,4:PL 54, 396.) St. Thomas Aquinas explains: "There is nothing to prevent human nature's being raised up to something greater, even after sin; God permits evil in order to draw forth some greater good. Thus St. Paul says: 'Where sin increased, grace abounded all the more'; and the Exultet sings, 'O happy fault,...which gained for us so great a Redeemer.' " (St. Thomas Aquinas, *STh III*, 1, 3, *ad* 3; cf. *Rom* 5:20.)[18]

How Relevant is All This to Me?

The history of the fall of man is the history of the beginning of the human race. It tells us *who* we are, *what* we are, and *why* we are what we are. It explains the beginning of temptations and human suffering, of our joys, our hopes, our desire for eternal happiness. This knowledge will help us in our daily struggle to bear sufferings and temptations.

I am writing for those who live an average life with its highs and lows and its alternating joys and sorrows. For those who are honestly seeking from God an explanation of "*Why?*" for their personal sufferings and the sufferings of the world. If we abandon ourselves to the fleeting emotions of joy or sorrow and forget to seek a rational approach based on our faith to our problems, we may end up denying the very existence of God or harboring a grudging resentment and a senseless anger against him -- and that means living in bitterness and near despair.

---

[18] Cf. CCC #412.

If, on the other hand, we build up a sound, rational foundation for our religious beliefs -- especially for the problem of suffering -- and if we learn to solve our problems and difficulties in a spirit of love for God, then even in the most crucial crises in our lives we will be ready to turn to him with confidence, and we will benefit by his help.

The clearer and deeper our knowledge of God's love for us and of the meaning of suffering, the easier it will be for us to accept God's will and to change our suffering into an instrument of good. The greater our knowledge of God and of his loving plan of salvation, the greater our love will be.

Personal Reflection

Does not my experience confirm what the Bible teaches about sin? I am often drawn toward a multitude of things that are morally wrong. Such desires certainly do not come from my Creator. Do I choose God or my personal pleasure? Have I forgotten what Jesus has done for me? I have scorned him and, like Adam and Eve, *I preferred to do my own thing.* But Jesus has not abandoned me. I feel in my conscience that he is always wanting me to do better, to make up for my past ingratitude and that he still loves me with his wonderful, forgiving, understanding love. If I do not want to be a monster of ingratitude, I must seriously endeavor to love Jesus much more than I do now. I must love Jesus above all else, focus my whole life on him, and reject whatever is against his will and harmful to my soul.

P R A Y E R
(By John Henry Cardinal Newman)

God has created me to do Him some definite service; he has committed some work to me which He has not committed to another. I have my mission. I may never know it in this life, but I shall be told it in the next. I am a link in a chain, a bond of connection between persons. He has not created me for nought. I shall do good, I shall do His work, I shall be a preacher of truth in my own place, while not intending it, if I do but keep His commandments and serve Him in my calling. Therefore, my God, I will put myself without reserve in your hands. What have I in heaven, and apart from you, what do I want on earth? My flesh and my heart fail, but God is the God of my heart, and my portion forever.[19]

Short Prayer

Jesus help me to love you always.

---

[19] *A Newman Prayer Book,* p.4

7

THE SUFFERINGS OF JESUS AND THE MYSTERY OF THE CROSS

The Suffering Servant of God

"Did not the Messiah have to undergo all this (suffering) so as to enter into his glory?" [1]

"If a man endures suffering all alone, the pain remains in him alone. But if another man looks at him and says, 'Brother, you are truly suffering a lot!' he becomes involved in the suffering of his friend through his eyes. If he is blind, through his ears. If he is deaf, through his hands. And if the other is far away and cannot touch him, see him, hear him, then he can guess it. This is what the Just One does: He absorbs all the evil that exists on earth and takes it into his own heart." [2] This is what Jesus did for us.

The above quotation is from a novel entitled, *"The Last of the Just Men,"* by Andre' Schuartz Bart, a French-born Jewish author, published in France in 1959. The theme of the novel is based on an old Jewish tradition that claims that the world rests on thirty-six just men who, from generation to generation, bear in themselves all the sufferings of humanity. These thirty-six just men constitute the expanded

---

[1] Luke 24:25
[2] Ravasi, p. 59.

heart of the world into which all our sufferings are poured as if into a receptacle.[3]

The background of this novel is in perfect harmony with the mysterious biblical figure of the Suffering Servant of God described by Isaiah: *"It was our infirmities that he bore, our sufferings that he endured. While we thought him as stricken, one smitten by God and afflicted, he was pierced for our offenses, crushed for our sins. Upon him was the chastisement that makes us whole, by his stripes we were healed."* [4]

For us Christians, the Suffering Servant described by Isaiah is Jesus who takes the sin of Adam and Eve, and all the sins of the world, upon his shoulders and volunteers to suffer to atone for them.

The Problem

In Chapter Five we have seen the universality of suffering that affects every human being from birth to death, in every society, through all time, after Adam's fall. We have also seen that human nature is always reluctant to suffer and that many people rebel against God because of suffering and fail to see him as their loving Father. We have also seen that suffering entered the world because of the sin of our first parents. These truths pose a problem that we must endeavor to understand in order to reconcile the reality of suffering with God's circle of love for mankind.

The problem is this: We believe in *the infinite goodness of God*, and at the same time, in *the presence of cruel sufferings in the world*. Superficially, it seems these two

---

[3] Ravasi, p. 59.
[4] Isaiah 53:4-5

beliefs contradict each other. How can an infinitely loving, all-powerful and all-knowing God create a world such as ours, with its tremendous injustices, its terrific cruelties, its endless physical, spiritual, intellectual, and moral sufferings? If we believe in the caring, loving God of the Judeo-Christian tradition, then we must also believe that the two beliefs do not contradict each other. But how can we reconcile them?

The Meaning of Suffering and Evil

What is the real meaning of *evil* and *suffering?* Evil has no simple definition that covers all its meanings and that is accepted by all. Evil can be many different things to different people. Basically, it is the opposite of "good" at all levels -- physical, moral, intellectual, spiritual. Evil is always something, either physical or moral, that is a source of suffering, harm, misfortune, destruction. *Moral evil* is something against the law of God, against the law of nature, and against the good of people -- something characterized by malice. *Spiritual evil* is something that adversely affects the ultimate good of the soul, our growth to maturity, and our love-relationship with God. *Suffering* can be physical, spiritual, intellectual, or emotional. It means the bearing of pain or distress and is the result of a physical or moral evil.

The problem is to reconcile the reality of suffering with God's love for us? Needless to say, from the beginning of its existence humanity has tried to explain away the problem of evil and suffering. Every culture, every religion, every philosophical school, even poets and writers have attempted to give some kind of explanation. Here, we will concentrate on understanding the solution offered by Christianity to our problem. This requires us to go back to square one: the consequences of original sin.

God Did Not Abandon Us After the Fall

Using anthropomorphic[5] language, we may say that after original sin God had three choices regarding us. Being all-perfect and, therefore, infinitely loving, just, and merciful, he had to find a solution which would reconcile both his justice and his mercy. *One solution* might have been to tell Adam and Eve: *"Sorry, I told you not to eat the fruit of that tree, but you willfully ignored my love for you and all I have done for you. You have brought upon yourselves the penalty for rejecting my love. As I warned you, you and your descendants will suffer and die. You shall never enter heaven. Depart from me for all eternity."* While man deserved this sentence, God's mercy and love would never consider it.

God's *second solution* would have been to tell Adam and Eve: *"I know you are poor creatures and you have been duped by Satan, so I forgive you. Let's forget what has happened. You can start all over again, and your children will inherit all the gifts and privileges I have given you."* This would have been splendid for us, but certainly not in accord with God's infinite justice, and it might even have encouraged mankind to do worse.

The *third solution* was to offer a *compromise*, and this is what God chose to do. Stated briefly, and remembering that we are using anthropomorphic language to explain God's profound mysteries, we might put it in the following way: God, himself, took the initiative to reconcile man to himself and devised an original and unique plan for our eternal salvation -- the Second Person would assume our human nature and become a human being, though retaining

---

[5] *Anthropomorphic* language attributes to God *human qualities.* This is the language of the Old and New Testaments, which speak of God as having a human body and human feelings.

his full divinity as the Second Person of the Trinity. As a man and being equal to us in everything except sin, he would take all the sins of humanity on himself; and by atoning for them through his sufferings, he would offer adequate reparation to God. Thus, God, would forgive our sins, grant us again the privilege of sharing in his life as true children; would re-open the gates of heaven to us and accept us again as members of his family.

Thus, the death and resurrection of Jesus constitutes a supreme act of love that only an infinitely loving God could conceive and implement. And so, as Isaiah prophesied: *"Through his wounds we were healed."* [6]

The Death of Jesus on the Cross: A Scene of Death and Life

It is shortly after the noon hour on Good Friday in Jerusalem in the year 33 AD. Just outside the city walls, on the barren hill of Calvary, three crosses stand against a dark and threatening sky. Three condemned men hang on them, about to die. A rabble-rousing mob moves around the central cross jeering and laughing at the dying man hanging upon it. A few women and one man stand at the foot of that center cross; one is the mother of the man hanging there. She and the others are crushed with sorrow; their faces show their anguish. They weep quietly. On the cross is a sign with an ironic inscription: *"This is the King of the Jews."* [7]

It is truly a macabre scene. Humanly speaking, it is a scene of tragedy and death. But is it really so? In the

---

[6] Isaiah 53:4
[7] Luke 23:38

eyes of God, this scene is *the* central and most important moment in the entire history of mankind. It is the triumph of love over evil, of life over death. Who are these three criminals? Why are they dying? What horrible crimes have they committed? The answers to these questions will give us a glimpse into the mystery of suffering and redemption.

The Cross in the Center

Who is the man hanging on the cross in the center? He is none other than the **Son of God made man.** He is the most fascinating, the most innocent, the most powerful and holiest man who ever walked the earth. A king trembled when he was born, yet humble shepherds came to worship him and wise men, guided by a star, came to adore him.

He is only thirty-three years old and has spent less than three years as an itinerant rabbi dedicated to doing good to others. He has given countless signs of his extraordinary power. With only a word he calmed the winds and storms at sea; he cured countless sick people; he made the blind to see and the lame to walk; he raised dead peoples from death; he inspired crowds to follow him; he moved sinners to repentance; he preached conversion and repentance, and above all love for one another. If he had wanted, he could have stepped down from the cross and wiped out all his enemies. But no, though the crowd taunted him, he did not do so. He chose to die on the cross because he had a job to complete and wanted to see it through; he wanted to prove to men that he was indeed the Son of God who had come to save them.

Rather than descending from the cross while still alive, he chose to die and later rise from the dead by his own power three days after his burial. Now, though he is the victim of the greatest miscarriage of justice the world has ever seen, he accepts death to save all men, even his killers.

Jesus' life on earth ended in apparent failure, and he died as a criminal. But his sufferings saved mankind from eternal ruin. He died because of LOVE -- love for people -- for all people -- those who have gone, those living now, those yet to be born ...people of all ages, race, color, and religion ...for you, even me. What did he accomplish? Through his sufferings and death he obtained from the Father the forgiveness of our sins; he opened again the doors of heaven and made possible eternal happiness for us. In order to win our love, he gave us the greatest proof anyone can ever expect: *"There is no greater love than this: to lay down one's life for one's friend."* [8] He did just that.

The Cross of the Bad Thief

Tradition calls him the "bad thief," and we have no other name for him. How bad he actually was is not for us to judge. He was probably a hardened criminal, and his attitude on Calvary certainly leaves much to be desired. He appeared to be one of those hard-hearted characters who lost all sense of understanding and compassion for others. His inner world was limited to his own little self. He lacked the most elementary humility; he didn't have even a spark of compassion for Jesus. As he turned to Jesus, his words were full of pride, arrogance, and selfishness: *"Aren't you the Messiah?"* he asked. But he had no faith. He was just baiting the jeering crowd; and like them, he was sarcastic. He continued speaking to Jesus: *"Save yourself and us!"* He was not concerned with Jesus' welfare, only with himself; he

---

[8] John 15:13

thought only of enjoying the admiration of the heartless mob. He was beyond hope. He hung right beside the Savior, but he was oblivious to the love shining in Jesus' eyes.

The Cross of the Good Thief

Dismas is the name that legend has given the "good thief" who died on Calvary. Someone once wrote of him: "He was a thief all his life right to the end -- he even stole heaven!" [9]

Reflect for a moment. This man was a criminal, a murderer like his companion on the other cross. He lead a sinful life and made other people suffer a great deal. Now he was paying with his life for his crimes. However, hearing his crucified partner in crime joining the mob in jeering Jesus, he came to Jesus' defense and openly condemned his friend: *"Have you no fear of the Lord at all, seeing you are under the same sentence? We deserve it after all. We are only paying the price for what we have done, but this man has done nothing."* [10]

He had a good heart; he felt compassion for Jesus and came to his defense. He recognized his own sinfulness; he humbled himself and found in his hardened heart a remnant of love and compassion for his innocent, crucified companion. Softly, he said to Jesus: *"Lord, remember me when You come into Your Kingdom."* [11] There was love, repentance and humility in his words.

Jesus' prompt forgiveness was total and absolute: *"Today you will be with me in paradise!"* [12] A few hours

---

[9] I am quoting from memory.
[10] Luke 24:40-42
[11] Matthew 37:24
[12] Ibid.

later, the good thief died with a bright vision of paradise in his mind as his mortal eyes closed to the light of this world. The bad thief died with darkness and despair in his soul because he had no love for others and failed to see the love of God for himself.

The Meaning of The Three Crosses

Here, we have three men with something in common: they are dying the same kind of death and undergoing intense physical and mental pain. But the similarity ends there. The consequences of their sufferings and of their spiritual attitudes are poles apart.

The bad thief remained proud to the end. He failed to repent for his sins and to accept death as an act of reparation. He had no humility and was only concerned with his own egotistical, little world. **It seems that his sufferings were of no good to him or to others.**

The good thief accepted his sufferings and death with humility. Recognizing his sins, he asked the Lord for mercy, and mercy he received in abundance. As he breathed his last, he soon entered into an everlasting life of happiness. **His sufferings, accepted with humility, were his gateway to Heaven.**

Jesus, who had no sin and had freely accepted to die on the Cross for love of others, accepted his painful death with perfect resignation to the Father's will. In his immense love for all, he died asking forgiveness for all, even his killers. **His sufferings, endured for others, saved the world.**

The three crosses on Calvary teach a most important and vital lesson: Suffering, accepted with love and humility for the sake of God, obtains forgiveness of sins for oneself and for others. In contrast, rebelling against God does not alleviate our pain; it leaves us in darkness, despair, and in hopeless stoicism; it is of no good to oneself or to others.

Calvary is really the beacon of light in the darkness leading us to the solution of our problem. **Suffering and evil can be changed into instruments of salvation for ourselves and for others.** Therefore, there is no contradiction between suffering and God's love for us. This is what St. John meant when he wrote: *"God so loved the world as to give his only son so that everyone who believes in him should not perish, but have everlasting life."* [13]

Personal Reflection

I close my eyes for a few moments and imagine that I am on Calvary at the foot of the cross on which Jesus is slowly dying. I see there Mary, John, and the little group of pious women. They fully share the sufferings of the Master. I am disgusted by the jeering, hostile crowd full of hatred, and by the crass remarks of the bad thief. I feel deep in my heart the awe of this moment. It is, indeed, the most important moment in the history of the world. I am moved to tears as I watch the slow death of Jesus, who has volunteered to die for the sins of the world. I know that I, too, am partly responsible for his death because my sins are on his shoulders. But there is a ray of light; the good thief asks for mercy, and mercy is granted him in abundance: he dies and goes to heaven. There is hope for me, too, here at the foot of the Cross: Jesus can forgive my sins and then my sufferings will be changed into instruments of good for my loved ones and for myself.

---

[13] John 3:6

PRAYER

With King David, I pray:

*"Have mercy on me, O God, in your goodness,
in your great tenderness, wipe away my faults,
wash me clean of my guilt, purify me of my sin.
For I am well aware of my faults,
I have my sin constantly in mind,
having sinned against none other than You,
having done what you regard as wrong."* [14]

Short Prayer

Have mercy on me, O Lord, my God, have mercy.

---

[14] Psalm 50

8

JESUS IS THE ANSWER
TO OUR PROBLEM OF SUFFERING

From Darkness to Light

Austrian-born poet Nedda Falzoleher (1906-1956) was stricken by polio as a child and spent fifty years of her life in a wheelchair. Through her teens and early adult years she was in such a state of depression that she wanted to be called "Nil," "nothing." But from the depths of despair and self-pity she began to open her soul to the world, then to others and, finally, to the light of God. Desperation gave way to light, and in her poems she sang of life as fascinating, even though living within a kind of prison to which she had been confined.

Slowly the idea of a mission matured in her -- the mission of the total offering of herself and her pains to God. In a beautiful poem entitled "Innocence," she sings of the power of love that flavors the confusing reality of everyday living, making sense even of death as it breathes life out of a tomb, and giving a greater splendor to the beauty of the heavens. With this vision in her mind, she walked the tortuous road of life and changed sufferings to blessings.[1]

Jesus' Physical Sufferings

Before we draw the final conclusion about reconciling suffering and God's care for us, let us further meditate on the sufferings of Jesus. His sufferings were not confined to

---

[1] Summarized from Ravasi, 92.

the last twenty-four hours of his life on earth. We must keep in mind that Jesus had two natures, human and divine; but he was one *person, the Son of God made man,* combining in himself divinity and humanity. It was because of this union that he had a perfect knowledge of who he was and of what he had to suffer. His sufferings began at the very moment of his incarnation and continued with varied intensity until he died on the Cross. Jesus' pain covered the whole range of human suffering -- physical, moral, emotional, intellectual, spiritual.[2]

Let's consider first his physical sufferings. He endured in his body all the discomforts of poverty and the hardships of ordinary life ...the growing pains of childhood, the routine of daily work, fatigue, famine and thirst, the discomfort of long journeys, endless hours of prayer on his knees night and day, the lack of rest as he was pursued by crowds interested only in his favors. Many spiritual writers believe that Jesus' pains were magnified by the fact that his perfect body, unstained by original sin was more sensitive to pain than that of ordinary mortals.

The last twenty-four hours of his life remain, probably, unparalleled for the atrocity of the spiritual and physical pain he endured. His body was tortured as he was tied up like a criminal in the garden of Gethsemane and from there, shuffled to the courts of Annas, Caiphas, Herod, and Pontius Pilate. The scourging was particularly severe because the soldiers inflicted on him the Roman type of

---

[2] Today, some liberal theologians hold the view that Jesus did not know who he was until late in his life, but the centuries-old, orthodox view handed down to us in the Gospels is that he always knew who he was.

scourging which placed no limits on the number of strokes.[3] It was the punishment reserved for rebellious slaves and murderers. This scourging all but exhausted the power of resistance of his delicate and sensitive body; it drained him of all strength as the skin on his back became a vast, painful, bleeding wound. As if all this were not enough, he had to endure the crowning with thorns. This was accompanied by the mockery of ignorant, foreign soldiers. They made a laughing stock of him, spat on his face, mocked him as the king of the Jews, and kept hitting the crown of thorns with a reed, thus driving them deeper into the skin on his head. Then came the long journey to Calvary, the terrific pain of the crucifixion as the nails pierced his hands and feet, and three excruciating hours of agony hanging from the cross. Each movement caused more pain while his blood flowed slowly to the ground and life ebbed away.

All through his life, and especially during the years of his ministry, Jesus had this harrowing picture constantly in mind, making his life one of continuous suffering. This is why he said: *"I have a baptism to receive. What anguish I feel till it is over."* [4] He was speaking of his own baptism of blood, the sufferings he had to endure to offer his Father the perfect *sacrifice* for the redemption of us all.

Mental and Spiritual Sufferings

Probably, Jesus' physical sufferings, even though ever present in his mind, represented only the least part of his sufferings. Through his entire life he suffered mentally, emotionally, and spiritually. As God, he saw events down

---

[3] In contrast, a Jewish scourging was limited to 40 strokes, but no more than 39 were administered for fear of breaking the Law.

[4] Luke 12:50

through the centuries, from the beginning to the end of the world. He saw people's ingratitude, he saw each and every one of our sins -- all the sins of humanity. His heart was wounded by our sheer ingratitude, our blindness to his love, our scorn, our perennial indifference to his appeals for love.

Throughout his life he heard the shouts of the crowd: *"Crucify him, crucify him!"* [5] Only God knows how many times he repeated the words of Psalm 69: *"Insult has broken my heart, and I am weak; I looked for sympathy, but there was none; for comforters, and I found none. Rather, they put gall in my food, and in my thirst they gave me vinegar to drink."* [6]

Rejection by his own people caused him agonizing spiritual pain. Imagine what he felt in his loving heart when his people chose Barabbas, the murderer, over him! Imagine how he felt when he was sentenced to death by the high priest, Caiphas, for telling the truth -- that he *was* the Son of God. Can we fathom the sufferings of his heart when he heard the howling of the crowd rejecting him as the promised Messiah? Or, when he heard the head of the Sanhedrin, the supreme religious authority of his country, proclaiming: *"We have no king but Caesar!"* [7] a pagan and a gentile? Again, when in their blind furor the blind religious leaders of Israel cried out: *"Let his blood be on us and on our children."* [8] With these words they abdicated their status as the chosen people of God.

All through his life Jesus suffered from his foresight of the indifference and ingratitude with which mankind would repay his love through the centuries to come. It was

---

[5] John 19:15
[6] Psalm 69:21-22
[7] Luke 19:16
[8] Matthew 27:25

this terrible, heavy feeling in his heart that made him sweat blood in the garden of Gethsemane. He felt in his soul the crushing weight of all the sins committed by people throughout all time because God *"made him who did not know sin, to be sin, so that in him we might become the very holiness of God."* [9]

Sentencing Jesus to death was an especially heinous crime and one of the greatest moral and legal injustices ever committed against an innocent man. They condemned him to death by using a political pretext[10] and because he had unmasked their hypocrisy. They were afraid to loose their prestigious positions and their personal income from the Temple's commercial activities.[11]   And yet, Jesus died praying for his enemies. Who else was ever so clean of any sin as Jesus was and suffered so much for the sins of others as Jesus did? Keep in mind that when we think of him suffering on the cross, we see only the tip of the iceberg, the culminating point of the cruel sufferings he endured throughout his lifetime.

Why Did Jesus Have to Suffer?

Several times throughout his public life Jesus said it was necessary for him to suffer and to die for the salvation

---

[9] 2 Corinthians 5:21. Romans 8:3. CCC #620.

[10] The pretext of avoiding trouble with Rome. They wilfully ignored that Jesus had taught his apostle: *"Give to Caesar what is Caesar's and to God what is God's."*

[11] Many of the Sanhedrin members were involved in the huge trading business of supplying animals for the daily sacrifices and other ventures. This is why they became very resentful when Jesus chased the merchants out of the Temple area. See Matthew 21:12.

of the world.   After the resurrection, he told the two disciples on the road to Emmaus: *"What little sense you have!   How slow you are to believe all the prophets have written about me.   Was it not ordained that the Messiah must undergo all this* (his suffering and death) *so as to enter into his glory?   Then, beginning with Moses and all the prophets, he interpreted for them every passage of the scripture which referred to him."* [12]

Here, Jesus states clearly that what was written in the Old Testament about the "Suffering Servant of God," especially in Isaiah, was actually written about him and that it was *necessary* for him to endure such excruciating pain in order to achieve the salvation of the world.

But, *why was it really necessary for Jesus to suffer?* Could not God find some other way to forgive humankind without making Jesus suffer?   These questions are all part of the mystery of our salvation, of suffering and redemption, and mysteries are beyond the boundaries of our human intelligence.   In front of a mystery we can only bow our head in humility and accept it in faith.   This does not mean abdicating our reason but simply recognizing that as human beings we have a limited intelligence, especially about spiritual matters.   Even though we cannot understand the ultimate **why** of the necessity for Jesus to suffer[13], what is really important for us to appreciate is that *"by his stripes* (sufferings) *we were healed."* [14]

Therefore, we must be grateful to God for helping us to understand that *love* and *suffering* not only can co-exist, but through Jesus' suffering they become an instrument of spiritual good.

---

[12] Luke 24:25-27

[13] As he told the disciples of Emmaus, Luke 24:26

[14] Isaiah 53:6

Nature and History Confirm
Jesus' Teachings on Suffering

To help us understand the mystery of the Cross, God, when creating the world, placed in nature many examples of how love and suffering can co-exist here on earth and of the good that comes from this co-existence. Perhaps, the most beautiful example of this truth is that of a mother suffering to bring a child into the world, and of her happiness in nurturing the creature of her womb.

In our daily lives, we can see many examples of the link between love and suffering -- a surgeon causes a patient to suffer but only to return that person to good health. To enjoy good health, we have to make sacrifices and abstain from many enjoyable but otherwise harmful activities.

In the Bible there are numerous examples of great social and personal benefits that came through suffering. The stories of Joseph, Tobit, Judith, and Esther are classic examples that illustrate this truth. The story of Joseph, son of the patriarch Jacob who lived around year 1630 B.C., is worth repeating.

Young Joseph was Jacob's favorite son causing a great deal of jealousy among his brothers. And out of jealousy, they decided to kill him. At the last moment, though, instead of killing him, they sold Joseph as a slave to a caravan of Egyptians who took him to Egypt. The envious brothers told Jacob that Joseph had been killed by a wild animal and even showed him the young man's tunic stained with blood. Jacob was heart-broken and deeply grieved his supposedly dead son.

Meanwhile, Joseph was experiencing great hardships in Egypt. As a slave, he was mistreated, cheated and finally framed and sent to jail. It seemed as though his life were at an end. One day, however, he was called to interpret a dream of the reigning Pharaoh. He was so successful in his interpretation that the Pharaoh elevated him to the position of second in command, after himself, over all of Egypt. Guided by the Spirit of God, Joseph saved Egypt from a nation-wide famine. It was because of this famine that his brothers, ignorant of his fate, came to Egypt to beg for food. When they were brought before him, Joseph recognized them immediately, but he hid his feelings and gave no sign of recognition. Only much later did he reveal to them his identity. He then assured them that they were fully forgiven and should not be afraid of him because of the evil they had done to him. He told them that *"it was really for the sake of saving lives that God sent me here ahead of you."* [15]

The moral of the story is that through his painful ordeal Joseph saved the Hebrew people from being destroyed by starvation; and thus, four centuries later, they were able to establish their own nation under Moses.

This beautiful, moving story should be read in the book of Genesis in its entirety. [16]   It is one of the events God used to prepare his people to accept the idea of a suffering Messiah who would become the savior of his nation. Examples such as this teach us that according to God's design all physical and spiritual sufferings, whether caused by humans or by the blind forces of nature, can be turned to our spiritual advantage.

Whether or not it works out that way depends on how we accept our crosses. This is the law of nature and of God: *"Amen, amen, I say to you, unless a grain of wheat falls to the ground and dies, it remains just a grain of wheat; but if it dies, it produces much fruit."* [17]   All great saints, artists,

---

[15] Genesis 45:5
[16] Genesis, chapters 37-48.
[17] John 12:14

scientists, writers, poets suffer a great deal before they produce immortal works of art or leave lasting legacies to mankind. Moral and bodily sufferings *do* refine a person's spirituality, stimulating the mind to achieve great results.

Jesus is the Answer to Our Problem of Suffering

Long ago, in the Garden of Eden, evil triumphed over love, death over life. But on Calvary, love triumphed over evil, life over death. Jesus did give us an answer: *he himself is the answer.*[18] From all that we have read so far, it is clear that God has not left us in darkness about the mystery of suffering and love. He did not give us a theory but a *person, JESUS*, who accepted out of love his sufferings and death and thus accomplished the salvation of the world. His Resurrection and Ascension to heaven are the fulfillment of his promise to his apostles: *"Amen, amen I say to you, you will weep and mourn, while the world rejoices; you will grieve, but your grief will become joy."* [19]

In brief, even though we cannot completely understand the mystery of suffering, especially suffering being turned into an instrument of good, the Bible gives us a clear and satisfactory explanation of God's wonderful plan of redemption and eternal life for us. Summarizing all that has been said so far, we can conclude that:

1) *Suffering was not created by God;* it is the result of Adam's and Eve's lack of love and rejection of God.

---

[18] From *Making Sense Out of Suffering,* ⊘ 1986 by Peter Kreeft. Publ'd by Servant Publications, Box 8617, Ann Arbor, MI 48107 p.156. Used with permission.

[19] John 16:20

2) After the sin of Adam and Eve, *suffering has become an integral part of every human life.*

3) *Jesus, the God made man, took the sins of all humanity on his shoulders* and through his sufferings obtained forgiveness for us from the Father and restored God's friendship to us.

4) *Our sufferings, accepted for his love, can be transformed into a source of blessings, into an instrument of purification for ourselves and of spiritual good for others; they help us atone for our own sins and bring us closer to Jesus our Divine Model.*

5) *Sufferings help us to share in Jesus' mission of building God's kingdom of love on earth.*

Personal Reflection

The way of the Cross (suffering leading to the glory of the Resurrection) is the way that Jesus chose for himself on earth and through which he obtained our salvation. For me, too, there is no other way to return his love except by following him on his way to Calvary so that one day I may rise with him to eternal glory. He told us clearly: *"Whoever wants to follow me, must deny his very self, take up his cross each day and follow me."* [20]

It is clear that there is nothing more pleasing to God, or more profitable for our spiritual growth, than to humbly accept the trials and tribulations of life, our own limitations, the environment in which we live, the unpleasant people we have to put up with, occasional poor health, and death in the end. These are our trials and crosses.

---

[20] Luke 9:3

Accepting them is the way to show Jesus our personal love for him, to repay him for all the sufferings he endured for us, and to make our life meaningful.

P R A Y E R

O my Jesus, I look at you hanging from the Cross. You are enduring undescribable sufferings that defy imagination. I know that you are suffering for me and worse still, I know I am responsible, at least in part, for your sufferings.

Jesus, I am sorry for my sins. Give me the strength to humbly accept from your hands all the crosses of my life and to offer them to you as proof of my love and gratitude.

Short Prayer

Jesus, help me to accept my crosses for love of you as you have suffered so much for me.

9

THE FRUITS OF JESUS' SUFFERINGS
His Gifts to Us from the Cross

"O God, where are your armies to defeat the furious battalions of your enemies? I do not see the flashes of your lightning nor your awesome majesty before which mountains melt like wax. I only see tortured flesh, blood spurting because of violence and an infamous and cruel death, a cross, and a crown of thorns. Is this your arsenal, is this all that you have to overcome your enemies? A cross and a crown of thorns are the 'arsenal' Jesus used to win our love and to unite us to him for all eternity." [1]

In the last few chapters we have reflected on the sufferings of Jesus and have seen that he is **the** answer to the problem of reconciling the apparent conflict between suffering and God's fatherly love for us. Just as important is it to realize deep in our hearts how great are the blessings that Jesus won for us through his great sufferings. These blessings are *his gifts to us from the Cross*, and we must endeavor to understand their importance because they reveal to us the depth and immensity of his love.

FIRST GIFT
Forgiveness of Sin through a Ritual Sacrifice

The key to understanding the concept of our redemption through the sacrifice of the Cross is to comprehend the

---

[1] From a sermon by the famous French orator, J.B. Bossuet (1627-1704) of Maux, France.

meaning of a religious sacrifice. The word *sacrifice,* in the sense of willingly doing or enduring something *unpleasant* for a good purpose, is fairly common in our everyday vocabulary. However, not many Christians are familiar with the idea of sacrifice in the sense of a *ritual sacrifice,* that is *an official religious offering made according to the particular ceremonial rite of a specific religion.* Comprehending this idea in depth is of the utmost importance because this is the very core of Christianity, of the death of Jesus, and of our redemption. Understanding the basic idea of a **religious sacrifice** is the indispensable key that will open our minds to a fuller understanding of the love of God for us, the Mass and the Eucharist, and all the benefits brought to us by Jesus' death.

Scholars agree that the practice of making offerings to a deity in the form of religious sacrifices goes back to the very beginning of humanity and is common to many ancient religions. People used such religious offerings to convey to the deity in a concrete manner their feelings of reverence, their repentance, their desire for reparation, and their petitions for help in their needs.

According to the Bible, Cain and Abel were the first humans to offer a "sacrifice" to God. *"Abel became a keeper of flocks, and Cain a tiller of the soil. In the course of time Cain brought an offering to the Lord from the fruits of the soil, while Abel, for his part, brought out one of the best firstlings of his flock."*[2]

If we visualize Abel and Cain in their primitive lives, without any formal religion, without priesthood, and without temples or places of worship, we can easily understand their desire to communicate with God in some concrete way. So

---

[2] Genesis 4:2-4

they thought of offering to God the very best they had from their flocks and harvest as a token of submission, reverence, reparation, and petition. This offering was their way of expressing their love for God.

According to the Bible, throughout the centuries following the primitive offerings of Cain and Abel, the practice of offering ritual sacrifices continued to flourish among the Israelites. The establishment of the Jewish nation under Moses and their covenant with God expanded this practice even further. Religious leaders, under the influence of God's inspiration, organized these ritual offerings and developed very detailed guidelines and rules.

Fr. John L. McKenzie, S.J., gives a scholarly definition of Jewish ritual sacrifices: "Sacrifices *(that is religious offerings -- Editor's note)* can be descriptively defined in general as a material oblation made to the deity by means of a consecration and consumption of the thing offered."[3]

The Passover ritual as prescribed by Moses[4] to remind Israel of their liberation from slavery prefigured the Sacrifice of the Cross and our liberation from the slavery of sin. It is worth analyzing it in detail.

"Every one of your families... the offering of a sacrifice is not a personal affair but an act of worship by the family or a community

must procure for itself a lamb, a year old, a male, and without blemish... designation of the victim and its qualifications.

It shall be slaughtered... the victim must be sacrificed, that is killed *during the evening twilight...*as a religious ceremony.

---

[3] McKenzie, John L., S.J. *Dictionary of the Bible.* Collier Books, Macmillan Publishing Co. New York. 1965. p. 754.

[4] Exodus 12:1-13

They... the family and those present, *shall take some of its blood and apply it to the doorpost and the lintels of every house in which they partake of the lamb...* blood was seen by the Jews as synonymous with life.

They shall eat its roasted flesh... eating part of the victim symbolized communion with the deity.

On the same night I will go through Egypt executing...judgment on all the gods of Egypt...but seeing the blood (on your houses) *I will pass over you...no destructive blow will come upon you."* The fruit of this sacrifice was their salvation as they escaped from the slavery of Egypt to the freedom of the promised land.

Most scholars agree that the essential elements of any sacrifice are:

A *victim*, a living being, such as a domesticated animal, or the first fruits of the harvest, offered by the family or community as homage to the deity in place of the persons who made the offering;

A *purpose*, such as to obtain salvation from some impending dangers, or as act of reparation, adoration, or petition;

The *ritual* or specific ceremonial (rite) for the destruction[5] of the victim, according to the different types of sacrifice such as thanksgiving, reparation and others;

A *priest,* or a person designated by the head of the community;

Communion with the deity by means of a sacrificial banquet at which parts of the animal offered to the god were eaten as a token of friendship.[6]

---

[5] The correct term is "immolation."

[6] Animal lovers may object to the slaughtering of animals for religious purposes. However, we must keep in mind that in those days such animal sacrifices were the best way to provide meat to

It is very important to note that most Jewish sacrifices involved the shedding of blood. According to Fr. McKenzie: "The common symbolic element of all Old Testament sacrifices is the manipulation of blood. The (victim's) blood is sprinkled on the altar, or dashed at the base, or smeared."[7] In the Jewish mind, blood represented life, and the shedding of the blood of the victim was the symbolic offering of one's life through the life of the animal that was transmitted to the deity.[8] In simple language, in their minds the meaning of sacrifice was this: Through the ritual slaughtering of an animal, the people told God that they were sorry for their sins; they recognized they were worthy of death because of their sins; but since he was merciful and did not want them to die, they deprived themselves of something very valuable in their lives, such as one of their best animals, and offered its life to him as a symbol of their repentance, their atonement, or their humble request for help. According to many biblical scholars, in certain types of sacrifices the officiating priest placed his extended hands over the head of the victim as if symbolically transferring to

---

the community, an extraordinary luxury for the ordinary people in those days. Very often, only the fatty parts of the animal were burnt on the altar of sacrifice, while the meaty parts were reserved to be eaten by the people. Sacrifices were intended not only as religious rituals but also as occasions for celebrating a feast and eating meat. The human element of personal enjoyment was always present.

[7] John L. McKenzie, S.J., *Dictionary of the Bible*. Collier Books, Macmillan Publishing Co. New York. 1965 p. 755.

[8] To describe the exact meaning of the shedding of the blood in Jewish and non-Jewish sacrifices is a very complex scholarly task. What I give here is only one of the various modern opinions.

the animal the sins of the person or communities offering the sacrifice.

After the building of the Temple in Jerusalem was completed, all ritual sacrifices had to be offered there by the priests[9] designated for this task. The head of a family would take an animal from out of his flock or would buy it and bring it to the Temple, where the offering was made. The priest would then burn some minor parts of the sacrificed animal on the altar, take a portion for himself, and give back to the family the largest share of the meaty parts to be consumed at a festive meal.

Jesus' voluntary death on the cross was a real Jewish sacrifice: as the High Priest of humanity,[10] being God and man, he was at the same time the *priest* and the *victim;* his death, caused by the shedding of his blood, represented the actual *sacrifice* or offering of the victim; the *altar* was the cross, and the *purpose* was the atonement for the sins of all mankind.

I have mentioned in the previous chapter that Jesus restored our friendship with God through his death on the cross. Now I have to add that the way Jesus accomplished our reconciliation with God was done specifically by offering himself as the *perfect victim* in this unique *sacrifice.* It was a sacrifice of adoration, of atonement, and of petition offered for us and in our name by the only *victim* acceptable to the Father. All other Jewish sacrifices from the time of Abel and Cain to the death of Jesus were only figures and symbols of Jesus' true sacrifice. The sacrifice of Jesus was the true sacrifice that won salvation for all mankind. The *Catechism* summarizes it all in a few paragraphs:

---

[9] Members of the Jewish tribe of Levi.
[10] Hebrew 8:1

Jesus freely and voluntarily offered himself for our salvation.   During the Last Supper he symbolized this offering and made it truly present: *"This is my body to be given for you."* (Lk 22:19).

The work of Christ 's redemption is that he came *"to give his life as a ransom for many"* (Matt. 20:28), that is, *"he had loved his own...to the end"* (John 13:1), so they might be *"delivered from the futile way of life [their] fathers handed on to [them]"* (1 Peter 1:18).

By his obedience to the Father, *"accepting even death, death on a cross"* (Phil 2:8), Jesus fulfills the atoning mission of the suffering Servant who will *"justify many, and their guilt shall he bear"* (Isa 53:11; cf. Rom 5:19).[11]

SECOND GIFT
The New and Everlasting Covenant: An Alliance of Love

The word "covenant" is a key to understanding the depth of the love of Jesus in shedding his blood for us. The Greek word for covenant means a testament, not in the sense of a last will, but as an agreement, a pact, an alliance. This is why we divide the Bible into the Old and New Testament[12] meaning the Old and New Alliance. The Hebrew society was based on the idea of alliances. In the early days of the Jewish nation the practice of making a covenant (an alliance) of friendship between two States, two communities, or two individuals and ratifying it with the shedding of

---

[11] Cf. CCC #621, 622, 623.

[12] The word "testament" in the sense of a "last will and testament" is not often used in the Bible.

blood of slaughtered animals[13] was very popular among the various people of the Middle East surrounding Israel. God, himself, used the same basic idea and format to establish an alliance of love between himself and his beloved people Israel. He solemnly promised help and protection in exchange for their love to be shown through the keeping of his Commandments.[14]

So among the Jewish people a covenant with God became a divinely guaranteed promise of special help, guidance, and protection on the part of God if the people kept their share of the bargain. Through the thousands of years of recorded history in the Bible, God made several such covenants with the Jews -- with Abraham, Moses, David and others. However, the people always failed in their obligations and abandoned God's ways. God finally promised to make a new and everlasting covenant.[15] This covenant would be *new* in the sense that God would use a new format and make new promises; it would be *everlasting* because God would never cancel it.

This new alliance of love between God, in the person of Jesus, and us, his followers and disciples, was made and sealed once and for all on Calvary through the shedding of the most precious blood of Jesus instead of an animal's blood.

Jesus' covenant is not a generic pact of reciprocal love between God and mankind; it is above all a personal pact between Jesus and each human being. When Jesus at the Last Supper told his apostles, *"This cup is the new covenant in my blood, which will be shed for you"* and added,

---

[13] These animal sacrifices were primarily intended to feed the people on solemn occasions.

[14] Exodus, 34:18.

[15] Luke, 22:20

"Do this in memory of me," [16] he asked them and all Christians through future centuries to renew their personal alliance with him and to make it their own. When we attend Mass, (the re-enactment of the Sacrifice of the Cross), Jesus reminds each of us of this personal alliance of love sealed in his blood on Calvary.

In the next chapter I will write more on the Mass as an alliance with Jesus. Here, I only wish to emphasize the meaning of the word *covenant* within the context of the Gospel: Jesus's gift from the cross establishing a personal alliance of love with each one of us.

THIRD GIFT
Restoration of God's Life to Our Souls and Forgiveness of Sins

Through his Sacrifice on the Cross Jesus not only offered a sacrifice of reparation to God and established a new covenant of love with us, he also restored to our souls the flow of divine life (technically *grace*) that we lost through original sin.

What exactly is "grace," namely, this *divine life* that Jesus has given back to us from the Cross? You may remember the similitude of the magnet and the three iron rings I used in Chapter Six. As long as the three iron rings (symbolizing the soul, the body, and the world) remain united to the magnet (God), magnetism (the life of God) is flowing through the rings, and there is peace and harmony. But if magnetism ceases to flow, the rings are separated from the magnet, and fall to the ground in disarray. Here on earth, if we loose God's grace, we may not experience

---

[16] Luke 22:19-20.

any sense of loss because our body distracts us from the things of the spirit, but once we are pure spirits, then being unable to see God will be a living hell.

As already pointed out, God's gift of divine life to Adam and Eve made their souls partially divine and capable of sharing in his divine life and nature. Thus, they became deified, truly similar to God, entitled to be called his children and heirs to his Kingdom. Original sin took away this very special characteristic; and man's soul, deprived of God's life and nature, was unable to share eternal life with him.

When Jesus offered his sacrifice on Calvary and brought peace again between God and us humans, the Father restored to us this special gift of friendship (grace) through Baptism, and made us again partakers in his divine life and nature. This is what grace does for us through Baptism: *it purifies us from all sins; it makes us a divine creation; adopted children of God; partakers in divine nature; members of Christ's body; heirs of the Kingdom with Jesus; temples of the Holy Spirit.*[17]

All these marvelous benefits that God offers us are truly Jesus' gifts of love bestowed on us from the Cross.

Human and Divine Adoption

We all are God's adopted children, and it is important to understand the difference between human and divine adoptions. For us humans, adoption is merely a legal fiction, as the lawyers call it. It does not bring about any physical change, nor does it create a blood relationship between the adoptee and the adopter. A blood relationship

---

[17] CCC, see words *Grace* and *Baptism*.

can only be established by generation between two beings of the same species. By natural law, living beings can only generate other living beings of the same species. We humans beget humans, animals beget animals, according to each respective species. We may love our favorite pet cat or dog or whatever -- but we can never bestow our human nature on it.

But what is impossible for humans is possible for God. At the time of creation, he made it possible for Adam and Eve to share in his very nature and life; so they, too, became like "gods" in a certain sense. This privilege was lost through original sin. But Jesus won it back for us, and so we can truly become children of God and share in his divine nature. It is because of this "sharing of nature" that we are his real children, that we can call God, "Father," and Jesus, "Brother." This divine gift is what we call grace. "Grace is *favor*, the *free and undeserved help* that God gives us to respond to his call to become children of God, adoptive sons, partakers of the divine nature and of eternal life." [18]

Do you realize what this means to us in our everyday lives? This loving relationship...

is the bond that unites us to God,
is the supreme good in life,
gives sense and meaning to our lives;
tells us who we are -- his children,
tells us where we come from -- from him,
tells us our eternal destiny -- eternal life with him.

Doesn't knowing this fill your heart with boundless love and gratitude!? You and I have been chosen to share in this great mystery, to receive this gift from our crucified Savior, our "brother" Jesus Christ.

---

[18] CCC #1996: Cf. Jn 1:12-18; 17:3; Rom 8:14-17; 2 Pet 1:3-4.

Personal Reflection

O my Jesus, I close my eyes to the things around me and to the world. I place myself at the foot of the Cross on Calvary, and I watch you slowly dye under a dark sky while your mother, Mary, and the few other friends silently weep. It is now almost three o'clock, and I see the jeering crowd beginning to disperse under the awesomeness of your tragic death. You are dying because we have sinned against you, and you freely offer your life to the Father in reparation for our sins. Now I know that because of your death the Father has forgiven my sins. You are opening the gates of heaven to me, and your own divine life flows again into my soul. I understand now that you are, indeed, *the way* to heaven. In return for your great love for me, I want to be your disciple and follow your example. I know there is only one way to do it: to love you and to accept the cross your Divine Mercy has assigned me to carry.

Yes, Jesus my love, I offer you all my sufferings. Unite my pains and sorrows to the immense sufferings you endured on earth so that I may learn to love you with all my heart.

P R A Y E R

O Lord Jesus, with the help of your grace make possible for me to do what cannot be done by nature, alone. You know well that I cannot endure much suffering and how easily I can turn away from you. I beseech you to help me with your grace to always accept your will with love and to suffer in a true spirit of gratitude for all you have done and have suffered for me. (Adapted from the *Imitation of Christ*)

Short Prayer
My Jesus, help me to do your will always.

10

THE FRUITS OF JESUS' SUFFERINGS
His Gifts to Us from the Cross, continued

FOURTH GIFT
Jesus' Death Helps Us to Atone for Our Sins

"Consciousness of sin and a sense of guilt can be transformed by love in a way that leads to salvation and spiritual growth. We live dreaming of celestial worlds, of angels, of purity and beauty while we are surrounded by the crude reality of a shameful world, where sin and crime and all that is ugly seem to triumph. Sensitive to the beauty around us, but tortured by evil in our souls, we weave together sin and salvation, heaven and earth, misery and splendor. We need to unburden our sufferings in him who sweated blood for us because he, alone, can change our sorrow into a source of liberation and of eternal life." [1]

The Meaning in Suffering[2]

For many people, the worst part of suffering is not so much enduring physical or spiritual pain but thinking that no good will come of their suffering and that they suffer in vain. Some people, when faced with suffering, adopt a stoic attitude of indifference to either pleasure or pain; but stoicism will never satisfy the human mind. Failure to see a purpose in suffering is the main cause of suicide among

---

[1] Ravasi p. 135.
[2] The first section of this chapter is a further explanation of Chapter 5 and other passages in this book.

many people, especially teenagers and the elderly. It also causes many people to lose their faith as they cannot reconcile the idea of a fatherly God allowing his children to endure so much senseless suffering. Yet Jesus offered mankind a new vision of suffering as an instrument for spiritual blessings for oneself and others.

Suffering as an Atonement for Sin

Jesus assures us that if we accept our sufferings with loving humility, they will become means of purification of our own sins. This means that crosses and trials can help us expiate our sins. A legitimate question then is: If Jesus offered adequate, even super-abundant reparation to God for our sins, why must we still suffer and atone for them?

Nature teaches us that the consequences of breaking physical or natural laws, such as eating or drinking to excess, overworking, abusing sex or drugs, are painful disorders afflicting body and soul. Every deliberate violation of God's laws is an offense against him, a rejection of his love, and an abuse of his gifts. And each brings with it its own penalty.

Obviously, any willful and deliberate offense against God carries *two unavoidable consequences:* First, *guilt,* that feeling of self-reproach as we become conscious of having committed a fault and have broken God's law. Secondly, a *penalty* to endure according to the gravity of each offense. Guilt is forgiven by God's mercy because of the sufferings of Jesus, but the penalty is our personal responsibility, namely, a suffering we have to endure.   Jesus has given us a practical demonstration of this truth through the death of the two criminals who were crucified with him. Recall the scene on Calvary.   The bad thief refused to accept his sufferings as an expiation for his sins; thus, he gained nothing and in all probability he lost heaven, too. In contrast, the good thief accepted his sufferings with humility and love and thus obtained forgiveness and the gift of everlasting glory. This episode teaches us that besides God's forgiveness, we still need to suffer. This suffering, accepted with love, becomes an instrument of purification and a source of spiritual growth leading us to a closer union with God.

It is a well-known truth that if we sin we must do penance. However, many people, even though they acknowledge their sinfulness, refuse to accept the penalty. Here is where love comes in. When we think of how much Jesus suffered to obtain God's forgiveness for our guilt, shall we refuse to accept the penalty? If we realize that the sufferings we endure are only temporary while the reward is eternal, should we not be grateful to God for his mercy and for the opportunity to purify our souls? Rather than complaining, we should reflect on all the blessings he has bestowed upon us throughout our lives despite our neglecting him.

People are inclined to look upon their sufferings as God's punishment for their sins and feel resentful. This is a great mistake. In many cases, it is we who cause our own sufferings by breaking the laws of God and nature. Why, then, do we blame God? Sometimes our behavior toward God is similar to the tantrums of little children who get mad when they do not get what they want. Aren't we acting like spoiled children when we complain and protest: *"Why me, Lord? Why me? After all I am not a great sinner. I have done a lot of good to many people. Why do you punish me like this?"* Sound familiar? This is our pride speaking. But faith, humility, and love should convince us that *"for those who love God, all things work together for good."* [3] Notice, it says *all things;* and, of course, suffering is the first thing to be turned into "spiritual gold" [4], provided we *love God.*

FIFTH GIFT
A New Dimension of Suffering: Helping Others

I venture to hope that what I have written above has convinced you that our sufferings in life are part of our personal purification from our sins. But the question now arises: What about the problem of the suffering of innocent persons, such as babies murdered in their mothers' wombs, of children who are tortured, abused, and killed, some even by their own parents? What about the sufferings of innumerable people who are stricken by cruel trials and misfortunes far beyond what seems reasonable, such as victims of unjust wars who die or whose lives are ruined forever, of persons languishing in prisons even though innocent of the crimes for which they have been convicted, of good parents with severely handicapped children, and of other countless cases of this kind?

To find a reasonable explanation for such seemingly unjust sufferings, we must remember that *not all human sufferings are a punishment for personal sins.* Pope John Paul II wrote: "It is not true that all suffering is a consequence of a (personal) fault or has the nature of a punishment." [5] If then there are sufferings which are not an expiation for our sins, what is their meaning? Are they in vain?

---

[3] Romans 8:28

[4] D. James Kennedy, *Turn It To Gold.* Servant Publications, Ann Arbor, Michigan. 1991.

[5] Letter on *Human Suffering,* #11.

Certainly not. Jesus has added a *new dimension to suffering* that gives it a higher purpose and meaning. *It is the dimension of our being associated with him in his work of salvation* and, therefore, being able to help others spiritually by offering our sufferings for their spiritual good. This point of doctrine requires a brief explanation.

According to the Gospel of St. John, Jesus told Nicodemus: *"For God so loved the world that he gave his only son, that whosoever believe in him should not perish but have eternal life."* [6] Pope John Paul II commented: "God gives His only-begotten Son so that man 'should not perish' and the meaning of these words 'should not perish' is precisely specified by the words that follow "but have eternal life." [7]

This was the redemptive mission of Jesus: *to suffer and die in place of mankind and thus save us from perishing* (from the eternal loss of God), *and secure for us "eternal life".* We share in his mission of saving people when we offer our sufferings for the good of other souls who are in need of spiritual help.

Pope John Paul II comments further: "The Redeemer suffered in place of man and for man. Every man has his own share in the redemption. Each one is also called to share in that suffering through which the redemption was accomplished. He is called to share in that suffering through which all human suffering has also been redeemed. In bringing about the redemption through suffering, Christ has also raised human suffering to the level of the Redemption. *Thus each man, in his suffering, can also become a sharer in the redemptive suffering of Christ."* [8]

---

[6] John 3:16
[7] Letter on *Human Suffering*, #11.
[8] Letter on *Human Suffering, #19.* (Author's underlining).

In plain words, the Holy Father is saying that through our personal sufferings we share in the worldwide saving mission of Jesus and that, as he suffered and obtained salvation for others so we, too, can offer our sufferings for the spiritual advantage of others and help bring about their salvation. Therefore, we must no longer regard suffering merely as a reluctant atonement for our sins but, rather, as a valuable instrument of doing good to others, especially relatives, friends and foes alike. This belief is a basic Christian doctrine. St. Paul teaches this explicitly when he writes: *"If we are afflicted, it is for your encouragement and salvation."* [9] Here he claims that the sufferings he is enduring are a source of comfort and spiritual help to his friends in their struggle for eternal salvation.

Living under the threat of persecution, the Christians of the early centuries of the Church were very much aware of this doctrine. Their slogan was: "The blood of martyrs is the seed of new Christians." The numerous martyrs were the inspiration for many conversions. Those truly heroic Christians saw a definite link between the sufferings of their martyrs and God's gift of faith to non-Christians.

Thinking of the spiritual good that our sufferings can do to others offers an additional, new and profound meaning to suffering. The elderly, the sick and infirm, the shut-ins, the bed-ridden, those serving time in jails whether guilty or not, people suffering from psychological problems and all those whose lives and sufferings seem a big waste should realize that their existence, far from being useless and a burden to others, is a vital instrument that will bring untold spiritual gifts to themselves, to their relatives and friends, and to all humanity.

---

[9] 2 Corinthians 1:6

Consider the sufferings of those parents who endure a living agony because their children have "gone sour" -- they have left the Church or are involved in drugs, are divorced, or may even be in jail. Instead of giving in to despair, these parents should find strength in the Christian belief that by persevering in daily prayers and sufferings they are actually redeeming and SAVING their loved ones by offering to God the most valuable gift of their cross. Jesus solemnly promised: *"Ask, and it shall be given to you."* [10] He cannot renege on his promise, but will infallibly grant what we ask for in his own time and manner.

We find a classical example of this truth in St. Monica,[11] the mother of St. Augustine.[12] Through her perseverance, her prayers, and the moral sufferings she endured for more than twenty years, she obtained from God the conversion of her wayward son and of other members of her family. She is a striking example of the power of suffering for the spiritual good of others, especially one's children and relatives.

In our pragmatic way, we often think that we can help others only by "doing" things -- writing a check to a good cause, feeding the poor, and generally doing good

---

[10] Matthew 7:7

[11] Born in the year 331, died in 387.

[12] Bishop and Doctor. St. Augustine was a philosopher, theologian, mystic, poet, writer, orator and saint. Born in Tagaste A.D. 354, he died as Bishop of Hippo, a Roman colony in North Africa, August 28, 430. "Augustine is undoubtedly the greatest of the Fathers and one of the great geniuses of humanity, whose influence on posterity has been continuous and profound." (Patrology, vol. 4., quoted by Charles E. Yost, SCJ, STL, *In His Likeness,* under "August 28". Priests of the Sacred Heart, Hales Corner, Wisconsin.)

deeds. This belief is *incorrect.* This type of "doing" is certainly good, but also as important is helping others spiritually through our sufferings. In so doing we share in Jesus' mission of saving all people. This is true love.

The possibility of helping others through our sufferings is part of the basic principle of human solidarity, that is, *helping one another.* Keep in mind that by nature we are social beings dependent on each other's help. This law is valid not only in the physical world but in our spiritual lives as well. Mankind has always believed in the efficacy of prayers for one another, regardless of the particular deity we pray to. Jesus has not only confirmed this, he has also given us the reason for it... namely, that we all are brothers and sisters in him, and he will never turn down our prayers.

SIXTH GIFT
Jesus: A Perfect Example of Endurance

"Christ suffered for you, leaving you an example that you should follow in his footsteps."[13] These words from a letter of St. Peter remind us that Jesus not only suffered but also set an example for us of HOW to endure pain. If God had not become human, we would still be in complete darkness about the meaning and purpose of suffering. This was the situation of the people of the Old Testament who were unable to see the acceptance of suffering as an act of love. In the book of Job, for instance, there is a great deal of talk about justice, retribution, respect, and submission to God, but not a hint that suffering can be an instrument of good for oneself and for others.

---

[13] 1 Peter 2:21

How different things are in the New Testament. In the *Acts of the Apostles* we read that Peter and John, after being flogged and excommunicated by order of the Sanhedrin, went out *"rejoicing that (they) had been found worthy to suffer dishonor for the sake of the name of Jesus."* [14] Note that being excommunicated meant becoming a social as well as religious outcast. In Jewish society it was the most shameful punishment of all. But the apostles *went out rejoicing!* They felt privileged to suffer for the sake of winning souls for Jesus. After receiving the Holy Spirit, the Apostles understood the value of suffering as an act of love; they felt privileged and honored to suffer with him who had died for them on the cross. They accepted with resignation and without complaining sufferings, persecution, and a violent death... martyrdom. All the apostles, with the exception of John, died martyrs. [15]

We may not be called to witness to our faith by shedding our blood, but we are called just the same to endure other kind of sufferings, perhaps equal in intensity to the sufferings of martyrs. What is important in the eyes of Jesus is not *what kind* of sufferings we endure, but *how we endure them.*

Have you ever reflected why crucifixes and crosses are so frequently and so copiously exhibited in Churches and Christian homes? Because they are a reminder of how *patiently* Jesus endured his sufferings for us, and a gentle reminder to strive to endure all kinds of pains and sufferings -- big and small, usual and unusual, physical and moral, pains of the heart and pains of the mind -- patiently and humbly as Jesus, our model, did on Calvary.

---

[14] Acts 4:41

[15] St. John did suffer persecution and exile, as did the others.

Personal Reflection

My Lord Jesus, I place myself in spirit at the foot of your cross. I hear you saying, "*I thirst!*" And I know that it is not just water you are asking for. You are thirsting for souls to be with you forever in heaven because you are dying for all people. You have taught me that if I accept my crosses with love they can help others spiritually. I know that life is a series of trials which follow one upon the other as the waves of a stormy sea. I must make a habit of seeing you, Jesus, in all my crosses and adversities, and I will bear them thinking of you on Calvary.

PRAYER

"Late have I loved you, O Beauty ever ancient, ever new, late have I loved you! You were within me, but I was outside, and it was there that I searched for you. In my unloveliness I plunged into the lovely things which you created. You were with me, but I was not with you. Created things kept me from you; yet if they had not been in you they would not have been at all. You called, you shouted, and you broke through my deafness. You flashed, you shone, and you dispelled my blindness. You breathed your fragrance on me; I drew in breath and now I pant for joy. I have tasted joy, now I hunger and thirst for more. You touched me, and I burned for your peace." (From the *Confessions* of St. Augustine.)

Short Prayer

Jesus, help me in joy and sorrow always to say:
Your will be done.

11

THE MASS
The Greatest Gift from the Cross

"Because, O Lord, in this immense desert I have no bread, no wine, no altar, I will spiritually rise beyond these human symbols to the splendor of your Real Presence. I, your priest, will offer you a sacrifice: the whole earth will be my altar, and I will offer you the work and the sufferings of the whole wide world. Down there at the far horizon dawn just begins to light up the last part of this Far Eastern world. On my paten,[1] O Lord, I will place the whole harvest of earth's labor, and I will pour in my chalice the juice of all the fruits that will be squeezed today." [2]

The Human Need to Offer Sacrifices

We cannot conclude our series of meditations on the gifts of Jesus from the Cross without reflecting on the greatest of them all: *The privilege to personally participate in the sacrifice of the cross through the Eucharistic celebration of the Mass.* This ritual offering is the very core of all Christian doctrine, the masterpiece of creation, the center of our spiritual life, the inspiration, the source of help we need in our daily life to grow in the knowledge and love of Jesus.

---

[1] The metal plate used by the priest to offer the host at Mass.

[2] Teilhard de Chardin, French Jesuit, poet and scientist (1888-1955) wrote these lines when visiting the desert-like Ordos plateau with a scientific expedition. Ravasi p. 301, *The Cosmic Mass.*

The Mass is undoubtedly God's greatest gift to mankind, even though it is so very little understood and appreciated.

In chapter nine, I mentioned that since the beginning of recorded history people of different nations and cultures have expressed their feelings of love, fear, gratitude, adoration, and respect for the deity through religious offerings, usually called religious (or ritual) sacrifices. This approach to God by means of sacrifices (offerings) is common to almost all people in every age because it is rooted in our very nature. Consider, for instance, the practice of giving gifts to friends to prove our love for them or as an apology to re-establish peace. We feel that words, alone, are not enough to convey our love, our gratitude, or repentance, and we need something more positive, more tangible, more visible. We need action. The same holds true in our relationship with God: the supreme act of worship of the deity has almost always been the offering of a sacrifice as the most acceptable way of saying something to God from the heart.

The Perfect Sacrifice of Love

Ritual bloody sacrifices in our Christian civilization have disappeared because we no longer need them. Jesus offered to the Father the one and only perfect sacrifice that humanity needed, and that is the sacrifice of Calvary which is spiritually re-enacted in every offering of the Mass.

Let us recall briefly what the sacrifice of Jesus on the cross did and meant for us. Father M. Eugene Boylan, an American Trappist, in his book, *This Tremendous Lover,* writes: "His acceptance of His death made it a sacrifice in which He was at once the *victim* and the *priest.* By that one sacrifice He merited (obtained) our salvation; He offered

God a satisfaction greater than that needed for all the sins of the world in all its history; He reconciled us to God; He redeemed us from the slavery of sin and our subjection to the devil; and He opened for us the gates of heaven. By it He merited for His own human nature the highest glory and the kingship of all the universe. For once, God received perfect worship from the inhabitants of this earth -- perfect interior worship and perfect exterior worship. A perfect sacrifice was offered to Him. The victim was His own son, whom He had given for the redemption of the world, and in whom He was 'well pleased.' All the worship we owe God was given to Him in that one sacrifice; all the satisfaction we owe God was given to Him there, also. All that we need from God, was merited for us there; and all the thanks we should give God are given there. *Nothing remains but to make that sacrifice our own,"* [3] by participation in the offering made by a priest in our name.

Our Participation in Jesus' Sacrifice

Jesus' suffering for us on Calvary manifested his boundless love for us; but as love is a two-way street, we must return love for love. How can we manifest our love for him? As I mentioned earlier, love is not love until we manifest it and *prove* it with deeds. Otherwise, it remains just a feeling. Therefore, there must be some practical way for us to tell God of our love in a way acceptable to him.

Throughout his life, Jesus told us of his love for us on many occasions; finally, he proved it by dying on the cross. This voluntary death for us was an act of sacrificial

---

[3] Boylan, p. 178.

love.[4] We, too, must love him in return with a sacrificial love and prove it by means of personal sacrifices acceptable to him. Namely, by doing what he, himself, asked us to do at the Last Supper. Let us re-read slowly and lovingly what Jesus said and did on that all important occasion:

"*Before he was given up to death, a death he freely accepted, he took bread and gave thanks. He broke the bread, gave it to his disciples and said: 'Take this, all of you, and eat it; this is my body which will be given up for you.'*

"*When supper was ended, he took the cup. Again he gave thanks and praise, gave the cup to his disciples, and said: 'Take this, all of you, and drink from it; this is the cup of my blood, the blood of the new and everlasting covenant. It will be shed for you and for all so that sins may be forgiven. Do this in memory of me.' *"[5]

What did Jesus mean when he spoke these words to his disciples? He wanted to perpetuate in a visible way the memory of his sacrifice of love and the shedding of his blood as it was to happen the following day on Calvary. So, by these words and actions, Jesus established a religious rite that would constantly remind all Christians of his death and resurrection. He took bread and wine, staple food of his nation, and with very simple words he changed the loaves of bread and the cup of wine into his living body and blood. The language he used is so simple and clear that it does not allow any other interpretation.

---

[4] Sacrificial love means a love proven by many sacrifices.

[5] There are four versions of this event in the New Testament: Matt 26:26-29; Mk 14:22-25; Lk 22:15-20; 1Cor 11:23-26. The substance is the same in all four versions, but there are slight variations of words. For practical purposes, I quote here the combined version used in the Roman Missal for the Consecration.

"THIS IS..." cannot have any other meaning than exactly what it says: *"THIS IS MY BODY. THIS IS MY BLOOD."* Obviously, he spoke of his body in a transformed, spiritual way of being, a total body (his flesh and blood) under the appearance of both bread and wine.

"DO THIS...," which means: *"Do what I have done,* change bread and wine into my body and blood." In fact, what Jesus had done was the symbolic representation of his forthcoming death. This is what he asked his disciples to do again and again to the end of time, *a symbolic representation of his death.*

"In memory of me." In other words: "When you do this as a remembrance of what I have done for you, remember how much I have suffered for love of you, unite yourself to me on the Cross, and accept your own crosses with love and resignation as I did."

It must be clearly understood that the renewal of the Sacrifice of the Cross at Mass is not a *new* sacrifice because there is no new victim, no *new* suffering on the part of Jesus, and no *new* physical shedding of blood. But it *is* a sacrifice, because the core of every sacrifice is the **offering of the victim,** and here Jesus, on the altar, *renews* the offering of his sufferings and death to the Father for our salvation as he had done on Calvary.

There is, however, an important difference in this renewal of the Sacrifice of the Cross on the altar: on Calvary, Jesus was alone and we were only present in his heart and mind as he offered his sacrifice in atonement for our sins. But now, if we are *actually present* (spiritually or physically) when Mass is being celebrated, we personally offer again the passion and death of Jesus to the Father as we unite ourselves to him and offer his sacrifice to the Father through the celebrant minister.

Jesus' Role at Mass

It is not easy to fully grasp what a conscious and intelligent participation in the Mass means to our souls, to our relationship with Jesus, and to the growth of our spiritual life. So bear with me as I try to explain more in depth this difficult point of doctrine -- Jesus' role and our role at Mass.[6]

Jesus on the cross is the one and only mediator between God and us who, in the whole history of the world, offered the one and only perfect sacrifice for our salvation. He fulfilled both the role of *high priest* (the person authorized to offer a sacrifice) and of *victim*, as he offered his own life to the Father. If we could verbalize what Jesus told his Father from the cross we might summarize it this way: *"Father, in my love for you and for the salvation of all the people of the world, I am now taking upon me all their sins. Therefore, I am offering you all my sufferings, even my very life in atonement for all these sins. As a representative of every human creature in the world I beseech you, Father, to accept the offering of my life, open the gates of heaven to all those who seek salvation and want to live with us for all eternity."*

In other words, in return for offering his life as a true "sacrifice" on the cross, Jesus obtained from the Father forgiveness for our sins and all the graces we need to achieve eternal salvation... if we want it. Jesus opens the gates of heaven but we must walk through them on our own two feet! Jesus does not want us in heaven if we do not

---

[6] This doctrine of the Church is based on Sacred Scripture, especially chapters 4 to 10 of St. Paul's letter to the Hebrews.

want to be with him. Our willing co-operation with his grace is indispensable.

The *Catechism* illustrates this point of doctrine in paragraph #1368, and I paraphrase it here: "As all Christians are part of the Mystical Body of Christ, that is in certain sense, his human family, so we as a family participate in the offering made by Jesus as the head of that family. Attending Mass means offering ourselves with him, and praying with him to the Father for all people. The sacrifice of Christ becomes our sacrifice as the members of his body; and our lives, our praises, our sufferings, prayers, and work are united with those of Christ and with his total offering. Christ's sacrifice, renewed on the altar, makes it possible for all generations of Christians to be consciously united with his offering.

"This truth was well understood by the early Christians. In the catacombs the Christian community was often represented as a woman in prayer, arms outstretched in the praying position. Like Christ who stretched out his arms on the cross, the Christian family through him, with him, and in him, offers itself and intercedes for all people."

As we have attempted to express in our human language Jesus' conversation with his Father from the cross, let us also try to express in our human language what his conversation with the Father might be whenever a Mass is celebrated. Jesus might say something like this: *"Father, as I offered you my sufferings and my life on Calvary, now I renew that offering for all the people in the world, especially for the benefit of the people physically or spiritually here present, and who are offering their life in union with my sacrifice."* [7]

This is Jesus' role at Mass -- as our priest and victim, he intercedes for us. What about our role?

Our Role at Mass

Many attend Mass to fulfill a duty, ignoring or paying little attention to what is happening on the altar. Their attitude is totally passive, and they ignore the fact that they are in church to do something very positive: to offer a sacrifice and to personally meet Jesus in a loving encounter in order to offer him to the Father through the actions of the priest for their salvation. The *Catechism* points out that at Mass we are not mere spectators watching the priest re-enact Jesus' offering of his death on the Cross. We are very much a part of that sacrifice, and we should consciously unite ourselves to Jesus in the offering of himself to the Father. Attending Mass means personally offering a *sacrifice* by doing in a symbolic way what Jesus did physically on Calvary.

The Offertory of the Mass

Let's now pause for a moment and compare the way the people of the Old Testament offered their ritual sacrifices with ours. When a Jewish family felt the need to express their respect for God or obtain his forgiveness, they would

---

[7] Please remember, this is anthropomorphic language that we are using to facilitate our understanding of the spiritual reality of Jesus' relationship with the Father.

go to their herd and choose an appropriate animal, or they would buy one. Then they would bring the animal to the temple to be slaughtered and offered, by the priest, on the altar to God as the visible expression of their feelings of love and reparation. The priest burned some parts of the animal on the altar, set aside a portion of meat for himself[8], and gave back to the family most of the edible parts of the roasted animal to take home to eat at a banquet. They believed that by eating the consecrated animal God, himself, was present at the table with them in a spirit of love and peace.

How different things are today! We still have the urge to offer something to God, but we do not have to find an animal as a victim. We simply go to Mass, and the victim we offer is the very Son of God who offers himself again, as he did on Calvary; but this time, especially for us and for all who are present. We cannot present ourselves to Jesus empty handed; we have to bring our personal offering to make the sacrifice relevant to us. The offering we must bring is our very life with its sorrows and joys, our sins to be purified, our good deeds done for his honor and glory -- for the good of mankind, for our special intentions, and for our spiritual good, as well as for our friends and foes.

Did you every think of the real meaning of the collection taken up in church at Offertory time? We all know that our contributions are necessary for the financial support of our parish church, but there is also another more profound meaning attached to it. The envelope you place in the collection plate, or the offering[9] you give a priest for the celebration of Mass for your intentions, represents a visible

---

[8] Priests officiating in the Temple could not engage in other occupations; they depended on such contributions for their living.

[9] Stipend.

gift, a little part of yourself which you offer to God with Jesus and through Jesus. Your Offertory donation symbolizes your direct, visible participation in the sacrifice of Calvary.

Then, as you see the priest raising the host and chalice as an offering to God, remember that you are part of it with all your good intentions and needs -- it is your personal offering to God through the ministry of the priest on the altar. After this offering, the priest joins his hands in prayer and says: "*Lord God, we ask you to receive us and be pleased with the sacrifice we offer you with humble and contrite hearts.*"

This prayer means that as the priest has offered to God the bread and wine that will be transformed into Jesus' body and blood as the victim of the sacrifice, he also asks the Father to "be pleased" to accept the offering of yourself and your life.

Consecration and Communion

The Consecration is the focal point of Mass, and it demands a very personal involvement. It is Jesus speaking to you directly. Listen to his voice so full of pathos and love, as he addresses you personally: "*This is my body for you, take and eat...this is the cup of my blood for you....take and drink.*"

Yes, these words are addressed *to you,* personally! You are there in the church pew, as the Apostles were present at the table of the Last Supper. Now, you bring with you all your good and bad qualities, your good and bad deeds, your weaknesses and spiritual victories.

Raise your head, look at him, the person who loves you most in this world, and tell him straight from the heart how grateful you are and how much you love him. Do not let your feelings of unworthiness hold you back. Remember that he is there to help you because you are a *sinner*, and he cares for you.

When the priest raises the chalice and says: *"This is the cup of my blood, the blood of the new and everlasting covenant,"* remember that Jesus is renewing his alliance with you. YOU AND JESUS are now partners in an alliance of mutual love. Yes, you and Jesus. As he has sealed this alliance with his blood for the forgiveness of your sins, now mentally renew your alliance of love with Jesus and offer yourself again entirely to him, asking him to make you as faithful to your pact of love as he is faithful to you.

Communion is the fusion of your soul with Jesus. It is the beginning of the eternal dialogue you will carry on with him in heaven through eternity; it is the beginning of your life with Jesus in heaven as you tell him of your enduring love. Ask him to make your love a reality -- no longer just a mere feeling -- to transform you so you may become one with him. This is the time to tell him, like the disciples of Emmaus, *"Lord, stay with us!"* [10] and meditate on the following verses from St. Thomas Aquinas:

"Godhead here in hiding, whom I do adore
Masked by these bare shadows, shape and nothing more,
See, Lord, at thy service low lies here a heart
Lost, all lost in wonder at the God thou art.

"Seeing, touching, tasting are in thee deceived;
How says trusty hearing? That shall be believed;
What God's son told me, that for truth I do;
"Truth himself speaks truly or there is nothing true." [11]

---

[10] Luke 24:29
[11] Translation by Gerard Manley Hopkins.

St. Francis de Sales summarizes the importance of the Mass in this way: *"The Mass is the sum of all spiritual exercises -- the most holy, sacred, and supremely sovereign sacrament and sacrifice of the Mass, center of the Christian religion, heart of devotion, and soul of piety, the ineffable mystery that comprises within itself the deepest depths of divine charity, the mystery in which God really gives himself and gloriously communicates his graces and favor to us."* [12]

Personal Reflection

The Mass is the most important element in my spiritual life and in my efforts toward an intimate relationship of love with God. Mass is truly *the ladder to God*, and since he gives me the opportunity to participate frequently in that sacrificial offering, why am I not making a greater effort to better understand and to participate in it more often? To make my attendance at Mass more fruitful, I must remember that I cannot go to Jesus empty-handed, that my entire life must be centered in the Mass, for it represents the real offering of myself to Jesus. He loved me to the point of death, and he now wants me and my love with all his heart.

---

[12] St. Francis de Sales, *Introduction to the Devout Life*, p. 103.

PRAYER
(by John Henry Cardinal Newman)

MY GOD, I know well you could have saved us at your word, without yourself suffering; but you did choose to purchase us at the price of your Blood. I look at you, the victim lifted on Calvary, and I know that your death was an expiation for the sins of the whole world.

My Lord, I offer you myself, in turn, as a sacrifice of thanksgiving. You have died for me, and I in turn make myself over to you. My wish is to be separated from everything of this world, to cleanse myself simply from sin. Enable me to carry out what I profess.[13]

Short Prayer

My Jesus, help me to offer the Sacrifice of the Mass
with ever greater love and understanding.

---

[13] *A Newman Prayer Book,* p.23

12

SEARCHING FOR HAPPINESS

"They [Mary and Joseph] were looking for him among their relatives and acquaintances. Not finding him they returned to Jerusalem in search of him." [1] *Probably, no other humans ever searched for God so anxiously as Mary and Joseph did when they lost Jesus on the way back from Jerusalem to Nazareth. In Christian spiritual literature their painful search for Jesus is a symbol of man's search for God through the centuries. The Psalmist writes: "My being thirsts for God, the living God. When can I go and see the face of God?"* [2] *This search still goes on today as intense as ever.*

Happiness

Throughout the previous chapters we have established the fact that God is love and that he loves us, that our supreme goal on earth is to love him as he alone can fulfill the desires of our heart and lead us to happiness, and that suffering, far from being an obstacle to our relationship of love with God, can be an instrument of spiritual growth.

However, the basic cravings of our human nature are not for God but for worldly and sensual satisfactions. We experience such cravings from birth because they are the natural expression of our self-love. So, *can we find happiness in our love for God?* The answer, obviously, is *YES*, because

---

[1] Luke 2:44-45.

[2] Psalm 42:3.

God is love and happiness itself, and *in finding God, we find spiritual and real happiness.*

But what *is* happiness? Happiness is very difficult to define. It is a much used, abused, and misused word. It is the goal of all our dreams and desires. Professor Kreeft writes: "...everyone seeks happiness -- in seeking anything, we are seeking happiness. Happiness is the last end, ultimate good, or *summum bonum* [supreme good] of everyone. No one seeks happiness as a means. No one wants happiness in order to attain riches, or power, or pleasures of the senses, or a good conscience, or knowledge; but we do seek all these things because we think they will make us happy. As Pascal puts it, 'this is the reason why one goes to war and why another does not. It is the motive for all we do, including those who go and hang themselves.' " [3]

There are different types of happiness. The most important distinction is between *natural* and *spiritual* happiness. Natural, sensual happiness is what we all know best and crave. In everyday conversations we use the word happiness to express joyful experiences and pleasant feelings such as contentment, gladness, and delight. These words are not synonymous; they express different types of natural happiness; they express the sense of *being satisfied.* The joy of newlyweds, the elation that comes from achievement or success in a field of endeavor, or the enjoyment of sensual pleasures all make us feel happy.

Many people think that feeling happy is the very purpose of life and that we have a *right* to be happy. "Life is to be enjoyed" is a basic tenet of our society. There are those who believe that the pursuit of happiness justifies their

---

[3] Kreeft, *Everything You Ever Wanted to Know About Heaven,* Pp. 206-207. Ignatius Press, San Francisco. 1990.

immoral actions. "It makes me feel good" is a justification offered by many seemingly decent people, as well.

Natural happiness is not the kind of happiness you will read about in this book. When we say that God is happiness itself, we are speaking of a totally different kind of happiness -- we are speaking of *spiritual happiness.*

Leaving aside the scholarly discussions of theologians and philosophers on the nature of happiness, I want to emphasize that here I am writing about strictly *spiritual happiness* in the sense of *a personal possession of a coveted spiritual good that can fulfill all our desires and aspirations.*[4] In other words, spiritual happiness in heaven will be possessing God. This kind of happiness is totally different from the transitory sensations of gladness and joy perceived by our senses that come from outside and are never permanent. Here on earth, spiritual happiness means a constant endeavor, sometimes even a painful one, to be intimately united to Jesus and living in love. Even as a fiance in love with his beloved betrothed enjoys thinking of his future marriage, so we, being in love with Jesus, enjoy doing his will, working for him, and doing good to others for his sake.

Only in God, love and happiness are synonymous, indivisible, and supreme. We will fully share in his happiness only when we become blessed spirits in heaven. However, those who live a life of intimate union with God here on earth will begin to share in his spiritual happiness now, even

---

[4] See NCE, vol. 6, word "*happiness.*" St. Thomas Aquinas described spiritual happiness as the vision and possession of God in heaven because he is the supreme and sovereign good that can fully satisfy all our spiritual desires.

though it will be in a rational rather than sensitive way and, then, only to a minimal degree.[5]

Jesus' sufferings in the garden of Gethsemane and on the cross offer a key to the understanding of happiness. He felt the repulsion of human nature against sufferings; but while agonizing in his body, he found strength and consolation in the clear vision of God's will and the salvation of mankind. Jesus' example teaches us that doing God's will can give us the same strength and consolation in the darkest moments of our lives.

Christianity Is a Religion of Joy

Christianity has been accused of being a joy-killer, a religion of doom, an enemy of pleasure, a foolish pursuit of a "pie in the sky." Such accusations are false and are due to ignorance of Christian doctrine. Christianity is a religion of joy and spiritual happiness; it is Christ's gift to us humans. Glancing through the pages of the gospel we find that at the birth of Jesus the Angel announced to the shepherds: "*I proclaim to you good news of great joy that will be for all the people.*" Later, at the beginning of his public life, Jesus went around to cities and villages and "*proclaimed the good news of the gospel's reign.*" [6] The very word *gospel* means *good news.*[7] Throughout his ministry in Judea and Galilee, Jesus spoke often of the joy of the good and faithful servant and

---

[5] I am writing about normal spiritual experiences and not about extraordinary spiritual phenomena such as the ecstasies and visions of mystics.

[6] Matthew 9:35.

[7] Webster's Dictionary.

of his *"sharing his master's joy."* [8] It makes no sense for true Christians to be sad. As heirs to the Kingdom of God, Christians should look beyond their present trials at the *mansion*[9] prepared by Jesus for his friends in heaven.

On the surface, there appears to be a contradiction between the kind of life of joy and hope promised in the gospel[10] to those who follow Jesus and his explicit request to take up our cross and follow him[11] to Calvary. But there is no contradiction. Jesus never promised to take away our sufferings; he simply promised to be at our side in time of suffering and to help us carry our cross with love because love alone can makes a sacrifice sweet. As he suffered for our sake and for love of us, so we, too, should accept our share of suffering for his love.

The Way of the Cross

It is a false assumption to believe that if we are good Christians we should receive some kind of preferential treatment from God and be spared at least unusual and exceptionally heavy crosses. Many passages of the Old Testament imply that if one lived a righteous life, kept the law, was good to his friends and neighbor, and said the prayers prescribed by the rabbis, one would certainly be blessed by God with a long and prosperous life on earth. The Jews of the Old Testament actually believed that any sickness, ill-fortune, and sufferings of any kind were a direct

---

[8] Matthew, 25:21.

[9] John 14:12

[10] *"Come to me all you who are weary...your souls will find rest, for my yoke is easy and my burdens light."* Luke 11:28.

[11] Matthew 16:24

punishment of God, while a righteous life was a guarantee of material prosperity and success. They looked upon unfortunate people (such as lepers) as people being punished and cursed by God because of their personal sins.

Today, many Christians still believe that a "good" person should be spared misfortunes and trials and should receive special graces and blessings. These people forget that throughout his life on earth Jesus constantly endeavored to correct such erroneous beliefs. By the example of his own way of life, in his public ministry, and especially in his Sermon on the Mount,[12] Jesus explicitly and repeatedly proclaimed that neither he, nor his mother, nor his disciples and followers would ever be exempt from the necessity of suffering during their earthly lives. He repeatedly warned his followers that they would have to endure suffering and persecution. The reward, a happiness beyond comprehension, would come later.

Our Quest for True Happiness

We are born with an innate desire for happiness, but we still risk choosing the wrong kind of happiness. The fact is that we are more attracted to the joys and pleasures of our bodies and minds than to the real but more remote spiritual happiness of our souls. God has given us the freedom to choose: *"The gate that leads to damnation is wide, the road is clear, and many choose to travel it. But how narrow is the gate that leads to life, how rough the road, and how few there are who find it"* [13] -- or choose to look for it.

---

[12] Matthew, chapters 5 to 9.
[13] Matthew 7:13-14.

This is the supreme choice we have to make in our quest for happiness. Which gate shall we choose?

There are two factors that we must consider in order to make the right decision: First, *God's Love For Us;* and second, *Suffering Is An Instrument of Love.* If we grasp the full import of these two factors, the right decision will be easily made.

God's Love for Us

This subject has been discussed in the earlier chapters, but here we will consider other aspects. The most impressive characteristic of God's love for us is his unceasing quest for *our* love. He not only loves us in spite of our ingratitude, neglect and even contempt for him, but he relentlessly pursues us with his love so we may open our minds and hearts to him. He paid for our salvation with his blood; he, therefore, wants us to live forever with him in everlasting happiness.

It is God's thirst for our love that inspired the British poet Francis Thompson to compose his famous poem *The Hound of Heaven.* Written during a two-year period in a Franciscan friary while recuperating from a "starved and homeless young manhood," Thompson eloquently expresses God's unrelenting pursuit of our love when he writes in part:

> *"I fled Him, down the nights and down the days,*
> *I fled Him, down the arches of the years,*
> *I fled Him, down the labyrinthine ways*
> *Of my own mind; and in the mist of tears*
> *I hid from Him, and under running laughter,*
> *Up vistaed hopes I sped:*
> *And shot, precipitated,*
> *Adown Titanic glooms of chasmed fears,*

From those strong Feet that followed, followed after
But with unhurrying chase,
And unperturbed pace,
Deliberate speed, majestic instancy,
They beat -- and a Voice beat
More instant than the Feet --
All things betray thee, who betray Me." [14]

If we could fully realize the depth of God's love for us, our love for him would be infinitely greater than it is. But most people do not take the time to study the "science of love." Please note that I could have written "theology of love." Unfortunately, today, theology has become in many cases a cold, lifeless and loveless human science. This is why I prefer the term *science of love* -- the most important of all sciences and the noblest pursuit in human life.

Regrettably, this science has never been of major concern to mankind. Dr. John C. H. Wu wrote: "The whole trouble about modern civilization seems to me to lie just in this: *There is too much love of science, and too little science of love."* [15] Natural sciences have made tremendous progress, and psychology has probed deep into the darkest nooks and corners of the human mind. But have we gone beyond the elevation and moral culture of Christianity? No. Christianity still continues to shine as the Morning Star and will continue to shine to the end of time. In fact, as Pope Pius XI pointed out: 'It might even be said that a knowledge of Nature will serve as an introduction to what is of far greater value, an understanding of things supernatural.' [16]   The

---

[14] Francis Thompson (1859-1907).

[15] *The Science of Love.* U.S. edition, p. 18.

[16] *St. Therese' of Lisieux: An Autobiography,* translated by Rev. Thomas N. Taylor (Burns, Oates & Washbourne, London), p. 268.

more science grows, the nearer we shall be to a living faith. ...Love has nothing to lose and everything to gain by the continual progress of civilization. Can science ever supersede Christianity, ...the Religion of Love *par excellence?*" [17]

The *science of love* is the study of God's love for us, our love for God and for our fellow man, of nature, of all created things. This is the only science that in time and eternity can quench our thirst for love and our need to love.

Suffering Is An Instrument of Love

Even though I have also written on this subject in previous chapters, I would like to comment further. The French writer Michael Tournier writes: " 'The light of the sun is the same for everyone, but the darkness of night is different for every person.' The library of God does not have sections for military victories -- men take care of these. It gathers, instead, the immense baggage of human suffering and records it in a complete book with its own plot. That volume is the book of life and suffering." [18]

The Polish writer Isaac Bashevis Singer wrote: "I believe that somewhere in the universe there must be an archive wherein all sufferings and the acts of sacrifice of all men are kept. There would be no divine justice if the story of even the most miserable human being did not ornate the library of God." [19]

Pope John Paul II in his Apostolic Letter, *The Christian Meaning of Human Suffering,* asks: "Why does evil exist?

---

[17] *The Science of Love,* p. 15-17.

[18] Ravasi, *Mattutino.* p. 54.

[19] Born in Poland in 1940, he died in the United States in 1978. Quotation from Ravasi, p. 53.

Why is there evil in the world? Both questions are difficult. Man does not put this question to the world, even though it is from the world that suffering often comes to him; but he puts it to God as the Creator and Lord of the world. And it is well known that concerning this question there arise not only frustrations and conflicts in the relations of man with God, but also that people reach the point of actually *denying God*. Whereas the existence of the world opens, as it were, the eyes of the human soul to the existence of God, to his wisdom, power, and greatness, evil and suffering seem to obscure the image, sometimes in a radical way, especially in the daily drama of so many cases of undeserved suffering when so many faults go by without proper punishment. This circumstance shows, perhaps more than any other, the importance *of the question of suffering*. It also shows how much care must be taken both in dealing with the question itself and with all possible answers to it."[20]

"...Jesus did three things to solve the problem of suffering. First, he came. He suffered with us. He wept. Second, in becoming man he transformed the meaning of our suffering: it is now part of his work of redemption. Our death pangs become birth pangs for heaven... Third, he died and rose. Dying, he paid the price for sin and opened heaven to us; rising, he transformed death from a hole into a door, from an end into a beginning." [21]

Being able to look at suffering as an instrument of love is the result of our intense and loving relationship with Jesus.

---

[20] ...*Human Suffering,* #9.
[21] From *Making Sense Out of Suffering,* © 1986 by Peter Kreeft. Publ'd by Servant Publications, Box 8617, Ann Arbor, MI 48107. p. 138. Used with permission.

From the "Imitation of Christ."

"Jesus has many lovers of his heavenly kingdom, but few cross-bearers. Many desire his consolation, but few his tribulation. Many will sit down with him at table, but few will share his fast. All desire to rejoice with him, but few will suffer with him.

"Many will follow him to the breaking of the bread, but will not drink the bitter cup of his Passion. Many revere his miracles, but few follow the shame of his cross. Many love Jesus when all goes well with them, and praise him when he does them a favor; but if Jesus conceals himself and leaves them for a little while, they fall to complaining or become depressed. Are not they to be called hirelings who always look for comforts? And they who think only of their own advantage, do they not show themselves to be lovers of self rather then of Christ?" [22]

Personal Reflection

God has created me -- yes, me, with all my good and bad qualities -- for the one and only purpose of making me *eternally happy* with him in heaven. This is why he has placed in my heart an unquenchable thirst for happiness. The only condition he has established is that I should *freely* decide to love him more than anything or anyone else. Can I say, "No" ?

---

[22] Commonly attributed to Thomas a' Kempis (1379-1471).

Jesus has made me a vital part of the eternal and worldwide circle of God's love. This is not ancient history, it is my personal, on-going story... the story of my personal relationship with my God, my Creator, my Redeemer, my divine Friend who died for love of me.

What is my love-response? Do I let my reluctance to suffer and gain self-control lead me away from my love for Jesus? Do I search for transitory, natural happiness disregarding the quest for true spiritual happiness?

The decision is mine. What shall it be?

P R A Y E R

God of our ancestors, Lord of mercy,
you have made all things by your word
And in your wisdom have established man
to rule the creatures produced by you,
To govern the world in holiness and justice,
and to render judgment in integrity of heart:
Give me Wisdom, the attendant of your throne,
and do not reject me from among your children.
For I am your servant, son of your handmaid,
a man weak and short-lived
and lacking in comprehension of judgment and of laws.
Indeed, were anyone perfect among the sons of men,
if Wisdom, who comes from you, be not with him,
he shall be held in no esteem...
Now with you is Wisdom, she knows your works
and was present when you made the world;
She understands what is pleasing in your eyes, and what
agrees with your commands.

Send her forth from the holy heavens
and from your glorious throne dispatch her
That she may be with me and work with me,
that I may know what is your pleasure.
For she knows and understands all things
and will guide me discreetly in my affairs
and safeguard me by her glory.[23]

Short Prayer
My Jesus, help me to carry my cross with you.

---

[23] Book of Wisdom 9:1-6, 9-11.

13

MARY, JESUS' FIRST DISCIPLE: OUR MOTHER AND MODEL

"The Son of God became man. He was conceived by the power of the Holy Spirit and born of the Virgin Mary."[1]

At a certain moment in time Mary becomes aware that Christ is her Son, her child and her God. She looks at him and thinks: 'This God is my Son; this divine flesh is my flesh, he is born of me. He has my eyes. The shape of his mouth is the same as mine. He resembles me. He is God, and yet he resembles me.' No other woman has ever had her God all for herself. A God-child whom she can embrace, and smother with kisses. A God who smiles and breaths. A God whom she can touch and who laughs." [2]

Mary is Unique

In the religious history of mankind Mary remains absolutely unique. Her's alone was the experience of conceiving a God-child who was to *"be called Son of the Most High,"*[3] of holding in her arms a God who resembled her in appearance, and of knowing the mystery of the Incarnation, experiencing it and living it as no other woman in the world ever could. Her's alone was the experience of being so close

---

[1] From the *Profession of Faith*

[2] A poem by an unknown author, quoted by Ravasi, p. 274.

[3] Luke 1:32

to the deity as to deserve the title of *Mother of God,* yet remain a humble human being.

The Role of Mary in the World

The great St. Ambrose[4] wrote of Mary: "She is not the *God* of the temple, but the *temple* of God." [5] In God's plan for the salvation of mankind, Mary's role has always been to lead people to Christ, her Son and her God.

Why do we Catholics, and some Protestants as well, honor Mary? There are any number of theological, historical, and traditional reasons. Innumerable books have been written about her by great saints, Doctors of the Church, and other famous writers. The tradition of honoring Mary goes back to the first century of Christianity in both the Eastern and Western churches. No other woman has ever done so much for so many people. She has molded hearts, influenced cultures and people, brought joy and inspiration to millions. She has been loved and revered as the mother of God and the first disciple of Jesus. Mary is the model of Christian life for all Christians.

Despite few occasions in history when fanatics promoted distorted forms of devotion to Mary, the Church has always upheld as correct the veneration[6] of Mary. We Christians *venerate* Mary, but we *adore* Jesus, her Son. What son would resent the honor paid to his mother?

---

[4] Bishop of Milan, Italy. Doctor of the Church. Born in the year 340, St. Ambrose had the privilege of converting St. Augustine to the Christian faith. He died in 397.

[5] Ravasi, *Mattutino.* p. 274-75.

[6] Veneration is theologically distinct from *adoration,* which is strictly reserved for God.

Let me emphasize that "what the Catholic faith believes about Mary is based on what it believes about Christ, and what it teaches about Mary illumines in turn its faith in Christ."[7]

In order to have a better knowledge of God's love for us, it is indispensable also to know Christianity's doctrine concerning Mary, who is central to the mysteries of the Incarnation and Redemption. Here, I will summarize the basic Christian doctrine about Mary under three headings: "Mary the Mother of God," "Mary our Mother," and "Mary the first disciple of Jesus and perfect model of Christian living."

Mary the Mother of God

Some readers might wonder: *"Is it correct to call Mary the Mother of God? After all, she was a human being created by God just like us. How could she generate God?"*

These are logical questions. As a matter of fact, during the first centuries of Christianity, Mary's motherhood of God was very much debated in both the Eastern and Western churches until it was finally settled by the Ecumenical Council of Ephesus on June 22, 431.

The Ecumenical Council of Ephesus declared that in Jesus there are two natures, but *one person* -- the second person of the Holy Trinity -- and that Mary generated Jesus, who is fully God and fully man at the same time. Even before the birth of Jesus, Mary, the "mother of Jesus," as she is called in the Gospels, is acclaimed by Elizabeth, at the prompting of the Holy Spirit, as "the mother of my Lord."[8] "In fact, the One whom she conceived as man by

---

[7] CCC #487

[8] Luke, 1:43; John 2:1; 19:25; Cf. Matthew 13:55.

the Holy Spirit, who truly became her Son according to the flesh, was none other than the Father's eternal Son, the second person of the Holy Trinity. Hence the Church confesses that Mary is truly 'Mother of God' (*Theo-tokos* [in Greek]). (Council of Ephesus [431]; DS 251)" [9]

It logically follows that as the mother of the Incarnate God she received from God many special, spiritual gifts and privileges to prepare her for her unique task. To become the Mother of the Savior, Mary was enriched by God with gifts appropriate to such a role.

The three special gifts granted to her in view of her role as Mother of the Son of God made flesh were: the privilege of being born without the stain of original sin (the Immaculate Conception), of conceiving a son without the cooperation of another human being (virgin birth), and her assumption into heaven.

IMMACULATE CONCEPTION. Pope Pius IX, in his 1854 Apostolic Letter, *Ineffabilis Deus,* declaring that the doctrine of the Immaculate Conception of Mary is an integral part of Christian beliefs, stated: "The most Blessed Virgin Mary was, from the first moment of her conception, by a singular grace and privilege of almighty God and by virtue of the merits of Jesus Christ, Savior of the human race, preserved immune from all stain of original sin." [10]

MARY'S VIRGINITY. Since its very beginning and in accord with the Gospel account, the Church believes "that Jesus was conceived solely by the power of the Holy Spirit in the womb of the Virgin Mary,...' by the Holy Spirit without human seed.' " [11] It is obvious, therefore, that the

---

[9] CCC #495

[10] Pius IX, *Ineffabilis Deus,* 1854.

[11] CCC #496, including quote from the Council of the Lateran, AD 649: DS 503; cf. DS 10-64.

virgin birth of Jesus is "a divine work that surpasses all human understanding and possibility. (Cf.Mt1:18-25; Lk1:26-38)"[12]

Commenting on these unique privileges, St. Irenaeus, Doctor of the Church,[13] writes: " 'Being obedient, she became the cause of salvation for herself and for the whole human race.' (Cf. *Adv. haeres.* 3,22,4:PG7/1, 959A). Hence not a few of the early Fathers gladly assert...: the knot of Eve's disobedience was untied by Mary's obedience; what the virgin Eve bound through her disbelief, Mary loosened by her faith (ibid). Comparing her with Eve, they call Mary the 'Mother of the living' and frequently claim: 'Death through Eve, life through Mary.' (LG 56; Epiphanius, *Haer.* 78,18: PG 42,728CD-729AB; St. Jerome, *Ep.*22,21: PL 22,408.)" [14]

THE ASSUMPTION INTO HEAVEN. This privilege means that, when Mary died, her soul and body were taken directly to heaven. This was a special participation in the Resurrection of her Son and an anticipation of the resurrection of men. [15] In other words, what God did for Mary is what he will do for all just souls at the end of the world; but he did it for Mary ahead of time in order to recognize her unique position as the Mother of his Son and as a proof of what he has prepared for all those who love him.[16]

---

[12] CCC #497. This doctrine is one to which Werfeld's famous saying applies: "For those who believe, no explanation is necessary; for those who do not believe, no explanation is possible."

[13] Bishop and Martyr (AD 130-207).

[14] CCC #494

[15] Cf. *CCC* #966.

[16] Even though the doctrine of the Assumption is not explicitly mentioned in the Bible, it is a long-standing belief that goes back to the first century after Christ. It has been uninterruptedly accepted by the majority of Christians throughout the centuries.

Mary Our Mother

When Mary, in her faith and humility, voluntarily agreed to become the Mother of Jesus, she also implicitly accepted her role of sharing in Jesus' sufferings for the salvation of souls. In fact, she cooperated by her obedience, her faith, her hope and her burning charity [love] in Jesus' work of restoring supernatural life to souls.[17]   This means Mary's freely accepted sufferings, united to the sufferings of Jesus, became part of Jesus' work of salvation of mankind. Mary's sufferings at the foot of the cross as the Mother of Jesus had a *unique and special value* in the eyes of God.

First of all, she suffered in a special way because she was the *mother* of Jesus. Her pains and sorrows were different from those of the other pious women who were there with her. Mary's sufferings as a mother, watching her Son dying such a tragic and unjust death, cannot be duplicated by any other human being.

Secondly, Mary did not suffer *for her own sins*, because she had none; she suffered for *our sins*! Thus, her sufferings, united to those of Jesus and offered to the Father, pleased him and were also instrumental in some way in generating new life in our souls, making us children of God and true heirs to his Kingdom. This is why, *in the order of grace,* she can be rightly called *our spiritual mother.*

Most of the early Fathers of the Church call Mary the "New Eve." The name *Eve* means "the mother of all the living". And by calling Mary the *new Eve* it is meant that she is the mother of the "whole Christ," [18] that is, all the re-

---

[17] Cf. CCC #968.
[18] John 19:25-27

deemed souls. The *Catechism* states: "Jesus is Mary's only son, but her spiritual motherhood extends to all men whom indeed he came to save." [19] As our spiritual mother, she constantly intercedes with God for our spiritual and temporal good.

Why do we believe in Mary's power of intercession with God? Because this belief is firmly rooted in the Bible. Abraham interceded for Sodom and Gomorrah, and God would have spared the two cities if even only a small number of just people were found. Moses interceded countless times for his people, and because of his prayers they were spared punishment and destruction. Many of the prophets and the great people of the Old Testament pleaded with God to save their people, as did Queen Esther and many other great leaders of Israel, and God heard their prayers of intercession.

If God heard the prayers of these holy people and granted their request on behalf of others, how then can God reject the prayers of the mother of his Son? Of course, Jesus is the one and only mediator, but God accepts also the prayers of intercession of all those who love him, and Mary is certainly the first.

Can we attain salvation if we do not feel inclined to pray to Mary? Certainly we can, because the only thing indispensable for our salvation is adoring and praying to God. He is the Lord, and Mary is his handmaid. However, traditional Christian piety throughout twenty centuries and the general teaching of the Church cannot be wrong in encouraging love and veneration for Mary, our spiritual mother.

---

[19] CCC #501

Mary Is the First Disciple of Jesus and a Perfect Model of Christian Life

The Gospels narrate that one day Jesus *"was still addressing the crowds when his mother and his brothers appeared outside to speak to him. Someone said to him: 'Your mother and your brothers are standing out there and they wish to speak to you.' He said to the one who had told him: 'Who is my mother? Who are my brothers?' Then extending his hand towards his disciples he said: 'Here are my mother and my brothers. Whoever does the will of my heavenly Father is brother and sister and mother to me.'"* [20]

Jesus was not disrespectful to his mother when he spoke like that. On the contrary, according to most Biblical scholars, Jesus paid his mother the greatest tribute of love and respect when he declared that *all those who obey his heavenly Father, are my mother and brothers;* as such, they are spiritually united to him. He used the terms *brother, sister, mother* to designate the *spiritual relationship* that makes souls dear to God, in the same way blood ties designate the natural relationship of one's brother, sister and mother on earth. This declaration of Jesus reveals in an indirect way all his love for his mother. Mary was especially dear to him because no other creature has ever done God's will as perfectly as she. [21] No one else is mother, brother or sister to Jesus as Mary is.

Mary was not only Jesus' beloved mother, she was his first disciple, as well. Jesus came into the world to teach us a new and better type of love for God and neighbor --

---

[20] Matthew 12:46-50

[21] *"I am the handmaid of the Lord. Let it be done to me as you say."* Luke 1:39.

different from the rather formalistic and fear-dominated kind of love generally practiced by the people of the Old Testament. And Mary was the first to understand and practice this *new* way of loving and serving. Jesus taught Mary his new way of worshipping *"the Father in Spirit and truth,"* [22] by his example, by his life style, and certainly through his long and loving conversations with her about the life of the spirit during the many quiet years of family life in Nazareth. Thus, Mary became the first and most authentic of the loving disciples of her own Son.

Being a perfect disciple of Jesus, Mary is also the *perfect model of Christian living* for everyone who wants to follow Jesus. Next to Jesus, Mary is the most attractive, the most beautiful, even the *easiest* model offered to us to imitate. Obviously, no one else can be like her, but everyone can endeavor to imitate her type of interior spiritual life.

She was so much and so deeply in love with God that sin never even touched her, and nothing could distract her from following God's will in both the decisive and commonplace events of life. St. Ambrose writes of her: "Charitable and full of consideration for all who surrounded her, ever ready to serve them,[23] never uttering a word or doing the least that could give pain, she was all loving and beloved of all." [24]

Mary practiced all Christian virtues to perfection. Her strong *faith* in God are most evident in how she faced her most difficult hours, when she consented to the words of the Angel, when Joseph doubted her fidelity, and when she stood at the foot of the Cross on Calvary. Her deep *humility*

---

[22] Jesus to the Samaritan woman. John 4:23.

[23] Remember the episode of Cana in Galilee... John 2:1-11.

[24] Quoted by A. Tanquerey, DD, in *The Spiritual Life,* p. 84-85. published by Desclee Co.

is an example to behold for all mankind. Even though she was fully conscious of the greatness of her status as Mother of the Messiah, she never claimed the slightest honor in recognition, and she accepted insults and mockery as the mother of the condemned criminal dying on the cross. When she was greeted by Elizabeth as *"the Mother of my Lord,"* she humbly replied: *"He has looked upon his servant in her lowliness."* [25] Last, but certainly not least, her **love for God and people** stood the test of exceptional crosses and tribulations -- she was totally dedicated to serve both.

What makes her even more fascinating as a model of Christian living is that in the order of nature she was a plain human being, like us. She was a girl, a bride, a mother, a widow, and she lived through these different stages of life maintaining her humility, her grace, her simplicity. We might say that for all appearances she was an *ordinary* woman, but whatever she did, she did it extraordinarily well, with extraordinary love, care, and dedication.

Personal Reflection

The Bible teaches us that Mary played a special and unique role in the life of Jesus. Believing in her power of intercession as the mother of Jesus and our spiritual mother is certainly according to Divine Revelation. That devotion to Mary has been practiced by Christians of the Eastern and Western Churches since the first century after Christ is also proof that this devotion is pleasing to Jesus. Even in most non-Christian religions, there is the idea of a

---

[25] Luke 1:42.

feminine person closer to the deity than the rest of mortals. Could Christianity then reject the devotion to Mary if it is defined and maintained in its subsidiary role to that of Christ?

If I am now practicing devotion to Mary, logic and common sense assure me that I should continue. If not, perhaps I should further explore this point of doctrine to share in the great blessings that accrue by believing in Mary's spiritual motherhood.

PRAYER
(From the *Divine Comedy* by Dante Alighieri)[26]

"Virgin Mother, daughter of thy son,
humble beyond all creatures and more exalted,
predestined turning point of God's intentions;

Thy merit so ennobled human nature
that its divine Creator did not scorn
to make Himself the creature of his creature.

The Love that was rekindled in thy womb
sends forth the warmth of the eternal peace
within whose ray this flower has come to bloom.

Here, to us, thou art the noon and scope
of Love revealed, and among mortal men,
the living fountain of eternal hope.

---

[26] *The Divine Comedy,* Canto XXXIII. Translated by John Ciardi. W.W. Norton & Co., Inc., New York. Dante attributes this prayer to St. Bernard. It has always been considered a masterpiece of faith and art.

Lady, thou art so near God's reckoning
that who seeks grace and does not seek thee
would have his wish fly upward without wings.

Not only does thy sweet benignity
flow out to all who beg, but oftentimes
thy charity arrives before the plea.

In thee is pity, in thee munificence,
in thee the tenderest heart, in thee unites
all that creation knows of excellence."

Short Prayer
Mary, mother of my Jesus, pray for me.

14

THE NEW COMMANDMENT:
"LOVE ONE ANOTHER
AS I HAVE LOVED YOU."

"I give you a new commandment: love one another. As I have loved you, so you also should love one another." [1]

On a large stone at the "Good Samaritan Inn" located on the old road from Jericho to Jerusalem as mentioned in the Gospel of St. Luke[2], an anonymous writer in the Middle Ages sculpted the following words: "If even priests and Levites will pass by and ignore your tragic anguish, know that Christ is the Good Samaritan, that he will always be merciful to you, and at the time of your death will carry you to the inn of eternal happiness."

In the previous chapters we have reflected on the love and care of God for mankind and the problem of reconciling such love with the presence of evil and suffering in the world. Now is the time to go forward. So far we have seen the first half of God's circle of love, now we have to reflect on the second half, and fully realize that the only way for us to express our love for God in a practical way is to love our neighbor: *"As I have loved you, so you also should love one another."* [3]

---

[1] John 13:34
[2] Luke 10:30-37
[3] John 13:34

Natural Love

It may seem redundant to write about love because there are so many books and manuals, written by Christian and non-Christian authors, about how to make friends and influence people, how to make a marriage last, how to get along with one another, and even how to make money by being kind to one another. Many of these books are useful in that they teach various techniques on how to express our love for others; but the motivation they offer is purely human, restricted to the love for the people we like, and totally unrelated to God. Many authors write of the solidarity of the human race, of brotherly love, of understanding and sharing, but only for human reasons and for one's own ultimate satisfaction. They often confuse selfish and carnal love, *eros,* with love of friendship, *agape.*

On the contrary, true love is the love that cares for the other more than for oneself, and it was *exemplified* by Jesus. The difference is that a purely human or philanthropic love of neighbor is self-seeking and self-centered while Christian love is unselfish -- it is sacrificial in nature and centered on Jesus. Human love is destined to perish; God-inspired love will begin on earth and will last for all eternity.

Christian Love

If we carefully analyze two episodes in the gospels, we will be better able to appreciate the complete picture of God's circle of love for mankind. Both episodes deal with love for God and neighbor; they complete each other and are of the highest importance to our growth in love.

In the first episode, St. Matthew reports that a scribe[4] approached Jesus and asked him the all-important question: *"Teacher, which commandment of the law is the greatest?"*

Jesus took this opportunity to emphasize the most basic point of his entire doctrine, *love*. Without a moment's hesitation he replied: *"You shall love the Lord your God with all your heart, with all your soul, and with all your mind. This is the greatest and the first commandment. The second is like it: you shall love your neighbor as yourself. The whole law and the prophets depend on these two commandments."* [5]

The second episode took place the very last evening of Jesus' life on earth; it is his last Will and Testament. At the Last Supper, after washing the disciples' feet, Jesus talked to them at length. It was a discourse full of pathos and tender love. At a certain moment, looking straight into the eyes of his apostles he said: *"I give you a new commandment: love one another. As I have loved you, so you also should love one another. This is how all will know you for my disciples: by your love for one another."* [6]

These words are among the most important words Jesus ever uttered. Through the centuries they have echoed in the hearts of billions of Christians; they have made Christianity *the religion of love;* they have brought joy and consolation to a large part of humanity.

Through his teachings on love, Jesus unveiled to the world a new and revolutionary doctrine, the very cornerstone of his revelation -- *that, for all practical purposes, love*

---

[4] A scholar of the Law who comprised both the civil and religious aspect of Jewish life.

[5] Matthew 22:34-40. See also Mark 12:29-31; Luke 10:25-28; Deuteronomy 6:4-5; Leviticus 19:18.

[6] John 13:34

for God and love for one another are linked together so intimately as to form only ONE commandment. Love for God and neighbor are *on the same level.*

Jesus called his commandment a **NEW** commandment. There is a lot of meaning in this simple adjective, *NEW*, that can be summarized in three sentences. *First:* Love for God and love for neighbor are linked together. *Second:* The meaning of the word *neighbor* is extended to include all mankind, even enemies and persecutors. *Third:* There is a new term of comparison -- before it was, *"as you love yourself;"* now Jesus makes it, *"as I have loved you."*

A NEW COMMANDMENT: Jesus links love of God and neighbor together because we all are God's children.

When Jesus said to the Jewish lawyer, *"The whole law and prophets depend on these commandments,"* he meant that love of God and neighbor is the very essence of the teachings of the Old Testament. Only through love can we attain the moral integrity God expects from us and thus achieve final salvation. According to God's plan we all are part of a circle of love, and love is the bond that unites us to God and with one another; this is why these two commandments are inseparably linked together.

We believe that we all are God's children, and share our humanity with Christ. Therefore, all humans are Jesus' family on earth in a very special way and must love one another as brothers and sisters. Throughout his entire life, in a thousand different ways, through parables and signs, by speaking simply and directly to the people, Jesus emphasized that *all people on earth are God's beloved sons and daughters,* the branches of the same tree, and that *he lives in each one of us.* The sense of solidarity and philanthropy towards one another is rooted in human nature because we are all human beings.   But Jesus told us to love one another because we are all God's children and Jesus' brothers and sisters and because he became one of us so that we might be one in him.

The traditional concept of the relationship of love in a well-ordered family is a good analogy of the relationship of love between Jesus and us, and between us and our neighbor. In an ideal family in which there is an intense community of love, an honor or an insult done to one of the members of the family is considered as done to all, and all rejoice or suffer because of it. This is why Jesus told us in no uncertain terms that *"whatever you do to one another is done to me."* [7]

On another occasion he said that even a cup of water given in his name will not go unrewarded.[8] When he appeared to St. Paul on his way to Damascus to arrest the new Christians in that community because of their newly found faith, Jesus said: *"Saul, Saul why do you persecute Me?"* [9] Actually, Saul (his name before his conversion) was persecuting the Christians, but Jesus said *"Me,"* because he identifies himself with all of us. It follows then that what is done to any one of our fellow humans is done to Jesus.

This doctrine is typical of the New Testament. God delayed the full revelation of his circle of love embracing all humanity until Jesus came into the world as a human being, because *he alone, could teach us this type of love and give us the help we need to practice it.*

---

[7] Read Matthew 25:31-46
[8] Mark 9:40; Matthew 10:42
[9] Acts 9:4

A NEW COMMANDMENT: The meaning of the word NEIGHBOR is extended to include all mankind.

Until Jesus came, the word *"neighbor"* among the Jews meant only kinsmen and fellow Jews; it was rarely extended to include servants and friendly foreigners living in their midst. It never included the gentiles (the non-Jewish population of the world), much less enemies and persecutors. The laws regarding interpersonal relationships were mainly concerned with refraining from hurting fellow Jews and with helping them in case of need. In practice, Jewish love of neighbor did not go much beyond what pagans were also practicing, namely, to be kind to one's friends.

Jesus, in his quiet way and in simple language, broadened the meaning of the word neighbor to comprise all mankind. All humans are God's creatures, and therefore, brothers and sisters of Jesus. *This is why we must see his human face in all our fellow men and women.*

The Christian who claims to be a son of the God who is *"kind towards the ungrateful and evil,"* [10] must extend love to all because God loves all. Let us keep in mind what Jesus said in his Sermon on the Mountain, *"My command to you is: love your enemies, pray for your persecutors. This will prove that you are sons of your heavenly Father, for his sun rises on the bad and the good, he rains on the just and the unjust. If you love those who love you, what merit is there in that? Do not tax collectors do as much? And if you greet your brothers only, what is so praiseworthy about that? Do not pagans do as much?"* [11]

---

[10] Luke 6:15
[11] Matthew 5:44-48

A NEW COMMANDMENT: Jesus changed the term of comparison from "as yourself"[12] to "as I have loved you.

Jesus' dialogue with the Jewish lawyer gives us only part of the new revelation he came to make to the world. Until Jesus came, the term of comparison used for loving one's neighbor was to love them *"as yourself."* But at the Last Supper, on the evening when he would face impending agony and death at the hands of his fellowmen, Jesus brought this commandment of love to new heights. He changed the term of comparison from "as yourself " to **"as I have loved you."** [13]

This literally means that love for one another should be modeled, as far as humanly possible, after the kind of love that God has for us, and more specifically, as exemplified by the kind of love of Jesus for his disciples. This is the type of love we must imitate in loving our neighbor.

How did Jesus love his disciples? William Barclay in his *Commentary on The Gospel of St. John*, writes that Jesus loved his disciples *selflessly,* because his one desire was to give himself and all he had for those he loved; *sacrificially,* because there was no limit to what his love would give or where it would go; *understandingly,* because real love is open-eyed, it loves not what it imagines a man to be, but what he is; *forgivingly,* because the heart of Jesus is big enough to love them as there were, and he held nothing against them; there was no failure that he could not forgive.

---

[12] As used in the Golden Rule, in the Old Testament, and occasionally in the New Testament.

[13] Only a few hours later, while hanging on the cross, he prayed for his killers and asked the Father to forgive them. Luke 23:34.

All enduring love must be built on forgiveness, for without forgiveness love is bound to die.[14]

It is important to emphasize the radical difference between the kind of love that God wants us to have for one another -- a selfless, sacrificial love -- and the purely human, self-centered type of natural love for neighbor promoted by secular writers.

Jesus' commandment makes Christianity the RELI-GION OF LOVE, the religion born in love, fulfilled in love, and destined to prepare us for eternal love. This is the only kind of love any of us needs if we truly want to be Jesus' disciples and some day attain eternal happiness.

Personal Reflection

Have I ever questioned myself seriously about how and how much I love my neighbor? Am I like most people who love only those who are kind and friendly to them? Do I have difficulty in loving for Jesus' sake all those who hurt me, who dislike me, those who get on my nerves, or who are practically unbearable? Do I forget that all these people are children of God, just like me? And that in all probability they are better than me in Jesus' eyes and that he loves them just as much as he loves me because he died for them, too?

If my answers to these questions are "yes", it means that I do not have the type of love for my neighbors that Jesus wants me to have. I should really try to love them as

---

[14] A summary of pp.149-150 of the Gospel of St. John, Vol. 2, in the Daily Study Bible Series by William Barclay. Westminster Knox Press, publr.

Jesus loves me and to think of them as my brothers and sisters. This is a matter of crucial importance. I must remember that on the day of my judgment I will be saved or damned on this question alone: *HOW MUCH HAVE I LOVED OTHERS?*

Everything else I do in my life means nothing unless I love my neighbor and do good to them *for Jesus' sake.*

P R A Y E R

My Jesus, I can visualize your eyes full of love as you tell your apostles: *"Love one another as I have loved you."* In the silence of my conscience you have repeated this command to me hundreds of times. I know that you love me with an enduring love, an understanding love, a self-sacrificing love, a forgiving love. Please, Jesus, help me to love others as you love me.

Short Prayer

My Jesus, help me to see you in all my neighbors.

15

AS I HAVE LOVED YOU

"As the Father has loved me, so I have loved you...
This is my commandment to you: love one another. It was
not you who chose me. It was I that chose you to go forth
and bear fruit." [1]

Jesus: A Model of Love of Neighbor

The great Dominican orator and scholar H. D. Lacorda-ire,[2] in a letter to some young friends, wrote: "Above all, be good. Goodness is what makes us most similar to God and it easily disarms men. You have in your soul the first seed of this virtue, but its furrows can never be cut deep enough. Constantly thinking kind and lovable thoughts about others ends up radiating goodness through your appearance. I never felt any attraction except to goodness shining through a human face. Human features that show high intelligence leave me cold, but the first person I chance to encounter who radiates goodness moves my heart and attracts me."

The purpose of this chapter is to focus your attention on *Jesus' love for people* as he manifested it during his earthly life. As an artist needs a model to create a masterpiece, we too need a model of true love of neighbor to imitate. Examples are always more effective than words.

---

[1] John 15:9, 12, 16

[2] Famous French orator (1802-1861) who for many years delivered scholarly sermons at Notre Dame Cathedral in Paris. Quoted by Ravasi in *Mattutino,* p. 337.

This is why when Jesus told his apostles to love one another he did not give them a "how to" manual but pointed to his own love for them as a *model to imitate.*

Let us keep in mind that Jesus is not a deceased historical figure. He is living in our midst as he lived with his apostles in Palestine. He is still talking to us today as he talked to his disciples when he was visible on earth. Today, he is telling you and me, personally, "love one another <u>as I have loved you.</u>" If we fail to do this, we cannot claim that we love God. St. John warns us: "If anyone says, 'I love God,' but hates his brother, he is a liar." [3]

Jesus Is All Goodness

Jesus possessed a magnetic and fascinating personality which drew people to him. People were attracted by his looks, his teachings, his love for his fellow man; they followed him blindly, making all kinds of sacrifices! The crowds that went with him into the desert, the apostles and disciples who gave up family and business to be with him, and Mary Magdalene sitting at his feet lovingly and admiringly, are only a few examples of the power of his fascinating personality. He simply radiated love of others, and people followed him, attracted by the force of his love and his total goodness. He was magnificent in his love and in his *holy* anger when he castigated the hypocrites and greedy leaders misleading his people. His wonderful, attractive personality was the result of the love that burned in his human heart and embraced not only his family and friends but all people and all things in the world.

---

[3] 1 John 4:20

Have you ever had the good fortune to meet one of those rare people who seem to radiate love for everyone and everything, who never utter a bad word about others, who are always ready to volunteer for difficult tasks, always freely giving of self, embracing saints and sinners alike in love, God-inspired love? These are the people who possess love of God and neighbor as Jesus did. They reflect the power of God's inspired love that the Holy Spirit breathes into souls. We all are attracted by human goodness more than by intelligence, power, or success. To attain it should be the goal of every Christian.

The Ingredients of Christian Love

In Chapter Thirteen of his first letter to the Corinthians, St. Paul, inspired by the Holy Spirit, gives us a superb and unparalleled analysis of what true Christian love of neighbor is and how to practice it. Let us re-read attentively three short verses from this famous letter which has been called the "Magna Carta" of love:

"Love is patient; love is kind. Love is not jealous; it does not put on airs; it is not snobbish. Love is never rude; it is not self-seeking; it is not prone to anger; neither does it brood over injuries. Love does not rejoice in what is wrong but rejoices with the truth. There is no limit to love's tolerance, to its trust, its hope, its power to endure." [4]

This passage is a faithful description of the kind of love Jesus has for us. It is a God-given road map to follow to attain the supreme good on earth and to live a life of love

---

[4] I Corinthians 13:4-7

with God and one another. Throughout the two thousand years of Christianity these words have offered a perfect description of what is meant by true love for neighbor.

Henry Drummond writes: "St. Paul, in these three short verses, gives us an amazing analysis of what this supreme thing is. I ask you to look at it. It is a compound thing, he tells us. It is like light. As you have seen a man of science take a beam of light and pass it through a crystal prism, as you have seen it come out on the other side of the prism broken up into its component colors -- red, and blue, and yellow, and violet, and orange, and all the colors of the rainbow -- so Paul passes this thing, Love, through the magnificent prism of his inspired intellect, and it comes out on the other side broken up into its elements. And in these few words we have what one might call the Spectrum of Love, the analysis of Love. Will you observe what its elements are? Will you notice that they have common names; that they are virtues which we hear about every day; that they are things which can be practiced by every man in every place in life; and how, by a multitude of small things and ordinary virtues, the supreme thing (in life) is made up?"[5]

This, then, is the "Spectrum of Love," the list of components that make up the nature and structure of Christian love as exemplified by Jesus:

PATIENCE: *Love is patient.*
KINDNESS: *Love is kind.*
BENEVOLENCE: *Love is not jealous.*
HUMILITY: *Love does not put on airs.*
RESPECT: *Love is never rude.*
UNSELFISHNESS: *Love is not self-seeking.*

---

[5] *The Greatest Thing in the World,* pp. 19-20.

GOOD TEMPER: *Love is not prone to anger.*
FORGIVENESS: *Love does not brood over injuries.*
HONESTY: *Love does not rejoice in what is wrong,*
but rejoices with the truth.

These are the virtues, Mr. Drummond continues, "that make up the supreme gift, the stature of the perfect man. Notice that all are in relation to men, in relation to life, in relation to the known today and the near tomorrow, and not to the unknown eternity. We hear much of love to God; Christ spoke much of love to man... The supreme good, the greatest thing on earth, the all-important thing, is not a thing at all, but *the giving of a further finish to the multitudinous words and acts which make up the sum of every common day.*" [6]

These are the ingredients that make up what we call **love of God and neighbor.** This is how Jesus loved his disciples, how he loves you and me, and how he wants us to love one another.

Characteristics of Christian Love

Christian love is properly called *charity;* however, we must keep in mind that when we are speaking of love for one another, the word *charity* is not used in the sense of helping others in need, but in the sense of a love for others inspired by God and rooted in his love for us. The *Catechism* defines it this way: "charity is the theological virtue by which we love God above all things for his own sake,[7] and our neighbor as ourselves for the love of God." [8]

---

[6] Ibid. p. 21.

[7] Not for fear of hell.

[8] CCC #1822.

Because of our imperfect nature, natural love is self-centered, therefore, unstable and dependent on emotion and physical attraction. However, true Christian love is enduring by nature. It is rooted in God and will not be extinguished even by death; it will continue forever as long as we remain united to its source, Jesus.

Obviously, in our daily lives, natural love and Christian love are easily mixed, and the dividing line between them is not straight and rigid. We are both human and divine, body and soul, matter and spirit, but fundamentally one being. So our love constantly fluctuates between the human and the divine. With God's help, however, and our own good will, we can endeavor to attain the right kind of love. Even the very natural kind of love called *eros*, which includes the normal and legitimate sexual love between spouses, can be brought up to the spiritual level as a form of total dedication, as we read in the history of Creation.[9] In the Song of Songs the spouse declares, *"My lover belongs to me and I to him."* [10] This is total dedication. It means that sex *(eros)* and love, as planned by God for the benefit of mankind, constitute a perfect harmony; and if they are separated and abused, they become harmful and are an offense against the dignity of the human being.

Christian Love and the Will of God

To attain a real growth in Christian love will remain for us only a dream unless we firmly understand how love of God and neighbor are linked together. We should love one another because such love is an integral part of God's

---

[9] Genesis, Chapters 1 and 2.
[10] Song of Songs, 2:16.

circle of love. If we do not have it, we cannot be part of God's family. Love *unites*, and as God loves all his creatures we, too, must love all of them if we really want to be united to him. Jesus' teaching on this matter is crystal clear: He taught us to pray, "...*Your will be done, on earth as it is in heaven.*" [11] We have seen in chapter thirteen that doing God's will is what made Mary the greatest and most glorious creature on earth, so we, too, should be united to him and do his will.

Let us re-read some of the more important lines of Jesus' discourse to his apostles at the Last Supper, as he also had us in mind:

"*As the Father has loved me, so I have loved you. Live on in my love. You will live in my love if you keep my com-mandments, even as I have kept my Father's commandments and live in his love... This is my commandment: love one another as I have loved you. There is no greater love than this: to lay down one's life for one's friends. You are my friends if you do what I command you.*" [12]

It is important to note that just before giving this new commandment, Jesus laid the foundation for it by telling his apostles: "*I am the vine, you are the branches.*" [13] In other words, when we are in a state of friendship with Jesus, we are, in fact, united by love to one another as the branches of a tree derive their nourishment and life from the roots.

The importance of this intimate union of love between the Father, Jesus, the Spirit and ourselves, leading to the unity of wills, was emphasized by St. Paul in his

---

[11] Matthew 6:10
[12] John 15:9-14
[13] John 15:5

teachings about all Christians being members of the "mystical body" of Christ[14] and by St. John: *"Beloved, let us love one another because love is of God; everyone who loves is begotten of God... whoever loves God must also love his brother."* [15]

Fr. Eugene Boylan sums it up this way: "We are bound to love all men. 'To love,' in this context, means to wish well to all men. Therefore, our *charity* (in the sense of *God-inspired love*, E.N.) must be sincere and interior, and we must will all men good equally insofar as we must will them all salvation. In practice, this means that we must not deliberately exclude anybody, friend or enemy, from our prayers, and that in a case of extreme necessity we should be ready to give them any help that is essential for them and which may be in our power." [16]

Personal Reflection

Can I say with complete honesty that I love my neighbor as Jesus loves me and as he wants me to love others? Have I ever asked myself if I look upon *all* my neighbors as brothers and sisters in Christ, or merely as people I can accept or reject at whim? Can I say that my mental attitude toward all the people around me is an attitude of love, respect, and willingness to serve as Jesus taught us to do? Do I love my neighbor, pleasant or unpleasant, for the sake of Jesus, seeing him in each of them? Do I always think of myself first, of my own inter-

---

[14] 1 Corinthians 10:16; Ephesians 4:7; and other passages.

[15] 1 John 4:7, 21

[16] *This Tremendous Lover,* Christian Classics, Inc. Chapter 16.

ests, my own pleasure, my own convenience, my own pride? What positive efforts am I making to increase my love for others, to do good to them? Do I reflect on the Last Judgment and the questions Jesus will ask of me? Perhaps I need to make some changes in this all-important area of my life.

PRAYER
A Christmas Prayer[17]

Night has come and the bright comet that guided the Wise Men from the East scintillates brightly. I am before you, Divine Child, with my head bowed and my hands joined in prayer. You, King of the Universe, have taught us that all your creatures are equal and what distinguishes them is only goodness, a treasure of immense value which is freely given to the poor and the rich. Jesus, teach me how to be good, how to keep only kindness and love in my heart, how to make your gift grow every day and to share it with others in your name.

Short Prayer

My Jesus, teach me how to love my neighbor.

---

[17] Composed by Umberto Saba (1883-1957), Austrian-born poet, quoted by Ravasi, *Mattutino.* p. 433.

16

PATIENCE: "LOVE IS PATIENT"

"Be patient, therefore, my brothers....See how the farmer awaits the precious yield of the soil. He looks forward to it patiently while the soil receives the winter and the spring rains."[1]

An Indian poem entitled simply, "Waiting!," describes how futile it is to force a flower to blossom before its time. One may shake it, beat it, bend, and squeeze it, but this will only break and spoil it. In contrast, the Maker of the flower, with a glance, will make life flow through the veins of the plant, and the flower will display its petals, bend with the breeze, and produce color and perfume. The poem concludes: "He who makes the flower blossom, is always at work, simply and silently."[2]

Jesus' Patience

Even in our post-Christian society, patience is still a much admired virtue. *"Patience is the virtue of saints"* is a popular saying, and *"the patience of Job"* is still a common household phrase in Christian families. But its opposite, impatience, is perhaps the most common of all human faults. This is why St. Paul places the virtue of patience at the top of the list of ingredients that make up love. Patience is an integral part of love, and it is very important for us to learn

---

[1] James 5:7
[2] Ravasi, *Mattutino*. p. 111.

what Jesus taught about it, how he practiced it, what the Bible says about it and, finally, how we should practice it in our relationship with God and humankind.

Jesus taught us patience by example as he practiced it in his relationship with the Father, waiting for the Father's hour to come, in everything he did. Think of the years he spent in Nazareth, thirty of the thirty-three years of his life. Thirty years in that little village working as the village carpenter and making a scant living. From our human viewpoint, we might say those years were wasted. However, they were thirty years of spiritual preparation, thirty years to teach us the most important lesson in life -- to wait patiently to do God's will in his own time and his own way.

Jesus had come to save the world, and he was eager to start his work: *"I have a baptism to receive. What an anguish I feel till it is over."*[3] Yet, he waited patiently for the time assigned by God to begin his public work. God's ways are not man's ways, and wait we must for God to act in his own time. This is why he taught us to pray *"...Your will be done on earth as it is in heaven."*

In his public life, Jesus practiced patience with all those he dealt with -- his disciples, the great crowds that demanded so much of him, the learned and the ignorant, his friends *and* his foes -- and he did so at all times, under all circumstances.

The fact that on a few occasions he showed anger in dealing with the scribes, the pharisees, and the vendors in the Temple does not mean that Jesus lost his temper. His was a *holy* anger in defense of his Father's rights, and his indignation was fully justified because he was defending

---

[3] Luke 12:50

God's cause. He was speaking for God, nor for himself as a man.

For three years Jesus constantly exercised patience with his disciples. They certainly loved him in their own way. They were well meaning, loyal, and devoted. But at the same time, they were uncouth, inconsiderate, motivated chiefly by their dreams of glory, jealous of one another, slow to understand each other, and slow to grasp the mission of Jesus and the feelings of his heart. This went on for three years, day and night, traveling the length and breadth of Palestine. Jesus never showed any impatience, because he loved them in spite of their limitations and did not want to hurt their feelings. He endured everything with limitless patience and was pleased with their good will.

Jesus also showed great patience in particularly difficult situations. When "the twins," John and James, and their mother came to ask that he allow them to sit one at his right and one at his left in his future kingdom, they were asking for the highest positions for themselves. Not only were they arrogant in their request, but they made their demand in the wrong place at the worst possible time -- they approached Jesus within sight of all the other apostles, late at night, when after a hard day of walking Jesus was about to pray -- on the day when Jesus had spoken to all his apostles about his forthcoming passion and death. They ignored Jesus' words, showing no sympathy, no empathy. But Jesus, without showing the slightest impatience and forgiving their insensitivity, their selfishness, and the late hour, dismissed them kindly with a vague promise... and probably a smile.

During his passion, when he endured the most excruciating pain, Jesus set for us an extraordinary example of patience. From the moment he was arrested in the Garden of Gethsemane until the moment he was nailed to the cross, he did not utter a word of complaint, resentment, or protest.   Isaiah describes his passion in these words: *"Though he was harshly treated, he submitted and opened not his mouth; like a lamb led to the slaughter or a sheep before the shearers, he was silent and opened not his mouth."* [4]

Recall briefly how much he suffered physically as he was dragged from the tribunal of the high priest to that of Pontius Pilate, then to Herod and back again, enduring his cruel scourging, his crowning with thorns, his painful trip to Calvary, his brutal crucifixion, his agony on the cross. Think also of his spiritual and mental suffering as he felt rejected by his own people, whom he had come to save, as he heard the people choosing Barabbas, a thief and a murderer, rather than himself, who had spent all his life doing good to others. As the shouts of the crowd -- *"Crucify him! Crucify him"* -- echoed in his mind and heart, he suffered silently, with dignity, accepting with love his Father's Will. Then, the first word he uttered from the cross was, *"Father, forgive them!"*[5]

St. Francis de Sales offers this reflection: "Look often with your inward eyes on Christ Jesus, crucified, naked, blasphemed, slandered, forsaken, and overwhelmed by every kind of weariness, sorrow, and labor. Remember that your sufferings are not comparable to his either in quality or quantity and that you can never suffer for his sake anything equal to what he has suffered for you. Think of the torments the martyrs endured and those so many people now endure that are incomparably more grievous than yours. Then say: 'Alas! are not my hardships consolations and my thorns roses in comparison with those who without help,

---

[4] Isaiah, 53:7
[5] Luke 23:24

assistance, or relief live a continual death under the burden of afflictions infinitely greater than mine?' "[6]

What an example for us! We are always tempted to lose our tempers and even to curse and swear when we are inconvenienced, when our pride is hurt or our reputation is at stake. Why not at such time take a crucifix in our hands and look at it? How can we complain and rage on about our personal misfortune while Jesus suffered so much for our love?

Patience in the Bible

In the Bible, patience is often presented as forbearance. Both virtues are very similar, but there is a difference between the two: *forbearance* means mostly self-restraint and control of anger, while *patience* has a broader meaning; it enables us to bear the trials and tribulations of life in a spirit of love and resignation to God's will.

As God is love, itself, so his patience with us is infinite and eternal. It does our soul good to often reflect on how much patience God has with us. Think of your indifference to his burning love, your neglect of him, your offenses when you abandon him to indulge your passions. No other thought can motivate us more effectively to practice patience with others than thinking of God's patience with us. It makes sense. As God exercises patience with us, so he wants us to be patient with his other creatures -- our brothers and sisters on earth when they offend us, as well as with the adversities inflicted on us by natural causes. We find in the Old Testament many references to God's ire, anger, and even

---

[6] *Introduction to the Devout Life.* Image Books, Doubleday. New York. p.131. (No publication date.)

vindictiveness. This terminology is the linguistic representation of human traits attributed to God[7] by the people of Old Testament.

It is enlightening to scan the Bible and discover how much God teaches us about patience. The picture that emerges is that of a fatherly God infinitely loving and tolerant with his erring children. The Bible presents God to us as *"a merciful and gracious God, slow to anger and rich in kindness and fidelity,"*[8] immensely patient with our stubbornness and infidelity, always ready to forgive those who turn to him.

Nehemiah's famous prayer referring to Jewish infidelity to God reads: *"You were <u>patient</u> with them for many years, bearing witness against them through your Spirit, still they would not listen."*[9] St. Peter says: *"The Lord is patient with you, not wishing that any should perish but that all should come to repentance."* [10] Sirach proclaims: *"The Lord is <u>patient</u> with men, and showers upon them his mercy."* [11]

The Old Testament deals with God's relationship with his chosen people, and we must keep in mind that what we read in the Bible about the Jews' stubbornness and infidelity applies to us, too! Let us never forget that the whole history of Israel's infidelity in loving and serving God is also the

---

[7] Anthropomorphism.

[8] Exodus 34:6

[9] Nehemiah 9:30

[10] 2 Peter 3:9

[11] Sirach, 18:9

history of our personal infidelity to God, of our stubbornness, and neglect of him.[12]

Patience and the Will of God

Patience is an eternal and unchangeable attribute of
God, but for us it is a virtue to be painfully acquired (with
God's help) by endeavoring to accept God's will out of love
and constant self-restraint from anger.

In order to learn how to bear patiently with our
neighbor, we must learn *to be patient with God* -- namely, to
accept our crosses *in a spirit of love* and look at God's loving
plan for the long-range good of our soul. We have to accept
his plans instead of our own, his delay in answering our
prayers, his apparent lack of support when everything seems
to be crumbling around us and we are on the verge of
despair. We can do this only with his help, and this is why
Jesus taught us to pray: *"...Your will be done on earth as it
is in heaven."* How often does it happen that we recite this
prayer with our lips while our hearts and minds say, *"...MY
will be done on earth...!"*

Unconditional acceptance of God's will is the first
step in our spiritual growth. This is religion: to love and,
therefore, to do God's holy will. *"Any one who loves me will
keep my word, and my Father will love him, and we will come
to him and make our dwelling place with him."* [13] Our
second step is to convince ourselves that God wants us to be
patient. St. Paul exhorts us: *"I plead with you...to live a life*

---

[12] If, while reading the Old and New Testaments, we keep in
mind that whatever infidelity the Jews committed against God is
a symbol of our own personal infidelity, we will draw greater
spiritual benefit by reading the Bible.

[13] John 15:23

worthy of the calling you have received with perfect humility, meekness, and **patience**, bearing with one another lovingly." [14] In his letter to the Colossians he insists: "Put on then, as God's chosen ones, holy and beloved, heartfelt compassion, kindness, humility, gentleness and **patience**." [15]

We must be patient not only when we face a just punishment but also when we suffer unjustly, as Jesus did. St. Peter, in his first letter, tells us: "What credit is there if you are patient when beaten for doing wrong? But if you are patient when you suffer for doing what is good, this is a grace before God." [16] Sirach also wrote: "Accept whatever befalls you, in crushing misfortune be patient." [17]

Reflect on these thoughts whenever you have to endure an offense or an insult from friends or foes. With God's help you can be patient and forgive them. Blessedness is the reward that God promises to those who are patient. Holy Scripture has it: "Blessed is the man who has patience and perseveres." [18]

The Practice of Patience

St. Paul warns us: "You need patience to do God's will and receive what he has promised." [19]

Years ago, a friend gave me a wall plaque with these words: "Lord, give me patience.... but hurry!" It still hangs on the wall in my office right in front of my eyes. At first glance the expression may sound a little irreverent, but it

---

[14] Ephesians 4:1-2
[15] Colossians 3:12
[16] 1 Peter 2:20
[17] Sirach 2:4
[18] Daniel 12:12
[19] Hebrews 10:36

means no offense; it does express, however, how hard it is for us humans to give up our will and to accept God's will. I confess that I still have to look at it many times a day, but I modify the words slightly: "Lord give me patience, and help me to do your will."

Patience, like any other virtue, can only be acquired by practicing it and by a determined will to succeed. The way to success is to develop a mental attitude that enables us to see Jesus living in others and to see God's hand in everything, in the big and small events of our daily lives. This basic Christian attitude of keeping our minds tuned to God's will is necessary in practicing not only patience but all the other virtues which are part of the spectrum of love described by St. Paul.

St. Francis de Sales, often referred to as the "patient saint," offers this motivation to stimulate us to practice patience: "We must often recall that Our Lord has saved us by his suffering and endurance and that we must work out our salvation by suffering and afflictions, enduring with all possible meekness the injuries, denials, and discomforts we meet."[20]

Henry Drummond wrote a simple but inspiring comment on this virtue: "Patience. This is the normal attitude of love, love passive, love waiting to begin; not in a hurry; calm; ready to do its work when the summon comes, but meantime wearing the ornament of a meek and quiet spirit. Love suffers long; bears all things, believes all things, hopes all things. For love understands, and therefore waits."[21]

What I have written about patience in this chapter must be understood and practiced using common sense.

---

[20] *Introduction to the Devout Life.* p.128.
[21] *The Greatest Thing in the World.* p.21-22.

This is an important warning, because even in our efforts to be good, it is easy to overdo it and indulge in exaggeration and irresponsibility. If parents, in order to practice patience, were to allow their children to run wild and do all kinds of mischief, they would not be practicing patience; they would be failing in their duty to educate and train their offspring.

We must remember, too, that our patience to endure contradiction and adversities is also dependent on the state of our health, on the type of temperament we have received from nature, on our mental well being and even on the presence of, or absence of, certain chemicals in our body. In cases of unusual irritability, it might be advisable to visit your family physician to find out if there is a physical cause. However, in our constant daily effort to learn patience, we must never lose sight of the fact that patience is love; and love can be manifested in different ways and at different times, sometimes even as a *holy* anger when it is a matter of upholding God's law. The secret of success is to not be discouraged when we fail but to keep trying. It is not those who never fail that are good, it is those who rise and start again after each failure. Perseverance is indispensable.

Patience is love. And love will bring peace and serenity to your soul; it will make your sacrifices sweet. As Martin Buber put it: "All suffering prepares the soul for vision." Let us meditate often on this beautiful parable that Jesus, himself, told us: *"A man scatters seed on the ground. He goes to bed and gets up day after day. Through it all, the seed sprouts and grows without his knowing how it happens. The soil produces of itself first the blade, then the ear. When the crop is ready he wields the sickle, for the time is ripe for harvest."*[22]

---

[22] Mark 4:27-29

Personal Reflection

Am I aware that my impatience with other people is often an expression of selfishness, of lack of love and consideration for others? Do I realize that in many cases my impatience makes other people suffer unjustly, that I am impatient because I think of *my* convenience only? Jesus exercised patience because he understood people, their limitations, and their backgrounds; he loved them as God and nature made them and not as he would have liked them to be. I must remember that I must accept God's plans for this world and bear with people as they are. There are times when I must wait for people to grow up or for events to happen without telling God what to do and without making my neighbor suffer. To make progress in becoming more patient, I must keep my mind tuned to God's will and develop the habit of seeing Jesus' human features in every person. I must remember that impatience means selfishness, patience means love, and my religion is love.

RESOLUTIONS

I resolve to nurture thoughts and feelings of patience in my soul so that I may always speak and act with patience in my dealings with everybody.

PRAYER
A CHRISTIAN PRAYER

I thank you, eternal Father, because you have not disdained me, your creature, nor have you turned your face away from me, nor have you ignored my desires. You, eternal light, have not disregarded the darkness in my soul; you, eternal life, have not despised me who am bound to die; you, divine physician, have not failed to see my infirmities; you, eternal purity, have not rejected me who am but mud; you who are infinite have not abandoned me who am so limited; you, eternal wisdom, have not despised me who am foolishness, itself.

Help me to remember your graces and favors and strengthen my will in the fire of your love. I realize that you loved me even before I existed and that you still pursue me with your ineffable love.

O abyss of love, eternal deity, most profound ocean. You are fire forever burning and never ceasing to exist; you are the fire that consumes in your heat every trace of my self-love; you are the fire that warms me and enlightens me. In this light I know I see your supreme and infinite Goodness above every other goodness. Happy Goodness, Incomparable Goodness, Most Valuable Goodness. Beauty above every other beauty. Wisdom above every other wisdom. To you be honor and glory.[23]

Short Prayer

My Jesus, help me to love others and to be more patient.

---

[23] This prayer is attributed to St. Catherine of Siena, but in reality it comes from an ancient collection of devotional prayers of popular nature, *The Book of Prayers,* by Dario Spada. Armenia. Free translation by the author from the original Italian.

17

"LOVE IS KIND"
THE KINDNESS OF JESUS

*"Merciful and gracious is the Lord, slow to anger,
abounding in kindness."*

*"The year was approximately 1230 BC. Moses, by
order from God, was alone on top of Mt. Sinai waiting for the
Lord to manifest himself.*

*"And the Lord came down in a cloud. The Lord stood
there with him and proclaimed his name, "Lord." Thus the
Lord passed before him and cried out, "THE LORD, THE LORD,
A MERCIFUL AND GRACIOUS GOD, SLOW TO ANGER AND
RICH IN KINDNESS AND FIDELITY, CONTINUING HIS
KINDNESS FOR A THOUSAND GENERATIONS, AND FORGIV-
ING WICKEDNESS AND CRIME AND SIN."* [1]

Jesus came on earth to complete God's revelation of
his love for us. He gave us his *new* commandment to love
one another and made such love the distinguishing characteristic of his followers. He taught love to us by words and
deeds and dedicated most of his public life to doing good
things to others. Every episode in his life is a lesson of love.
It is love and kindness that make him the most fascinating
man in the history of mankind -- to know him is to love him.

As I have stated elsewhere, my aim is to help people
to *know* Jesus and to *fall in love* with him. Let us reflect
more in depth on some special episodes in the Gospel that
reveal his immense kindness to friends and foes alike.

---

[1] Exodus 34:2-7

Seeing his love in action will help us to better understand how to love our neighbors.

Cana of Galilee

The miracle of *changing water into wine* at the wedding in Cana of Galilee[2] is a classic example of Jesus' kindness. Notice that the first miracle he performed was neither to raise a person from the dead, nor to cure a hopelessly sick person, but simply to please a young couple on their wedding day and to prevent ruining the celebration. Notice also that the miracle was performed without the knowledge of even the spouses. Jesus loved seeing people happy and enjoying themselves because he loved them for their sake and not for his own satisfaction.

The Samaritan Woman

The episode of the *Samaritan woman* and her conversation[3] with Jesus is another fascinating example of Jesus' kindness and tact. He did not wait for the sinner to come to him; he took the initiative and sought her out. He was weary from the journey, thirsty and exhausted, but he ignored his tiredness to talk to one of his children who had gone astray, one who had much potential for good.

Jesus did not reproach or scold her. He simply asked her for a favor -- *"Give me to drink"* -- and he spoke to her as a friend in spite of the traditional enmity between Jews and Samaritans. She probably would have refused to talk to any

---

[2] John 2:1-11
[3] John 4:4-42

person about religion or her personal life, but Jesus acted only as a friend who did not judge or condemn, but one who understood.   To win her to God, Jesus disregarded the barriers of religion and nationality, risking his reputation by talking in public to a woman of bad character.   When she tried to evade his questions and in jest asked him for a drink of his kind of spiritual water, Jesus brought her to her senses with a simple request -- *"Go and fetch your husband"* -- making her realize her sinfulness.   It was Jesus' kindness that conquered her and made of her a missionary to her town. Kindness always conquers.

The Woman Caught in Adultery

This episode[4] is probably the greatest revelation of Jesus' sensitivity, understanding, and kindness.   It was a dramatic occurrence because a human life was at stake. On one side were the accusers, lawyers, and pharisees who wanted to see Jesus disgraced; on the other side, a woman who was being destroyed physically and morally. Jesus was in the middle. His love went out to the poor woman in her anguish. At the same time, he was profoundly disgusted by the revolting hypocrisy and bad faith of the plaintiffs who would stoop so low as to use God's law to go against him and to destroy a precious human being.

Jesus did not honor the accusers with an answer; their hatred placed them beyond reach.   He was only interested in saving the poor woman's life.   After the accusers left in silence and shame, Jesus turned to the still trembling woman and with great kindness and compassion

---

[4] John 8:1-11

told her: *"You may go. But from now on, avoid this sin."*
What a relief! Just moments before she had faced a horrible
and ignominious death and now she was free. All because
a man loved her for her own sake -- for her immortal soul --
and wanted to win her chaste love.

On the Road to Naim

At Naim[5] in Galilee, we see a totally different scene.
Jesus met a funeral procession on its way out to bury a dead
young man -- the only son of a widowed mother. The crowd
was exceptionally somber and many were weeping. The
mother, a fairly young woman, followed the casket crying
and lamenting desperately as only a mother can. Jesus
knew the situation, and the sight of the poor mother moved
his heart with immense pity. He saw not only that particular
mother, but his own mother at the foot of the cross, and all
the mothers in the world through all ages crying over their
physically or spiritually dead children.

In his special love for all women and mothers, he
gently told the weeping woman: *"Do not cry."* Then he
approached the coffin, told the coffin bearers to stop, and
with his divine authority said aloud: *"Young man, I bid you
get up."* Immediately, the young man arose to a sitting
position and began to talk. Jesus simply took him by the
hand and gave him back to his mother.

This is Jesus' kindness: a kind deed to an unknown
weeping woman[6] without even waiting for her to ask.

---

[5] Luke 7:11-15
[6] Unknown to him as a man, not as the Son of God.

Jesus' Kindness to Peter

Jesus reveals the magnitude of his kindness especially when dealing with sinners. As our brother, he knows the depth of our misery, the frailty of our nature, the violence of our passions; and because he wants our ultimate happiness, his kindness is unlimited.

Who can forget Jesus' kindness to Peter after his denial?[7] In a moment of weakness Peter told a string of lies to the maid servant questioning him and even swore that he did not know Jesus. In spite of the fact that he had a privileged position in the little community of Jesus' disciples and that he had received more graces and favors from Jesus than any of the other apostles, he lied shamelessly. His sin of ingratitude was great indeed, but Jesus neither reproached him nor condemned him. And when on that very night Jesus, as a prisoner being dragged from one tribunal to another, passed by, he simply turned and looked at Peter. Only a glance; a glance of deep sorrow and disappointment. That's all. But it was enough to remind Peter of his sin and *"going out, he wept bitterly."*[8] A few days later, Jesus asked Peter three times to affirm his love and then officially proclaimed him the head of his apostles. Jesus' kindness excelled in forgiving sins to repentant sinners.

---

[7] Luke 22:16

[8] A tradition in the Apocrypha claims that since that night Peter always shed tears whenever he heard a cock crow in the early dawn.

Mary Magdalene: the Woman Who Loved Much

The story of Mary Magdalene's love for Jesus, as recorded by St. Luke,[9] is another beautiful, if not the most beautiful and most touching example of Jesus' kindness. It manifests his deep understanding of a woman's heart.

Picture the entire scene in your mind. Driven by her new love for Jesus and wanting to give him a public sign of her sincere conversion, Mary Magdalene enters the banquet hall where Jesus is sitting at table with the leaders of the city. She knows them all -- many of them were her clients. She knows their arrogance and contempt for women, and she knows most of their shameful secrets. She knows that in the eyes of these vulgar and proud males she is merely a "thing", an object to be used for carnal satisfaction and then discarded and thrown away. She knows the contempt with which she is going to be received and yet, inspired by her new, chaste, and tremendous love for Jesus, she is ready to face anything because her love is as strong as death. Her newly acquired humility and knowledge of herself, coupled with her unlimited trust in the love of her Master and Savior, give her unprecedented confidence to defy male arrogance.

Entering the banquet hall with her precious alabaster box of perfumed ointment, she disregards the whispers of surprise and the ogling of the guests. She goes straight to Jesus' place. *"Standing behind his feet, she began to wash them with her tears and wipe them with the hairs of her head, and then she kissed his feet and anointed them with her ointment."*[10]

---

[9] Luke 7:36-50
[10] Luke 7:38. (Revised Standard Version)

Her action was a noble and public affirmation of her new love and her new life. But this gesture of love was lost on the guests. They could not understand her repentance because their warped minds could think only of sex and money. Even the host of the party, Simon, who had invited Jesus for the festive meal, felt nothing but contempt for Mary Magdalene.

Jesus, touched to the core of his heart by this manifestation of repentance and love, came quickly to her defense. Talking loud enough to be understood by all, he told Simon a short parable about a man who had two debtors, one owed him a large sum and the other a paltry one, but neither could pay because they had no money. So the rich man forgave both their debts. Then Jesus asked Simon: *"Which of the two loved him (their master) most?"* Simon answered correctly: *"He to whom he forgave most."*

Jesus turning to Mary Magdalene, told Simon:
"Do you see this woman? I came into your house. You did not give me any water for my feet, but she wet my feet with her tears and wiped them with her hair. You did not give me a kiss, but this woman, from the moment she came in, has not stopped kissing my feet. You did not anoint my head with oil, but she has anointed my feet with perfume. Therefore, I tell you, her many sins have been forgiven -- because she loved much." Then Jesus, turning to her, gently said: *"Your sins are forgiven... Your faith has saved you. Go in peace."*

Who can fathom the depth of relief, of love, of gratitude that swept Mary Magdalene's soul because of Jesus' kindness? Not a word of reproach for the past, not even a warning for the future, only a total and complete forgiveness. The guests were silent and astounded. No one had ever witnessed a similar scene before or had heard similar words. With head held high and shoulders straight, Mary

Magdalene walked out with dignity and peace of mind. The kindness of Jesus had made a new woman of her.

Learning How to Love Others

It is a basic psychological principle that the intensity of our love is always in proportion to the attraction we feel for the object we love. Once we begin to realize the depth of the love of Jesus for us, there can be no other being who can ever attract us as profoundly and as totally as he who is the very "human face" of God. The history of Christianity is replete with examples of men and women, famous and unknown, young and old, who have performed heroic deeds for friends and foes, because they saw God in them.

Let us not forget that to love Jesus means *to see his face in every human face,* in every human creature who walks the face of the earth, no matter how revolting or unlovable, because Jesus considers as done to himself whatever we do to others for his love.[11]

To do this, we must strive to acquire the habit of seeing Jesus in our neighbor and act accordingly.[12] We cannot do this by ourselves. We need help. Prayer is indispensable if we hope to achieve this goal. In our search for God and spiritual maturity, we are not striving to acquire merely a human habit of goodwill towards others, but the real God-inspired love that he, alone, can give us.

Jesus said: *"I am the vine, you are the branches. Whoever remains in me and I in him will bear much fruit*

---

[11] Matthew 25:40

[12] Always in accord with God's law and using common sense.

because without me you can do nothing." [13]   The reason so many Christians fail to be kinder and to spread kindness is because they do not pray enough to obtain from God the gift of loving people in a Christian way. This is also the reason why, in spite of so many books and manuals on love, there is still so little true love in the world. Kindness motivated only by human concerns cannot change the world, but *true* love of God and neighbor can change the face of the earth.

The key to increasing our kindness is a constant effort to get closer to Jesus, abandoning ourselves into his loving, protecting arms, pursuing the kind of love described by St. Paul: *"Nor heights, nor depths, nor any other creature will be able to separate us from the love of God in Christ Jesus."* [14]   Jesus said: *"Ask and it shall be given to you."* [15] This is a divine promise, and Jesus will never fail to keep his promise if we turn to him with humility and confidence.

Personal Reflection

The gospel is the greatest book in the world because it contains the eternal message of life Jesus brought to the world, the "good news" for all mankind, the way to salvation, the whole teaching of Jesus in words and example. We would not have been able to fully understand God's message if Jesus, himself, had not given us practical examples of love for others. If I have neglected reading the gospel daily, it is now time for me to begin to do so, reading slowly, a few lines every day, to better know his heart and what is really important in life.

---

[13] John 15:5
[14] Romans 8:39
[15] Matthew 7:7

The gospel, the Word of God, is devoid of any rhetoric; it is simple, transparent, and uncompromising. It shows us Jesus' life in all its splendor and suffering... it tells us his words of peace and meekness, of tenderness and love.[16]

RESOLUTIONS

The reason Jesus was so kind and gentle is that he looked at people as creatures of the same Father and as brothers and sisters in his humanity. I resolve, therefore, to foster in my mind and heart kind thoughts and feelings toward others so that my words and actions may reflect externally my interior love for God and for them.

P R A Y E R

O Jesus, I cannot even *begin* to imagine the depth and strength of your kindness to us your creatures: it is infinite. But you have also placed in my heart a spark of such kindness, and I beg your help in making it grow so I may imitate you by being kind to all my neighbors, whether they be kind or unkind, with no regard for my personal feelings... and to do it all for the love of you alone.

Short Prayer

Jesus, teach me to be kind to *all* your children.

---

[16] See Ravasi, p. 38.

18

"LOVE IS KIND"
HOW TO PRACTICE KINDNESS

"The greatest thing a man can do for his Heavenly Father is to be kind to some of his other children." [1]

It was a cold, snowy day in Assisi (Italy) in the winter of the year 1206. Young, handsome, aristocratic Francis, the "beau" of the younger set of the city, was living a marginal spiritual life and uncertain whether or not to give himself entirely to God. One day, as he climbed the hill back home, he saw a half naked leper by the roadside asking for help. Shocked to the core of his spirit, Francis was tempted to ignore him and run away. The genteel, sophisticated young man loathed the very sight of this leper, but a stronger inner force pushed him toward the poor man. Suddenly, he remembered: the leper is Christ begging for food and love. He immediately took off his expensive winter coat and wrapped it around the shivering body of the poor creature, gave him all the money he had, and overcoming a deep repugnance, he bent down and kissed the purulent wounds. That kiss was for Francis the decisive moment of his total conversion to God. His commitment to a life of service and dedication to God was made forever.

---

[1] Drummond, p. 22

The Beauty of Kindness

When St. Francis of Assisi bent down to kiss a leper, he performed an act of *heroic kindness*. Even though we may not be called to perform such heroic acts, we cannot fail to admire St. Francis' kindness, his gentle and loving nature, and his love for God. Love of God means that we must constantly remember "to treat each human being with dignity, with reverence, keeping in mind that each person uniquely bears something of God's image. Every human being -- the visible image of the invisible God." [2]

Here is a beautiful page from Henry Drummond's booklet on love: "Kindness is love active. Have you ever noticed how much of Christ's life was spent in merely doing kind things? Run over it with that in view, and you will find that he spent a great portion of his time simply making people happy, doing good turns to other people. God *has* put in our power the happiness of those about us and that is largely to be secured by our being kind to them.

"'*The greatest thing a man can do for his Heavenly Father*,'" someone once said, '*is to be kind to some of His other children.*' I wonder why it is that we are not all kinder than we are? How much the world needs it. How easily it is done. How instantaneously it acts. How infallibly it is remembered. How superabundantly it pays itself back -- for there is no debtor in the world so honorable, so superbly honorable, as Love. 'Love never faileth.' Love is success. Love is happiness. Love is life. Where love is, God is. He that dwelleth in love, dwelleth in God. God is love. Therefore, *love*. Without distinction, without calculation, without procrastination, love. Lavish it upon the poor where

---

[2] Fr. Andrew Anderson, *The Florida Catholic.* March 20, 1996.

it is very easy; especially upon the rich, who often need it most. Most of all upon our equals, where it is very difficult and for whom perhaps we do least of all.

"There is a difference between *trying to please* and *giving pleasure.* Give pleasure. Lose no chance to give pleasure. For that is the ceaseless and anonymous triumph of a truly loving spirit. "I shall pass through this world but once. Any good thing, therefore, that I can do or any kindness that I can show to any human being let me do it *now!* Let me not defer it or neglect it, for I shall not pass this way again." [3]

I invite you to read and re-read this page more than once so that its deep thoughts and motivating ideas may sink deeply into your heart and mind.

Why Are We Not Kinder?

I believe that when it comes to kindness and generosity the American people, as a nation, are second to none. I have lived and worked for almost 90 years on three continents -- Europe, Asia, and the Americas -- and I believe I am qualified to express an unbiased opinion in this matter. When it comes to sympathizing and offering help to the victims of disastrous events, nobody can beat the USA! It is one of our national characteristics to always side with the "underdog". However, when it comes to being kind and generous to others in our daily lives, unfortunately, we are not much better than the rest of the world.

Drummond asks: *"Why is it that we are not all kinder than we are?"* It is a very important question, and it de-

---

[3] Drummond, pp. 22-24.

mands an answer because our own happiness in life and beyond depends upon it.

As we have already noted, most human sufferings and miseries are man-made and are inflicted on humans by fellow humans. True, there are also many sufferings caused by physical laws of nature -- age, weather, sickness -- but the greatest part of all the evils and suffering that afflict us are the result of lack of love and kindness to one another.

Pause for a moment and reflect how you have probably caused misery and suffering to people around you. Think of your impatience, especially with your family. Think of how much suffering you cause because of your selfishness, your insensitivity, your criticism and blame of others, your negative attitude and lack of interest towards so many people. Why is this so?

Lack of kindness is due to innumerable causes, and it is imperative to analyze and correct them. Let us summarize briefly the negative factors that cause lack of kindness, and then find ways and means to foster kindness.

Causes of Lack of Kindness

The are many causes for lack of kindness. We will examine the major ones.

LACK OF GOODWILL. Most of us do not have the will nor the determination to love others as Jesus told us to do -- actually we seldom think about this problem at all.

William Barclay writes: "Most people have an instinctive desire for goodness, but that desire is *wistful and nebulous* rather than *sharp and intense,* and when the moment of decision comes they are not prepared to make the effort and the sacrifice that real goodness demands.

Most people suffer from what Robert Louis Stevenson called *'the malady of not wanting.'* It would obviously make the biggest difference in the world if we desired goodness more than anything else." [4]

SELF-SACRIFICE. Loving all people in a Christian way means self-sacrifice. Why should we sacrifice ourselves for other peoples' sake? Self-love is one of the strongest instincts controlling our personality, our actions, our thoughts, our feelings, our whole behavior. *This is human nature as we have inherited it.* We were created to be happy. Therefore, to give up pleasure is always painful.

Contemporary society, forgetting God and the life of the spirit, tells people to "enjoy yourself, pamper yourself, do your own thing, put yourself first in everything, forget others." However, Jesus tells us: *"Whoever would save his life will lose it, but whoever loses his life for my sake will find it."*[5] This passage of the gospel is the key to understanding the entire plan of God for our lives. Jesus' words, *"Whoever would save his life will lose it,"* mean that those who are interested only in themselves and do everything for personal advantage and enjoyment are wasting their lives and, in the end, will come to nothing. In contrast, " *Whoever loses his life for my sake will find it."* Those who follow Christ, and for his sake care for others more than for themselves, will, in the end, achieve eternal life with God. This is what Christianity is all about.

---

[4] Reproduced from *the Gospel of Matthew*, Vol. 1, p. 100 in the Daily Study Bible Series by William Barclay. Used by permission of Westminster John Knox Press.

[5] Matthew 16:25

LACK OF MOTIVATION. The third and probably most important cause of lack of kindness is that we do not reflect enough on the right motives that should urge us to be kind to others. Let me explain.

Most of the major religions urge their followers to love one another. Philosophers and writers, even the _media_, encourage love for one another. But all of them fail to give us any compelling motives why we should do so and, of course, never mention love for enemies and other unpleasant people. We are rational creatures and we need motives to move us to act. When it comes to avoiding evil and doing good, love is an infinitely more powerful motivation than fear. We need a compelling love, such as the love for God, to act against our natural inclinations. But in our secular society, God is never mentioned in connection with solving social problems. This is why so many plans, laws, and huge amounts of money intended to correct evils end up in miserable failures. Sacred Scripture has it: _"Unless the Lord builds the house, they labor in vain who build."_[6]

Positive Suggestions
Fostering Kind Thoughts, Words, and Deeds

The best way to overcome _negative_ thinking about others is to foster _positive,_ kind thoughts. We cannot make a lemon sweet by taking the acid out of it; we do it only by adding sugar. To overcome our selfishness and to be willing to make sacrifices for others, we must _fill our hearts and minds_ with kind feelings and loving thoughts that lead us to speak kind words and perform kind deeds.

---

[6] Psalm 127:1

KIND THOUGHTS AND FEELINGS. Father Pierre E. Lachance, O.P., writes: "Nothing makes us more God-like than kindness. To acquire so amiable a virtue we must cultivate it at its source: in our hearts. As Jesus said: _'The mouth speaks from the abundance of the heart.'_[7]

"Our external behavior reflects our interior world where our character is formed. The thoughts we approve or reject determine the kind of person we are. He who controls his thinking is in control of his life. If we learn to think as a Christian, we shall act like a Christian, hence the importance of prayer, meditation, and spiritual reading. The thoughts and values we entertain and live by represent the real 'me'.

"Kind thoughts show that we are in touch with God and reflect the goodness of God.

"Finally, the habit of thinking kindly inspires a more profound view of things. We are not prone to judge superficially. We see the goodness in people that often lies beneath the surface. In this, we become more like God who, even when we fail, sees our struggles, our generous efforts, our basic good intentions.God loves us as we really are in the secrecy of our hearts.

"How can we develop the habit of kind thoughts? I would mention two things: First, be humble;[8] second, develop the habit of charitable interpretations.

"Kind interpretations offer an excellent way to develop the habit of kind thoughts. Jesus teaches us not to judge.[9] When we see that one behaves wrongly, it would be foolish to pretend otherwise; but we have no right to

---

[7] Matthew 12:34

[8] We will develop and explain the concept of humility in Chapter 20.

[9] Matthew 7:2

judge the intentions of the heart, which no one but God can see. Nor must we make rash judgments based on insufficient evidence. In such cases, we must withhold judgment and simply say: I don't know.

"We can go one step further: we can avoid being curious about everybody else's business and looking for gossip. Remember the words of Jesus: *'As you judge, so you will be judged.'* " [10]

The practice of charitable interpretations will help us develop the habit of spontaneous kind thoughts. This habit is not easy to acquire and requires time to develop. However, we have to try. And let us not forget that we have a kind Father in heaven who will bless and reward us according to the sincerity and perseverance of our efforts, not according to our success. No one is dispensed from making a serious attempt to think kindly of others: this is love for neighbor.

KIND WORDS. Our love for others remains a mere personal, ineffective feeling until we manifest it outwardly by words, looks, gestures, and deeds. Without such external manifestation, love remains only a personal feeling. This is why *kind words* -- spoken or written -- are of primary importance in manifesting our feelings and helping us to fulfill Jesus' command to love one another. Unfortunately, words can also be used to express hatred and to sow the seed of discord and death. Our tongue can give life, joy, encouragement, or it can cause suffering, despair, even death. The apostle James writes: *"No human being can tame the tongue. It is a ruthless evil, full of deadly poison."* [11]

---

[10] Lachance, Fr. Pierre E., O.P. *The Anchor*, Diocese of Fall River, MA. "About Kind Thoughts." July 22, 1994.

[11] James 3:5

However, true love of God can make the tongue an instrument of life and goodness. Once we have filled our minds with feelings of love, we will naturally *"speak from the abundance of the heart,"*[12] as Jesus said. Just think! what kind words can do:

- *They can make us more God-like* and help us to spread a ray of sunshine around us.

- *They can give happiness* to others and make their lives less dreary.

- *They can reconcile enemies* and destroy long-standing enmities, giving us peace of mind.

- *They can dispel doubts* and misunderstandings and bring people to discuss their problems with sanity.

- *They can help us to spread peace* and bring us all the blessings promised by Jesus to peace-makers.[13]

- *They can bring us peace of mind and soul* and make our lives more happy and serene.

- *They can help us to thank people* for their generosity and reward them for their kindness.

In fact, "there is hardly a power on earth equal to that of kind words" [14] because they are a living expression of that love, which is as strong as death.

Besides using kind words, we can also manifest our love through written words -- love notes, thank you notes -- by a smile, a gift of flowers or of sentimentally valuable objects, by body language, and by any other conventional means that convey to others our inner feelings of love, respect, esteem.

---

[12] Matthew 12:34

[13] Matthew 5:9

[14] Lachance, Fr. Pierre E., O.P. *The Anchor,* "About Kind Words." July 29, 1994. p. 14.

KIND ACTIONS. The power of *kind words* is greatest when accompanied by *kind deeds* that are inspired by genuine love. Jesus' description of the Last Judgment[15] emphasizes kind deeds as the *one* and *only criterion* for admittance to God's Kingdom. Christianity has always believed that the importance of *corporal works of mercy*, such as feeding the hungry, clothing the naked, visiting the sick and others, is shared by the correspondent *spiritual works of mercy* as well, such as teaching the ignorant, counseling, consoling, guiding.

Some people think that kindness shows weakness and that certain qualities such as force, violence, and brute strength are more useful to society. Jesus thought different-ly, and these people are vastly mistaken. Love and kindness are the virtues that help humans to achieve their best potential as God's creatures. If only we all could be more God-like the earth would be transformed into a kind of heaven. Violence can only make it more like hell.

Personal Reflection

I begin to see now how difficult it is to be kind and to love all people with the same kind of all-embracing, universal, and truly spiritual love, without distinctions or restrictions, with which Jesus loves me. He said that people will recognize us as his disciples if we have love for one another. Unfortunately, no one can point to me and say: "See how kind he (or she) is to people. He (or she) is a true Christian."

---

[15] Matthew 25:31-46

It is also true that I do not love others because I hate sacrificing myself, and my faith and love are not strong enough to see the face of Jesus in others. Perhaps I have never attached much importance to being kind to others, except friends. I do strive to avoid sin, I do help others occasionally, but I have never considered being kind to others, friend or foe, to be the most important and most basic teaching of Christ. It never occurred to me that the greatest thing I can do for my Heavenly Father is to be kind to some of his other children.

It is time to change. I must make a real effort to acquire the habit of seeing Jesus in others, good and bad, pleasant and revolting, and *remember constantly that what I do to others is done to Jesus.* I must seriously begin to examine myself daily, to learn how many times I fail to be kind to Jesus.

RESOLUTIONS

Confucius said that even the longest trip of ten thousand miles begins with the first step. I also have a long journey ahead of me to reach the goal of acquiring a genuine love for God and neighbor. My first step in this direction will be to care for the happiness of people around me and to perform every day some kind deeds to manifest my love for them.

P R A Y E R

Lord Jesus, as you love me so much, so I, too, must love my fellow men and women. Help me, please, to love others in deed and truth, and not merely talk about it. Help me, please, to mend my ways and to live in harmony and

peace with all, no matter the cost.   Dwell in me, Lord
Jesus. Teach me to always speak wisely, kindly, compas-
sionately, always forgiving others as you have forgiven me
and never closing my heart to my brothers and sisters in
need.

God be praised for ever and ever.

Short Prayer

Jesus, teach me to be kind.

19

BENEVOLENCE: "LOVE IS NOT JEALOUS"
Overcoming Envy and Jealousy

"For as long as there are jealousy and quarrels among you, are you not of the flesh? And is not your behavior that of ordinary men?"[1]

JESUS' TRIAL BEFORE PILATE. It is early morning when the Roman governor is called in haste to quell a near riot. He hates the Jews' endless religious squabbles. He wants to get this trial over with as quickly as possible. He sits on his gubernatorial chair surrounded by a host of aids and interpreters. Standing before him is Jesus, in chains. Outside the palace, a jeering, howling mob is venting its hatred on the harmless prisoner chanting in staccato time: "Crucify him, crucify him." Pilate, the astute Roman diplomat feels that Jesus is innocent and knows "that it was out of envy that the chief priests had handed him over,"[2] but for political reasons and fearing for his own future career, he condemns Jesus to die -- a victim of jealousy.

Envy and Jealousy

Envy and jealousy are not synonymous, even though some dictionaries treat them as such. They do, however,

---

[1] 1 Corinthians 3:3
[2] Mark 15:10

have some aspects in common. Dr. William Schofield writes: "Envy relates to prestige, property, and power; jealousy relates to perceived threat to an intimate personal relationship, real or desired. For instance, he who suffers the pangs of envy is not necessarily the victim also of jealousy."[3]

Both envy and jealousy are as old as humanity itself. Envy was very much a part of the sin of Adam and Eve, and it was the main reason why Cain murdered his brother, Abel. Jealousy, on the other hand, is the sense of fear and anger we experience when we are afraid to lose some good we treasure very much. A common case of jealousy is the worry and apprehension that a loving spouse experiences when in doubt as to the fidelity of the other partner. Such fear poisons our lives. Jealousy has been called the "jaundice of the soul."

Envy and jealousy both stem from the darkest recesses of our fallen human nature. Indulging in them is irrational, unchristian, and can be the cause of much suffering for ourselves and, worse, for innocent people. Both are markedly selfish and are the product of distorted self-love. They usually prevail in our spiritual life when love for God is absent or ineffective.

Envy and Jealousy in the Bible

The Bible is the story of God's efforts to rescue wayward mankind from its evil ways. It contains all kinds of stories about sin and vice, including many examples of envy and jealousy and their tragic consequences.

---

[3] Dr. Schofield holds a PhD and is a Professor Emeritus of the Departments of Psychiatry and Psychology, Univ. of Minnesota, Minneapolis, MN. From a private letter of April 22, 1995.

The most striking example of these two pernicious vices is the crucifixion of Jesus. His death was the result of the envy and jealousy of the ruling classes of his day. The scribes and pharisees envied Jesus for his power to attract crowds and recruit followers; they were jealous of him because they feared he would destroy their position as national leaders and, thus, ruin their large financial interests.

Other examples include the murder of Abel by his brother Cain, mentioned above, the first recorded crime in the history of mankind; the persecution, kidnapping, and selling of Joseph as a slave to the Egyptians by his older brothers because they envied him the favors he received from their father. Think also of King Saul, who persecuted his son-in-law, David, out of sheer jealousy because David was more popular than himself; in the end, Saul lost his reign *and* his life.

In the New Testament we read of St. Paul who was persecuted, imprisoned, scourged, and finally sent to Rome in chains as a prisoner because of the jealousy of the scribes and pharisees. The gospel records for us the beautiful parable of the prodigal son. You would certainly think that this young man was an ungrateful wretch. But did it ever occur to you that his elder brother was even more despicable? Even though he was supposed to be the "model son," the "good kid on the block," he certainly did not behave like one -- he was off sulking outside the banquet hall, jealous of the attention his brother was receiving. This show of bad temper killed the joy of the aging father for the return of his younger son and ruined an otherwise joyous celebration for all the guests. These stories exemplify the tragic consequences of envy and jealousy.

The Evil Effects of Envy and Jealousy

Indulging deliberately in feelings of envy and jealousy often leads to dislike, even hatred, of the people we envy. As a result, we speak badly of them, make false accusations, and even spread false information to ruin their reputation. Another evil effect is the spreading of dissension and division among members of the same family, the same organization, or even within the same religion. We all probably know pitiful stories of enmities between members of the same family, quarrelling among themselves over some inheritance. If not controlled, envy and jealousy, may lead to a real lust for power and success with disastrous results for one's life.

History attest to the fact that human nature and its basic instincts have changed little down through the centuries. However, God's revelation of divine love has done much to help us toward a better understanding and practice of the virtues of goodness, unselfishness, and generosity -- the very opposites of envy and jealousy.

The Insanity of Envy and Jealousy

If we analyze the origin of envy and jealousy in the light of God's plan for us, we cannot fail to realize how senseless and irrational such feelings are.

We know that God loves us all, and that all he expects from each of us is to love him and to fulfill the role in life that he has appointed us to do. All that matters in life is how much we love God and our neighbor according to the gifts we have received. A similitude can help us to better understand this:

Life on earth can be compared to a stage play where the most applauded actor is not the one that plays the part of a king or queen, but the one who plays his part best, even if it be the part os a servant or slave. So, too, in the life of the spirit, we will not be rewarded by God according to the worldly dignity of our status in life, but according to the way we lived our own life. This is why it makes no sense to envy others for the gifts they have, for their achievements, or for their social position. Remember, the more that is given to us, the more will be expected of us.

It makes no sense to question God as to why he gives certain gifts to us and different ones to others. We have only a very limited, myopic view of the world, while God, in his infinite knowledge and wisdom, sees the eternal, universal picture. How can *we* criticize *his* judgments?

To better understand this point, look upon the love and hatred, the joy and sorrow, the life and death of all the men and women in this world as an immense embroidery designed and woven by God himself, according to his own design. Here on earth, we see only the reverse side of the embroidery, the confused and seemingly purposeless mass of tangled, knotted, multi-colored threads, going off in all directions. But God sees the front side, the finished design and the beauty of his handiwork. Only when we will be with God forever will we see the wonderful design he has worked; then, we will understand and thank him. Here on earth we must humbly fulfill the role God has appointed to us, and believe in his promises, trusting that whatever happens to us is truly for our ultimate good.

Controlling Envy and Jealousy

When we experience symptoms of envy and jealousy, we must react vigorously and reflect on the situation from

God's point of view. We must analyze the evil prompting and, with the help of prayer, reject unchristian feelings. Can we kneel in prayer in front of a crucifix and tell God we love him while at the same time we hate a fellow human, who is our brother or sister, because he is wealthier than us? What really matters in life is not how much we possess, it is how much we *love*.

Perhaps we do not attach much importance to our feelings of envy and jealousy; maybe we seldom if ever mention them in confession. However, indulging in destructive thoughts and feelings, even in a mild form, prevents us from loving our neighbor as we should. They have a very negative effect on our spiritual life and prevent growth in our love for God because they deprive us of much needed help from him.

We cannot always prevent bad feelings from arising in our hearts, but we must react fast, striving to control them by fostering kind thoughts for those people who are the object of our envy or jealousy. If the opportunity arises, we must be especially kind to them, remembering that what we do to them is done to Christ himself.

"Love envieth not," Henry Drummond writes. "Envy is a feeling of ill-will...a spirit of covetousness and detraction. That most despicable of all the unworthy moods which cloud a Christian's soul assuredly waits for us on the threshold of every work, unless we are fortified with grace of magnanimity. Only one thing truly need the Christian envy: the large, rich, generous soul which 'envieth not.'"[4]

---

[4] *The Greatest Thing in the World*, pp. 24-25.

Personal Reflection

Do I frequently experience feelings of envy and jealousy? How strong and frequent are they? If they are too frequent and intense and seem to control most of my life, it may be that I have a natural tendency toward jealousy and envy, and I may need help. I must resign myself to bear this cross throughout my life and be determined to conquer it vigorously. Indulging in envy and jealousy can lead me to spiritual ruin. With prayer and time, and when my spiritual life becomes more intense, I will find it easier to overcome these feelings. Practicing goodness means that I must develop the habit of *seeing* Jesus in my neighbors and *loving* Jesus in them. This is true Christianity.

RESOLUTIONS

I resolve to react promptly whenever I experience feelings of envy or jealousy for other people by praying interiorly for them, loving them with benevolence; I will continue to do so every time I am inclined to think unkindly of them.

PRAYER

Jesus, my Lord, I humbly ask you to teach and give me generosity of spirit so that I may love all friends, enemies, and sinners with a great and benevolent heart, like yours. Grant me the grace to see your face in every human face, so that I may not yield to the temptation to envy or be jealous of anyone because all of us are your children and brothers and sisters. Help me to share the joys and sorrows of other people, beginning with the members of my family and embracing all, friends and foes, good and bad, because you are the Father of us all.

Short Prayer

Lord, Jesus, teach me to always be
kind and generous.

20

HUMILITY: "LOVE DOES NOT PUT ON AIRS"

"Come to me...for I am meek and humble of heart."[1]

One day "the disciples came up to Jesus with the question: "Who is of greatest importance in the kingdom of God?" He called a little child over and stood him in their midst and said: "I assure you, unless you change and become like little children, you will not enter the kingdom of God. Whoever makes himself lowly, becoming like this child, is of greatest importance in that heavenly reign."[2]

The characteristics of a child are simplicity, trust, and forgiveness. These are the virtues Jesus says we need to become citizens of the kingdom of heaven.

The Humility of Jesus

Humility is the most basic and essential element of love; it underlies all other virtues. It is also the most difficult virtue to understand and to practice because its objective is to overcome inborn pride and distorted self-love. It is also difficult to define and hard to describe. We may have an insight into this virtue by reflecting on Jesus' humility as he taught it by his words and example.

"Take my yoke upon you and learn from me, for I am meek and humble of heart, and you will find rest for your-

---

[1] Matthew 11:29
[2] Matthew, 18:1-4.

selves." [3] With these words, Jesus invites us to look at him as our *role model* in the practice of humility.

The figure of Jesus that emerges from the sketchy pages of the gospels is that of a man who attracts people because he is immensely good, kind, wise, and lovable. Jesus taught us a great deal about all virtues, but his most precious teachings are about humility, the core of goodness and love. To endure humiliations was an essential part of Jesus' mission because he came to make reparation for Adam's sin of pride. St. Paul briefly summarized this concept when he wrote: *"Though he was God... he took the form of a slave and... humbled himself, obediently accepting even death, death on a cross."* [4]

Jesus' free choice to be born a cave for animals was the beginning of his earthly life of humility. As he grew in age, he practiced it in Nazareth for thirty years living the life of an ordinary child and adolescent, and later as an adult, working as a carpenter, all the while hiding his divine origin and powers. He showed humility when he requested John's baptism and thus associated himself with public sinners and tax collectors. Often, after performing a miracle, he requested people to tell no one; he refused to accept honors; he went into hiding because the people wanted to make him king. These are but a few of the innumerable examples of Jesus' humility, and the gospels are filled with such examples.

Jesus also demonstrated his humility in the way he accepted rejection and suffering. When his own people in Nazareth refused to accept him and decided to throw him from a cliff, he simply walked away from them without even a word of condemnation or resentment. When the crowds

---

[3] Matthew 11:29
[4] Philippians 2:6-8

left him after his speech about eating his flesh and drinking his blood, he did not utter a word of complaint. Even when his apostles criticized him for not hurrying to go to Bethany to cure his sick friend, Lazarus, he showed no resentment.

But where Jesus' humility shines in all its greatness is the way he endured his passion and death. Isaiah wrote of Him: *"Though he was harshly treated, he submitted and opened not his mouth; like a lamb led to the slaughter or a sheep before his shearers, he was silent and opened not his mouth."* [5]

When an arrogant servant in the house of Caiphas slapped him in the face, Jesus simply asked with dignity: *"If I have said anything wrong, produce the evidence; but if I spoke the truth why do you hit me?"* [6] When *"Herod and his guards treated him with contempt and sent him back to Pilate"* [7] dressed as a fool, Jesus did not utter a word. Even on the cross, rather than expressing indignation for that supreme travesty of justice, he simply prayed: *"Father, forgive them."*

When Jesus spoke to the Jews about humility, repentance and a contrite heart, they understood very well what he meant. The Jews, as "the chosen people of God," through three thousand years of preparation for the coming of Jesus, learned humility, expiation, and repentance through their dependence on God. The prophets and the writers of the Psalms speak of humility as a manifestation of filial respect, obedience, contrition, and meekness.

Jesus confirmed the old Jewish concept of humility and emphasized its importance as an indispensable element in our love for God and neighbor. He spoke of himself as "meek and humble," as the Son of God who had come to

---

[5] Isaiah 53:7
[6] John 18:23
[7] Luke 23:11

obey, to serve, and to accept the humiliation of the cross in order to do his Father's will. When he, the Son of God, stooped down to wash the feet of his apostles, he was humility personified.[8]

By all his examples he taught us that humility is indispensable to his followers, and those who do not have it cannot be his disciples. *"Whoever exalts himself shall be humbled, but who humbles himself shall be exalted."* [9]

The Parable of the Pharisee and the Tax Collector[10]

The masterful portrait of the proud pharisee and the humble tax collector created by Jesus in this famous parable is the best practical description of what pride and humility really are. St. Luke reminds us that this parable was *"addressed to those who believed in their own self-righteousness while holding everyone else in contempt."* [11]

With an unparalleled graphic description, Jesus outlines the loveless figure of the pompous, self-loving pharisee. He has gone up to the temple to pray; but he does not pray, he only recites a testimonial to his ego. *"With head unbowed,"* he boasts about himself, *"I give you thanks, O God, I am not like the rest of men -- grasping, crooked, adulterous -- or even like this tax collector. I fast twice a week, I pay tithes on all I possess."* [12]

This is the prayer of a man who thinks only of himself, who refuses to recognize his sins and has no love but for himself. He even implies that God should be grateful

---

[8] John 13:4-5
[9] Matthew 32:12
[10] Luke 18:9-14
[11] Luke 18:9
[12] Luke 18:9-12

to him for his good deeds. His proud words cannot please God because he has no love for him and only praises himself. He proudly believes that all his good qualities are the fruits of his doings, and he feels nothing but contempt for his fellowmen, especially for people he considers beneath himself.

How different is the behavior of the tax collector. He is a public sinner. In the opinion of his people, he is a worthless wretch preying on the poor and defenseless people for his personal profit. Among the Jews, tax collectors were the lowest of the low, the most contemptible of people and at the same level as prostitutes. But the tax collector of this parable is now repenting. Realizing his sinfulness, in contrast with the pharisee, he asks for mercy. And mercy he obtains in abundance.

Visualize for a moment this outcast as *"he kept his distance, not even daring to raise his eyes to heaven. All he did was beat his breast and say, 'O God, be merciful to me a sinner.' "* [13] He recognizes and admits his sinfulness; he offers no excuses and is truly sorry for his misdeeds. It is this kind of humility that moves the heart of God. This is why Jesus concluded the parable with a declaration of approval and blessing: *"Believe me, this man went home from the temple justified, but the other did not."* [14] In plain language, the tax collector had made peace with God and had become God's friend, while the pharisee had displeased God and remained steeped in his own sinful pride.

It is a good habit for Christians to nurture feelings of humility like those of the tax collector, because humility always draws God's forgiveness and blessings.

---

[13] Luke 18:13
[14] Luke 18:14

What is Humility?

In this day and age, humility is a much disparaged virtue. Like the pagans of old who had no knowledge of Christian humility,[15] many people today consider humility a weakness and seldom mention it. If it is mentioned, it is usually done with contempt instead of admiration. Many scholars, including psychiatrists and psychologists, cannot reconcile Christian humility with self-respect, self-esteem, self-confidence, and all the other "selfs" that are necessary for a successful and happy life. Before attempting to explain how such reconciliation is possible, I must briefly describe what humility is.

During Jesus' trial before Pontius Pilate, the Roman Governor asked Jesus an interesting question, *"What is truth?"* and with a shrug of his shoulders he left the hall. So Jesus never answered that question, and we are still asking: *What is truth?* However, the Bible answers this question in no uncertain terms: God is truth; therefore, *humility is truth.* This statement requires an explanation.

Humility is the opposite of pride. Pride inclines us to believe that whatever good qualities we have or whatever we achieve is due to ourselves -- our ability, our power, our intelligence and know-how. It attributes all the good there is in us to ourselves as if God did not exist. Such belief practically denies God's existence. In contrast, humility inclines us to see and evaluate ourselves as we really are in the eyes of God, not in our own eyes, because he, alone,

---

[15] Even in pagan (non-Christian) cultures, however, there were some exceptional philosophers, such as Plato, Aristotle, Seneca, and Cicero, who recognized that a true knowledge of self, deprived of pride, is the only way to truth and to the deity.

truly knows us as he made us, and his judgment is the only true judgment.

Looking at oneself from God's point of view means trying to see oneself as God sees us, with all one's foibles and wickedness, unlimited misery, weakness and evil inclinations. Of course, we realize that there is also some good in all of us; but we have to recognize that whatever is good comes from God as a gift, because without him we would be nothing and would have nothing -- we would not even exist. It is obvious, then, that the evaluation of ourselves prompted by pride is false, while God's evaluation of us is *the truth*. We are what God sees in us.

An excellent spiritual exercise to help develop Christian humility is this: in a moment of spiritual solitude and deep recollection, look at your inner-most spiritual self as God sees you. Look at the ulterior motives you have even when doing good. Look at your past and present deficiencies, your secret passions and desires, all the skeletons in your closet, your lack of love for God and neighbor, your real self. You may be shocked by what you see. Be convinced that if God had not given you all the gifts you have, if he had left you to the mercy of your evil inclinations and desires, you could conceivably be a criminal or a worthless being.

Then look at the good there is in you, at all that you have achieved, all that you possess -- intelligence, wealth, success, good deeds -- whatever you call a blessing, and remember that all these good things come from God. You would not have them without his gift of life and all the other gifts he has bestowed upon you. Seeing yourself in all your spiritual nudity is perhaps not a very pleasant sight, but it is definitely *the truth!*

How can we reconcile such lowly feelings about ourselves with the self-confidence and self-esteem we need to overcome difficulties and to make our lives meaningful? For those who believe in God there is no contradiction whatsoever. In Christian history there are innumerable examples of people who achieved great humility and, at the same time, great success in life. We can see this happy combination of humility and Christian greatness in the lives of countless men and women who, through two thousand years of Christianity, achieved tremendous success, yet, possessed great humility. Among them you will find people in all conditions and walks of life... kings and popes, famous and not-so-famous people, learned and ignorant, rich and poor, young and old... people who remained celibate or professed virginity, or married and with many children.

Some names that come quickly to mind are, St. Francis of Assisi; St. Augustine, who converted to the faith as an adult; St. Henry, the King; St. Bridget of Sweden with nine children; Mother Seton, who was married, widowed, and a convert; Blessed Kateri Tekakwitha, a young native American girl; Mother Teresa of Calcutta; and such famous scientists and writers as Pascal, Dante, Galileo, Isaac Newton, and countless others. These are the real heroes of mankind, the people who achieved great success both in the eyes of God and of the world, who remained humble and glorified God while doing great things for the good of humanity. Humility is *not* a cause of failure in life but a stimulus to real success.

Sigmund Freud stated that religion is a "universal obsessive neurosis" and the cause of many psychological problems. Today, this doctrine is regarded as false even by psychiatrists. What may cause psychological problems and undesirable effects is not religion but a false interpretation of religion. Trying to see ourselves as God sees us is neither weakening our ego-development nor destroying our faith in a strong ego. It is only a question of establishing the right relationships between our mind, soul, and imagination and our feelings of love and submission to our God, who is our loving Father and Creator. *"With God, all things are possible."* [16] This is true Christian faith.

Humility: A Basic Necessity

Spiritual maturity, that is, attaining a life of love and union with God, is the ultimate goal in the life of every Christian who understands his faith. If we have even the slightest wish to secure this supreme good in order to make our lives meaningful, we must be convinced that humility is the gateway to such a life. Actually, it is the first step on the ladder of love leading to intimacy and union with Jesus.

Without humility we are proud; and pride, like that of Adam, inclines us to push God aside and make ourselves the center of everything. Humility, on the other hand, re-establishes God's order within us. It brings us back to reality and opens for us the gateway to spiritual greatness and immortality. This is why St. Peter exhorts us: *"Wrap yourselves in humility... because God refuses the proud and will always favor the humble."* [17] Our relationship with God is based on humility, the consciousness of our limitations, and our dependence on him.

Is this something unworthy of and degrading to humans? Certainly not. On the contrary, it is the most intelligent thing we can do because humility is the acceptance of God's plan for us as his loving children. Pride is characteristic of Satan; humility is characteristic of Jesus. Which one will we choose?

---

[16] Matthew, 19:26
[17] 1 Peter 5:5. The Jerusalem Bible.

Practicing Humility

Humility is a habit[18] that we must acquire by practice. We cannot become humble by reading about it or wishing for it. We have to go through the hard knocks of humiliation to develop an humble attitude of mind and heart. But how? Through prayer -- by asking for it from the Lord through constant and insistent prayer. Humility, as taught by Jesus, is a Christian virtue beyond the reach of our human efforts, and God grants it to those who ask for it with loving perseverance.

We must endeavor to develop a *humble mental attitude* in our relationship with *God* and our *neighbor*:

WITH GOD -- With feelings of *love and joy,* we must acknowledge his infinite perfection and our absolute nothingness: *"For you alone are the Holy One, you alone are the Lord, you alone are the Most High."*[19] With the deepest *gratitude,* we must recognize him as the source of all blessings. With feelings of *dependency,* we must admit our inability to do any good by ourselves and our dependence on him for everything.

WITH OUR NEIGHBOR -- We must rejoice in their successes, empathize with their failures, regard them as better than ourselves in the eyes of God. *"Never act out of rivalry or conceit; rather, let all parties think humbly of others as superior to themselves."*[20] This will lead us to *humility of mind,* a confidence in God and a readiness to ask for and follow the advice of competent persons, and to *humility of*

---

[18] Occasional acts of humility do not make one a humble person. Humility becomes a virtue only when, like all other virtues, it is practiced regularly.

[19] Liturgical prayer.

[20] Philippians 2:3

heart, which helps us to avoid seeking honor and glory for our own satisfaction and pride and to esteem others more than ourselves in the eyes of God.

If, when we suffer a humiliation, we can say with the Psalmist, "It is good for me, Lord, that I have been humbled,"[21] then we surely are on the right path.

Personal Reflection

Jesus told his apostles, "When you have done all you have been commanded to do, say: 'We are useless servants. We have done no more than our duty.'"[22] This is the attitude of a true Christian, but is it mine, too? Humility does not come naturally, but pride does. We inherit pride, and if I do not learn to control it, it may handicap my growth in the love for God and neighbor.

How do I react when I am humiliated? Angry? Depressed? Vindictive? How often do I pray to the Lord for the gift of humility? Do I ever remember that all I have -- life itself, intelligence, wealth, success, good health, family, a blessed country, everything -- are all gifts of God, freely given? Do I ever try to see myself as God sees me?

RESOLUTIONS

I resolve that when I pray I will remember the humble attitude of the tax collector in the temple, and I will try to imitate his feelings of humility.

---

[21] Psalm 118:71
[22] Luke 17:10

P R A Y E R
(from Psalm 51)

"Have mercy on me, O God, in your goodness;
in the greatness of your compassion, wipe out my offense.
Thoroughly wash me from my guilt, and of my sin cleanse
me. For I acknowledge my offense, and my sin is before
me always. Against you only have I sinned and done what
is evil in your sight. My sacrifice, O God, is a contrite spirit;
a heart contrite and humbled, you will not spurn."

Short Prayer

Lord, *"I am a useless servant."* Teach me to be humble.

21

RESPECT FOR OTHERS:
"LOVE IS NEVER RUDE"

*"The Father already loves you because you have loved
me, and have believed that I came from God."* [1]

"There is a Rabbinic tale of a certain Rabbi, Simon ben
Eleazar. Simon was coming from his teacher's house, and he
was feeling uplifted at the thought of his own scholarship and
erudition and goodness. A very ill-favored passer-by gave him
a greeting. The Rabbi did not return the greeting, but said:
'You raca. How ugly you are! Are all the men of your town
as ugly as you?' 'That,' said the passer-by, 'I do not know.
Go and tell the Maker who created me how ugly is the creature
he has made.' And there the sin of contempt was rebuked." [2]

Respect for People and Things

In listing the ingredients of love, St. Paul stated:
"love is never rude." Biblical translators use different words
to convey to us what St. Paul had in mind. They speak of a
love that is polite, charming, gracious, courteous, tactful,
sensitive, generous and so on. All these qualities can be
summarized in one word, *respect.* Love is not real love if it

---

[1] John 16:27.
[2] Reproduced from *the Gospel of Matthew,* Vol. 1, p. 139, in the
<u>Daily Study Bible Series</u> by William Barclay. Used by permission
of Westminster John Knox Press.

is lacking this most important characteristic.   A rude, unpleasant, and contemptuous love is no love at all.

Henry Drummond uses the word "courtesy" to translate the Greek "never rude" and explains: "Courtesy is love in society, love in relation to etiquette. Politeness has been defined as love in little things. And the one secret of politeness is *Love*. The old translation reads: *'Love does not behave itself unseemly.'*" [3]   William Barclay writes: "In Greek, the word for *grace* and for *charm* are the same. There is a graciousness in Christian love which never forgets that courtesy and tact and politeness are lovely things." [4]

I prefer to use the words *respect* and *respectful* to designate the opposite of *being rude*, because we can only love what we respect. When St. Paul included not being rude among the ingredients of love, he was referring to an old, well-established Jewish tradition: that of respect for others.

The moral of the rabbinic parable at the beginning of the chapter is that lack of respect is caused by a lack of love. Rabbi Simon was so conceited and proud of his knowledge that he had no respect for the seemingly ignorant country bumpkin. Forgetting that the Law commands, *"Thou shalt love..,"* he despised the poor passer-by and looked down on him with contempt. He responded to the kind greeting of the poor man with an insult, and called him "raca," which means silly, fool, idiot. Not satisfied with this, he also manifested his contempt for the people of the village of the passer-by. In so doing, the proud Rabbi broke the God's law twice, while the lowly and humble man showed a sense of

---

[3] *The Greatest Thing in the World.* pp. 26-27.

[4] Reproduced from, *the Letters to the Corinthians*, p. 121, in the Daily Study Bible Series by William Barclay. Used by permission of Westminster John Knox Press.

true religion -- he forgave the insult. He taught the Rabbi a good lesson, reminding him that all human beings are God's creatures, and he who criticizes them, criticizes their Maker.

Respect is the Basis for Human Relationships

Joseph Conrad stated a great truth when he wrote: "A man's *real life* is that accorded to him in the thoughts of other men by reason of respect or natural love." [5] Whatever we are able to achieve in life depends on the respect we win from others. Interpersonal relationships are of such vital importance that if we do not enjoy respect from others, we can achieve little or nothing at all. No man is an island. We are essentially social beings, and we cannot live without the help of others. Our whole life is dependent upon interpersonal relationships, from infancy to old age. Through childhood we are dependent upon our parents and family and, later, on our teachers and classmates. In our adult lives we are dependent upon not only the families we have created, but also our fellow workers and all those people who will "wheel us around" in our golden age.

It all boils down to the fact that we will be loved and treated by others as we love and treat them. This is one of the basic principles of life that is often neglected and disregarded. Selfishness creates misery for everyone, and its evil consequences are widespread. *Respect* for each other, for animals, for the environment is, on the other hand, the root that produces the fruits of love.

---

[5] Joseph Conrad, 1857-1924, *Under Western Eyes* (1911). Quoted by John Bartlett, *Bartlett's Familiar Quotations*. 15 ed. p.684

Respect in Married Life

The human relationship which suffers most from lack of respect is that between husband and wife. Lack of respect is the main reason why today in our country almost fifty percent of all marriages wind up in the divorce court.

How can a husband and wife build up and maintain respect for each other? By overcoming the temptation to criticize each other and by thinking and appreciating the good qualities that are present in each of them. Some marriage manuals advise spouses to build a *spiritual pedestal* for each other. If this suggestion is carried out with true Christian spirit, it is an excellent way to help married couples maintain and foster married love. What does it mean to "build a spiritual pedestal?"

The road to divorce begins when spouses discover each other's faults that they had ignored during courtship but which now seem unbearable in married life. Most of the time such defects are caused by lack of self-discipline or selfishness on the part of one or both sides and a lack of understanding of the nature of marriage which demands a complete gift of self to each other. Instead of praying together for guidance and talking things over with each other to resolve their problems as mature adults should do, they begin criticizing each other. This causes a lack of respect for each other and leads to quarrels and insults. And as the initial romantic feelings cool and the excitement of the early years of married life wanes, each spouse becomes more irritated by the other. They can no longer see the good qualities of the other, only their faults. Life together becomes impossible and divorce follows, with all its tragic consequences for the spouses themselves and, above all, for the children.

The best way to avoid the disaster of divorce is to keep alive the fundamental Christian idea of marriage as a total gift of self to one another and to continually foster the growth of that mutual respect that originally attracted one to the other. It can be done if each spouse works seriously at correcting his or her own defects for the sake of pleasing the other and if each reflects on the positive attributes, good qualities and deeds of the other partner.

It may help to make a list of the good qualities of one's spouse, such as being a generous provider, a faithful spouse, a good parent, and so on. These good points may be considered as so many bricks in the building of the *spiritual pedestal* we mentioned above. As love and admiration for each other grow, by continually adding new "bricks" (good points), the spouses will be able to discuss each other's deficiencies and negative qualities in a spirit of love and work toward smoothing out the rocky road of married life.

John Giba, a close personal friend, in an article on *The Secret For A Long And Happy Marriage,* writes: "A successful marriage is a relationship between two people based on love, loyalty, and a mutual respect for each other. Such a marriage demands a mysterious blend of independence and loving dependence. It is a giving-receiving relationship. Like the two halves of a whole, they complement one another, fulfill each other's needs, and make up for their mutual deficiencies. In a word, they are equal but different with each having his and her own opinions, feelings, and needs. And it must be realized that at times each may require their own privacy -- space."

These wise words are the fruit of the writer's long and happy marriage of over fifty years.

We all know that a successful married life takes work and at times can be very difficult, but let's not forget that prayer and love can conquer everything because *"for God all things are possible."* [6]

Respect for Children

Respect for children is another important characteristic of Christian love. Such respect, as taught by Jesus, [7] is not only an extremely important element of family life but an indispensable necessity for imparting a true Christian education to one's children.

Children need to feel respected and loved to build up their own self-respect and self-confidence, two necessary and basic elements for normal growth and healthy development. A common and tragic mistake often committed by parents and teachers is to believe that a child will be stimulated to study, to behave, to perform well if he is ignored, ridiculed, blamed and punished for anything that may go wrong. Under this kind of treatment, even a healthy child will become depressed and rebellious and take refuge in a totally passive attitude.

Another common mistake made by parents is to let their children do what they want for fear of inhibiting their child's personality and creativity. Such theories, in spite of their popularity, have been proven wrong. They are utopian and unrealistic. Parents seem to forget that children need discipline, administered with love, patience, training, and spiritual guidance, as much as they need food, clothing, a sense of stability, and a loving environment.

Parents (and teachers, too) who treat children like pawns on a chessboard, who have no respect for their

---

[6] Matthew 19:26
[7] Matthew 19:13; Mark 10:13; Luke 18:16

individual personalities, and who try only to impose their own will on them, should be aware that they are acting contrary to common sense and contrary to the teachings of Christ. And what they call love for their children is nothing but masked selfishness.

If Christian parents want to fulfill their most sacred duties as teachers and educators of their own children, they must develop the habit of seeing in them a reflection of Jesus' image. Therefore, they must make the child feel esteemed, wanted, and loved, even during a just reprimand. In families with children who have different degrees of intelligence, the parents should abstain from any form of preferential treatment, particularly during the formative childhood years. Pushing the less gifted children aside while putting the more gifted ones on a pedestal can ruin the less gifted for life, leaving indelible scars on their hearts and souls. Such preference also gives the more gifted child the false notion that he or she is better than others, leading to an attitude of superiority and lack of humility.

The Power of Respect

Henry Drummond writes: "God has put in our power the happiness of those about us, and that is largely to be secured by our being kind to them." [8] We have this tremendous power to either give happiness to those who live with us and around us or to make them miserable. It all depends on the respect we have for them. Respect for others is uplifting. It makes people feel good and loved. This basic respect is what makes our love all-powerful and brings happiness, confidence, and joy to all those around us.

---

[8] *The Greatest Thing in the World.* p. 22.

Personal Reflection

Am I inclined to be kind only to people who are attractive to me or who can do me some good? Am I indifferent, even hostile, to people whom I do not like? This attitude is certainly not what Jesus has taught me. I have to read again the *Sermon on the Mount,*[9] where Jesus gives us the concentrated essence of true respect and love for others. It is the highest moral code ever proposed to mankind, and it gives us all the necessary details to practice it in our relationships with others. If I really want to grow to spiritual maturity and enjoy all the benefits it brings in time and eternity, I must read and re-read these beautiful chapters from St. Matthew's Gospel.

RESOLUTIONS

I resolve to extend respect for others to all people with whom I will have personal contact every day of my life, beginning with those who are near and dear to me, extending it to those I don't know, and especially to those whom I dislike most. I will treat with respect (even those crazy drivers on the roads!) all people regardless of race, religion, or sex, because I know that all are children of God, like I am.

---

[9] Matthew, Chaps. 5-10

PRAYER
(by John Henry Cardinal Newman)

LEAD, Kindly Light, amid the encircling gloom
    Lead Thou me on!
The night is dark, and I am far from home -
    Lead Thou me on!
Keep Thou my feet: I do not ask to see
The distant scene -- one step enough for me.

I was not ever thus, nor pray'd that Thou
    Shouldst lead me on.
I loved to choose and see my path, but now
    Lead Thou me on!
I loved the garish day and, in spite of fears,
Pride ruled my will: remember not past years.

So long Thy power hath blest me, sure it still
    Will lead me on,
O'er moor and fen, o'er crag and torrent, till
    The night is gone;
And with the morn those angel faces smile
Which I have loved long since and lost
awhile.[10]

Short Prayer

Jesus, teach me to respect all people
as your beloved children.

---

[10] *A Newman Prayer Book,* p.32

22

UNSELFISHNESS:
"LOVE IS NOT SELF-SEEKING"

"No one should be looking for his own advantage, but everybody for the advantage of the other person." [1]

Terror reigned among the innocent prisoners in Block 14 in the Auschwitz Nazi concentration camp on July 11, 1941. One prisoner had managed to escape and now the other inmates were cowering in terror waiting for the authorities' reprisal. It came soon and in a tragic way. They all knew the rule: for every prisoner who escaped, ten would die. Ten men were picked at random and condemned to die. Among them was a young man whose only fault was that he practiced his religion. He had left at home a young wife and child. Now the thought of dying drove him to despair. He wept, he screamed, he entreated the camp guard to let him live, but all to no avail. His fellow prisoners, though accustomed to such scenes, were all in tears or in futile raging. Then a 47-year old Franciscan Friar stepped boldly forward and asked the commanding officer to let him die in the place of the young father. The Nazi officer agreed, and the young man was spared. Shortly afterward, Father Maximilian Kolbe was killed by an injection of carbolic acid. We now venerate this heroic priest as **Saint Maximilian Kolbe**. In the midst of the tragic horror of that infamous camp, once more the words of Jesus

---

[1] 1 Corinthians 10:24

*were fulfilled: **"No one has greater love than this, to lay down one's life for one's friends."** [2]*

Primacy of Unselfishness

Unselfishness is among the most important attributes of Christian love because it aims directly at controlling distorted self-love.

God created us to choose freely between *love for him* above everything and everyone else, or *love for self* and other creatures more than for him. If we did not have such a choice, we would be like robots programmed to love God only, and there can be no merit in that.

By nature we are inclined to love ourselves more than God. God is an invisible Spirit, and our instincts draw us to visible and earthly pleasures rather than to the supernatural. It is such attraction, if left uncontrolled, that causes so much evil and suffering in the world. Actually, the story of man's spiritual relationship with God on earth is the story of self-love prevailing over love for God. This is why many of the evils we suffer are man-made and stem from unrestrained selfishness.

True, not all sufferings in the world are caused by distorted self-love. There are, for instance, "the suicidal missions of the Japanese Air Force during World War II and the 'ethnic cleansing' in the Middle East wars that are examples of selfless devotion to cause and the fruit of religious fanaticism rather than to self-love." [3] But generally

---

[2] John 15:13

[3] Private letter from Dr. William Schofield of April 22, 1995.

speaking, sufferings inflicted on others by self-love are a regular occurrence in everybody's life.

Jesus' Example of Unselfishness

Unselfishness is the primary characteristic of Jesus' mission on earth and of his personal love for us. He is the model we have to imitate in order to live a true Christian life. Jesus sacrificed himself to the point of becoming equal to us in everything, except sin, in order to be our model. *"Though he was in the form of God..., he emptied himself and took the form of a man, being born in the likeness of man..., (and) humbled himself obediently accepting even death, death on the cross."* [4] No one can do more than give up his life for the good of others, and Jesus did just that.

Throughout his earthly life Jesus had a very clear set of priorities. His Father came first, we humans second and he, himself, third. His whole life on earth was a continuous example of the most dedicated unselfishness the world has ever seen. He gladly undertook the saving of mankind, he assumed a body and accepted death to atone for our sins and to obtain forgiveness. *"Behold I come. To do your will, O my God, is my delight."* [5]

Throughout his first thirty years of life, from his humble birth in Bethlehem and his exile in Egypt to his hidden life in Nazareth, Jesus lived selflessly for us. Later, he revealed the goal of his earthly life: *"The Son of Man did not come to be served but to serve and to give his life as a*

---

[4] Philippians 2:6-8
[5] Psalm 40:8

ransom for many." [6]   This is why he taught his apostles: *"Whoever is the greatest among you, let him serve the others."* His three years of public life were all spent in the service of others as he *"went about doing good work and healing all who were in the grip of the devil."* [7]

He never thought of himself, but of us. For our sake he submitted himself to temptation. He experienced hunger, thirst, tiredness, incredible psychological pain to the point of perspiring drops of blood. For us he gave up his right to life and accepted mockery, torture, and a trial that was the greatest travesty of justice the world has ever seen. His death on the cross is the greatest example of unselfish love man has ever witnessed in the history of the world. Can we then ignore him when he asks us to imitate his unselfish love and to love others as he loves us? He said: *"You shall love the Lord, your God, with all your heart... and soul... and mind."* [8] Then he added: *"If I washed your feet -- I who am your Teacher and Lord -- then you must wash each other's feet. I give you a new commandment: love one another. Such as my love has been for you, so must you have love for one another."* [9]

Love: Motivation and Reward

There are two reasons that can move humans to love God: *one* is fear of punishment, hell; or the desire of reward, eternal life. The *second* is to love God for his own sake, for what he is: the eternal being and supreme beauty who created us for an eternal life of love with him. Once we

---

[6] Matthew 20:28
[7] Acts 10:38
[8] Matthew 22:37
[9] John 13:14,34

shed our mortal body, we will feel the full attraction to him much as a piece of iron is irresistibly attracted to a magnet.

The first way is tainted with selfishness, but it is still acceptable to God who knows the frailty of our nature. The second way, the way we should try to follow, is the way God has planned for us as his intelligent beings.

Dr. Schofield comments that today, many scientists believe that "all behavior is shaped and governed by the principle of consequences, that is, reward and/or punishment, or the anticipation of such based on experience. Therefore, in the end, our love of God is controlled by the anticipation of punishment or reward, and it is basically of a selfish nature... In my view, the appeal of the Christian message is sullied, or diluted, by the promise of a personal reward. What greater act of selfishness can there be than to have my behavior governed by the promise of eternal perpetuation of my *self*, or the threat of punishment?" [10]

With all due respect to my good friend Dr. Schofield, in this case it seems to me that "the principle of consequences" is much too generalized and it exceeds its limits. In other words, this principle does not apply to actions motivated by *true* love. A mother who spends sleepless nights caring for a sick child does not think of reward; she acts out of love, and all she cares for is the well-being of her child. *True* love is not motivated by reward because love IS a reward in itself. When we truly love another person, we want the happiness of that person, and to see that person happy increases our love. The enjoyment we experience in loving is built into the very nature of love. We love because we are attracted to the person we love, and the enjoyment

---

[10] From personal letter of April 22, 1995.

that accompanies such love is the immediate result of love itself, not a reward.[11]

However, we have to make a distinction: the way we love God on earth is *not* the same way we will love him in heaven. Here on earth love can be tainted by selfishness, and the vision of God is only a matter of faith, but in heaven, as pure spirits, we will enjoy the characteristics of *spirits* and will see God as he is, in all his love, splendor, and beauty. We will love him for his own sake and will find in his love the perfect fulfillment of all our needs and desires -- a *fulfillment*, not a reward.

The Consequences of Selfishness

As I have already mentioned, the media and "pop-psychology," floundering in secularism and naturalism continually urge us to enjoy ourselves, pamper ourselves, do our own thing, be happy, enjoy life... forget others! In short... *ME* first, *ME* always.

What are the consequences of such thinking? Dr. Ravasi describes the effects of such a pernicious philosophy of life. "Our civilization under the pretext of overcoming psychological complexes and removing inhibiting brakes, praises and encourages blind sexuality, the following of instincts, the removal of every rule and norm. Lack of self-control is regarded as a cool life-style, a sign of superiority, of freedom, of lack of taboos. We must give the child whatever he wants, teenagers need not exercise their will or be concerned with self-control, the adult need not worry

---

[11] It is important to keep in mind that here I am speaking of love as *agape,* not *eros.*

about spiritual growth and development, the elderly person can do whatever he or she likes. The end result of such pagan attitudes is a disproportionate number of persons who are abnormally selfish, arrogant, uncouth, frustrated, intolerant of the least sacrifice, not to speak of the spreading of crime among people of all ages and social condition, and the general decay of moral values, of art and culture. St. Augustine used strong language in describing the evil effects of selfishness: *'Self-love to the point of disregarding God, is what makes the world a Babylon.'* " [12]

Loving God More than Oneself

Loving ourselves or other creatures more than God means relegating God to second place, distorting the primary purpose of life, making ourselves the primary object of our love, and putting ourselves in the place of God in our order of priorities. Can there be anything more senseless and ludicrous than this? When we think of the frailty of our existence and of the evil inclinations and limitations of our human nature, how can we declare our independence from our loving Creator? On the contrary, if we are convinced that we are God's children and are all brothers and sisters, then it makes sense to love Jesus more than oneself and to sacrifice oneself for the happiness of others. This is what he wants us to do because this is what he did.

Let me repeat that it is in the nature of love to rejoice in making the other person happy even at the cost of a personal sacrifice. This is what we call "self-sacrificing love". It is the type of love Jesus had for us, that parents

---

[12] *Mattutino.* p. 100-101.

have for children, and it is the characteristic of every true love on earth. Only in heaven will we will taste pure happiness because our time of trial will be over.

Love and Self-Discipline
Controlling our Human Drives through the Mind

Love and self-discipline have to co-exist; they are not at odds with one another. Many psychiatrists and psychologists agree on this point because we truly live in a state of warfare between the contradicting desires and inclinations of soul and body, of spirit and matter.

Buddhists and Muslims believe in this doctrine, too. A medieval Muslim mystic commenting on the difficulty of self-control once wrote: "The Holy War is made up of ten parts: one part consists of fighting against the enemy, and the nine remaining parts in waging war against oneself." [13] We must practice self-denial if we are to prevent our selfish inclinations from leading us away from God. Jesus told us exactly that: *"If any one wants to come after me, he must deny his very self, take up his cross, and begin to follow in my footsteps."* [14]

The New Catholic Encyclopedia explains: our passions "must be checked, disciplined and integrated into the coherent work of love. Unless our spirit truly and vigorously assumes the ascendancy, man's lower drives run riot in their strident search for satisfaction. But, as part of the larger work of love, even their curtailment and frustration in particular instances can contribute to overall growth." [15]

---

[13] Ravasi, *Mattutino*. p.100.

[14] Matthew 14:24

[15] NCE. Word, *self-love*.

M. Scott Peck, M.D., in his book, *The Road Less Traveled,* teaches a great Christian truth when he writes that seemingly being compelled "to give up one's self and one's life represents a kind of cruelty on the part of God or fate, which makes our existence a sort of bad joke and which can never be completely accepted. This attitude is particularly true in present day Western culture in which the self is held sacred and is considered an unspeakable insult. Yet the exact opposite is the reality. It is in the giving up of self that human beings can find the most ecstatic and lasting, solid, durable joy of life. And it is death that provides life with its meaning. This 'secret' is the central wisdom of religion." [16]

Jesus Our Helper

Of the nine ingredients of love,[17] unselfishness is the most difficult and the least practiced. Self-renouncement is truly difficult, and only a heartfelt love for Jesus can help us to do it.

Henry Drummond writes: "Nothing is a hardship to love, and nothing is hard. I believe that Christ's 'yoke' is easy. Christ's 'yoke' is just His way of taking life. And I believe it is an easier way than any other. I believe it is a happier way than any other. The most obvious lesson in Christ's teaching is that there is no happiness in having and getting anything, but only in giving. I repeat, *there is no happiness in having or getting, but only in giving.* And half the world is on the wrong scent in pursuit of happiness. They think it consists in having and getting, and in being served by others. It consists in giving and in serving others.

---

[16] *The Road Less Traveled,* p. 72.
[17] See Chapter 15.

He that would be greater among you, said Christ, let him serve. He that would be happy, let him remember that there is but one way -- it is more blessed, it is more happy, to give than to receive." [18]

In other words, only when we have really fallen in love with Jesus and he has become the most loved and adored person in our lives, the beginning and end of all we think and do, then with his help we will be able to practice self-denial and to see his reflection in every human being and love them all, friends and foes, for his sake.

Personal Reflection

There is no doubt that "giving up of self" is painful, but we are the disciples of a crucified God and we must share his sufferings. All the true followers of Jesus, like Mary, the Apostles, and all the Saints and all true Christians, have practiced unselfishness to a heroic degree. But, I am no saint. How can I do it? I must begin to pray and ask for Jesus' help, more often and more insistently. Out of all the prayers in the world, the prayer to help us grow in his love is certainly the one that Jesus cannot fail to grant us. I have to do it.

RESOLUTIONS

I resolve that whenever I shall have a reasonable opportunity to sacrifice myself for others, I will not think of them or of me, but only of Jesus, whom I want to please.

---

[18] *The Greatest Thing in the World.* p. 28.

PRAYER
(by John Henry Cardinal Newman)

"TO POSSESS you, Lover of Souls, is happiness, and the only happiness of the immortal soul. To enjoy the sight of you is the only happiness of eternity. What can give me happiness but you? To see you, to contemplate you, this alone is inexhaustible. You indeed are unchangeable, yet in you there are always more glorious depths and more varied attributes to search into; we shall ever be beginning as if we have never gazed upon you. How far am I from acting according to what I know so well! Rouse me from sloth and coldness and make me desire Thee with my whole heart." [19]

Short Prayer

Lord Jesus, help me to practice self-denial
for your sake.

---

[19] *A Newman Prayer Book,* p.1

23

GOOD TEMPER:
"LOVE IS NOT PRONE TO ANGER"

A VIGNETTE FROM THE GOSPEL.- (From the parable of the Prodigal Son.[1]) Henry Drummond writes: "Look at the Elder Brother, moral, hard-working, patient, dutiful -- let him get all the credit for his virtues -- look at this man, this baby, sulking outside his father's door. 'He was angry,' we read, 'and would not go in.' Look at the effect upon the father, upon the servants, upon the happiness of the guests. Judge of the effect upon the Prodigal -and how many prodigals are kept out of the Kingdom of God by the unlovely character of those who profess to be inside? Analyze, as a study in Temper, the under-cloud as it gathers upon the Elder Brother's brow. What is it made of? Jealousy, anger, pride, uncharity, touchiness, self-righteousness, cruelty, doggedness, sullenness, - these are the ingredients of this dark and loveless soul. In varying proportions, also, these are the ingredients of all ill temper."[2]

Love and Good Temper

"*Love is not prone to anger.*"[3] Contemporary biblical versions offer various translations of this verse of St. Paul, such as "*love is not provoked,*" or "*love is not irritable,* or "*love is not quick to take offense,*" and so on. Translated into the

---

[1] Luke 15:11-31.

[2] Drummond, *The Greatest Thing in the World.* pp. 31-32

[3] 1 Corinthians 13:5.

positive form as Drummond does, "*good temper,*" reflects even better the mind of St. Paul.

It is not surprising to find *good temper* in this God-inspired list of ingredients of love because it really is the *sum total of many other virtues* and the visible expression of love for neighbor.

Love, or lack of love, has a determining influence on our behavior. Our good temper is *love in action* as much as our bad temper shows lack of love. In most cases the presence or the absence of love for others makes the difference between good and bad temper and determines our attitude towards things and persons.

It is not my intention to discuss here ancient and modern theories on the psychology of temperament; however, I would like to quote some interesting observations made by Dr. Peck in his book, *The Road Less Traveled.* He uses the phrase "self-discipline" instead of self-sacrificing love or mortification, as we find in most Catholic spiritual writings; but all three mean substantially the same thing: voluntary self-control and repression of anger. Without self-discipline there is no good temper.

Dr. Peck writes: "The energy for the work of self-discipline derives from love, which is a form of will. It follows, then, not only that self-discipline is usually love translated into action, but also that any genuine lover behaves with self-discipline, and any genuinely loving relationship is a disciplined relationship. If I truly love another, I will obviously order my behavior in such a way as to contribute the utmost to his or her spiritual growth." [4] This is Christianity in action if we do it for the love of God.

---

[4] *The Road Less Traveled,* p. 155.

The Evil of Bad Temper

Before we discuss good temper further, we must consider the evil of bad temper. Obviously, the kind of bad temper about which I am writing here does not consist of impulsive and occasional acts of impatience caused by poor health or by exceptional circumstances. What I wish to emphasize here is habitual selfishness which makes us self-centered and interested only in ourselves, causing much suffering to others.

The scene of the sulking elder brother as described in the parable of the prodigal son points out the disastrous effects of bad temper on others. The comments of Henry Drummond on this parable of Jesus are very realistic. Drummond writes: "We are inclined to look upon bad temper as a very harmless weakness. We speak of it as a mere infirmity of nature, a family failing, a matter of temperament, not a thing to take into very serious account in examining a man's character. And yet here, right in the heart of this analysis of Love, it finds a place; and the Bible again and again returns to condemn it as one of the most destructive elements in human nature.... You will see then why Temper is significant. It is not in what it is alone, but in what it reveals. This is why I take the liberty now of speaking of it with such unusual plainness. It is a test of Love, a symptom, a revelation of an unloving nature at bottom; it is the intermittent fever which bespeaks un-intermittent disease within, the occasional bubble escaping to the surface which betrays some rottenness underneath, a sample of the most hidden products of the soul dropped involuntarily when off one's guard. In a word, the lightening from a hundred hideous and un-Christian sins. For a want of patience, a want of kindness, a want of generosity, a want of courtesy, a want of unselfishness, all are instantaneously symbolized in a flash of Temper." [5]

To make people suffer because of our selfishness means breaking the basic and all-important commandment of Jesus: *"Love one another."*

This is no small sin. Drummond explains: "The peculiarity of bad temper is that it is the vice of the virtuous. It is often the one blot on an otherwise noble character. You know men who are all but perfect, and women who would be entirely perfect, but for an easily ruffled, quick-tempered, or 'touchy' disposition.... No form of vice, not worldliness, not greed of gold, not drunkenness itself, does more to un-Christianize society than evil temper. For embittering life, for breaking up communities, for destroying the most sacred relationships, for devastating homes, for withering up men and women, for taking the bloom off childhood, in short, for sheer, gratuitous misery-producing power, this influence stands alone... There is really no place in Heaven for a disposition like this. A man with such a mood could only make Heaven miserable for all the people in it." [6]

One might think Mr. Drummond's description of the evil effects of bad temper are exaggerated and unreal. However, I believe that were he to write it today he would paint an even darker picture. In these last few years we have all been shocked and horrified by the growing number of abused children and women who suffer and die because of the lack of self-control on the part of violent and bad-tempered parents or spouses. Abusive or violent behavior is due to many causes, but its roots are always to be found in uncontrolled selfishness, lack of genuine love and of self-control. When we realize that the number of cases of abuse

---

[5] *The Greatest Things in the World*, pp. 29, 32-33.

[6] Ibid. p. 30-32.

reported by the media are but a fraction of all those that actually occur, we cannot help being appalled by the evils of uncontrolled bad temper and its presence at every level of society.

Sociologists may explain this epidemic of parents and spouses taking out their temper on the members of their families as a cultural phenomenon and the result of our technological and soul-less society; however, these tragic cases of bad temper are also due to the loss of family values and a condoning of evil by our society. Let us not forget that love for one another is the key to a beautiful and peaceful life.

Unfortunately, millions of people suffer every day because of a bad-tempered parent or employer or teacher or some other person in a position of authority. Who can count the number of children whose personalities remain warped and adversely affected throughout their lives because of an unhappy childhood caused by the quarrels and bad temper of their parents? Who can count the number of failures in any walk of life because of some bad-tempered, irresponsible teacher or employer?

If we reflect on this ocean of misery and suffering caused by bad temper worldwide, beginning perhaps in our own families, office, school, or factory, we cannot fail to agree with Mr. Drummond that *"for misery producing effects, bad temper stands alone."*

Love: The Remedy for Bad Temper

Lack of true, self-sacrificing love is always one of the basic causes of bad temper, and this type of deficiency cannot be cured simply by saying, *"No."* Mr. Drummond explains: "It is not enough to deal with the Temper. We must go to the source and change the inner nature, and the angry humors will die away of themselves. Souls are made sweet not by taking the acid out, but by putting something in -- a great Love, a new Spirit -- the Spirit of Christ. Christ, the Spirit of Christ, inter-penetrating ours, sweetens, purifies, transforms all. This only can eradicate what is wrong, work a chemical change, renovate and regenerate, rehabilitate the inner man. Willpower does not change man. Time does not change man. Christ does. Therefore, 'Let that mind be in you which was also in Christ Jesus.' Some of us do not have much time to lose. Remember, once more, that this is a matter of life or death. I cannot help speaking urgently, for myself, for yourselves. 'Whoso shall offend one of these little ones, who believes in me, it were better for him that a millstone were hanged about his neck, and that he were drowned in the depth of the sea.' That is to say, it is the deliberate verdict of the Lord Jesus that...*It is better not to live than not to love.*" [7]

What kind of love must we have to make life worth living? Based on the revelation of God's love for us through Jesus, we know that without Christ there can be no true, God-inspired love. He, alone, can give us the supernatural help we need to love all humans as he loves us. We can do so only when we see him in all people, pleasant and un-pleasant, and in the good and bad events that make up our lives. We can succeed in loving all the people all the time only if we see Christ in them.

Dr. Peck is right when he writes that self-discipline is the result of love -- actually, it is love in action. We must realize, however, that this is not the kind of love that brings us joys all the time. It requires a self-denial that only too

---

[7] *The Greatest Thing in the World.* pp. 33-34

often is painful to practice, but love can make sacrifice sweet, even though it does not diminish the pain. This is why it is said that the *life of man on earth is a warfare*. And Jesus said: *"Take up your cross and follow me <u>daily</u>."*[8] Spiritual growth and habitual good temper cannot be achieved without much struggle and pain.

Personal Reflection

Am I prone to anger, to brood over offenses, to be irritable if things are not done my way? Am I one of those people who think that bad temper is a harmless habit? Do I care about sparing others needless suffering because of my personal comfort and convenience? Do I have the habit of seeing Jesus in my neighbor? This is a habit not easy to acquire, but how serious am I in trying to master it?

RESOLUTIONS

I will regard bad temper as a very serious defect than can handicap my spiritual growth. Therefore, I will try to live each day unselfishly, dedicating my every action to pleasing others in order to please Jesus, who is living in them.

---

[8] Matthew 10:24

P R A Y E R

Lord God, my Father and my Savior, I humble myself before you as I recognize my inner failure to see you in all people, in all things, and in the events of my life. I humbly ask for your grace to help me recognize your Divine and human face in the faces of the people around me, good and bad, friend or foe, pleasant or unpleasant, so that I may treat them as kindly as I would treat you personally. You alone, O Lord, can help me to do this, and I beg for your help.

Short Prayer

Help me Jesus to see you in all people.

24

FORGIVENESS: "LOVE DOES NOT BROOD OVER INJURIES"

"To err is human; to forgive is divine" [1]

A VIGNETTE FROM THE GOSPEL. *Visualize the Crucifixion of Jesus on Calvary, the day of his death. It is about noon, but there is no sun. Threatening, dark clouds accumulate at the horizon, and they throw an ominous, eerie light. Three large crosses stand tall and dark in the ghastly light. Three half naked men hang on them, agonizing in pain and waiting to die. Two of them are common criminals. The one in the center is Jesus, the Son of God who bears on his shoulders the sins of all humanity, yours and mine included. He wears a crown of thorns, his face is bloodstained, every muscle, every bone in his body is torturing him. He raises his head as if to speak. The soldiers and the hostile crowd expect him to scream, to curse, to protest. But he does not. He resignedly looks at the sky and simply prays: "Father, forgive them; they know not what they do." [2] In his last, dying hour, Jesus does not think of himself, he does not seek revenge; he thinks of us, of you and me, and he asks the Father to forgive us for crucifying him through our sins. Let us bow our heads in humility and contrition.*

---

[1] Alexander Pope, English poet, (1688-1746).
[2] Luke 23:34.

Love and Forgiveness

Forgiveness is an indispensable attribute of love. A refusal to forgive is a refusal to love our enemies.

Look at the world today. Two thousand years after Jesus came and told us to forgive and love one another, hatred, revenge, and cruelty are as prevalent among Christians as well as among non-Christians as if Jesus had never walked the earth. Hatred and selfishness prevail everywhere and they are, at least in part, the cause of local wars, genocides, social injustices, and the death of millions of people. Rwanda, Bosnia, Palestine are all tragic examples of the havoc created by lack of love and forgiveness.

At the personal level, we have only to look around us to discover how much hatred and dislike of others are present everywhere and how much sufferings they cause.

Why Is Forgiveness So Difficult?

Dr. Scott Peck writes: "A big part of growing is learning to forgive. We go through life blaming others for our pain. And blame always begins with anger. Anger is a powerful emotion that originates in the brain." [3] He explains that in our brain there are clusters of nerves centers called "neural centers", and one of these centers controls the emotion of anger. When it is stimulated by the dislike of somebody or something we react with anger.

Anger is a powerful emotion that is an integral part of our physical makeup and of our instinct for preservation. We need it for our very survival. But the lack of control of our anger can lead to our destruction. We must learn to

---

[3] *Further Along The Road Less Traveled.* p. 17.

control it for our own sake and for the sake of those around us. Our spiritual growth is blocked if we do not control anger and are not willing to forgive.

There are psychologists who claim that since anger is a part of our instinct of preservation any inhibiting of it is harmful to us. These psychologists seem to forget that even though we may experience anger in much the same way that some animals do, we are not brute animals; we have an intellect, we have a soul, and we have a free will that makes us responsible for our actions. Above all, we have the power to love, and love can make the control of anger and forgiveness possible, even a source of joy.

Jesus' Forgiveness

Throughout his life, Jesus condemned revenge and urged forgiveness. He alone can ask us to do this because it is he alone who can give us the help and the motivation we need to do it.

Jesus did not mince words when he stated emphatically: *"You have heard the commandment: 'You shall love your countryman but hate your enemy.' My command to you is love your enemies, pray for your persecutors. This is proof that you are sons of your heavenly Father for his sun rises on the bad and the good, he rains on the just and unjust."* [4]

What does Jesus mean by *"love your enemies?"* [5] Love of enemies is not the same kind of love with which we love God or our relatives or even our friends. Love for God and friends comes from the heart while love of enemies is an

---

[4] Matthew 5:43-45

[5] Reproduced from *the Gospel of Matthew*, Vol. 1, pp. 172, 173, in the <u>Daily Study Bible Series</u> by William Barclay. Used by permission of Westminster John Knox Press.

act of the will -- we force ourselves to do it out of our love for Jesus. In fact, forgiveness is a victory over love of self. Love of enemies is possible only when we understand true Christian love, when we see Jesus' presence in all people; we, thereby, willingly foster feelings of tolerance and benevolence toward those who hurt and injure us. Our instincts incline us to hatred and revenge, but with Jesus' help we can conquer them. St. Paul says: *"What will separate us from the love of Christ? Will anguish, or distress, or persecution, or famine, or nakedness, or peril, or the sword?... nor height, nor depth, nor any other creature will be able to separate us from the love of God in Christ Jesus our Lord."* [6] This kind of love is the force that enables us to act as Christians and fosters in us goodwill towards our enemies.

There is a great difference between *experiencing* feelings of anger and *giving in* to such feelings. There are times when it is impossible to completely suppress our feelings of hurt. Only the passing of time may diminish their intensity; but even time may not uproot them completely.

In his mercy, the Lord, who alone knows the depth of our frailty and wicked inclinations, will take into consideration our goodwill. For our part, we can say that we love our enemies when, for the sake of Jesus, we pray for them and wish them eternal salvation. As long as we can mentally do this, we have won the battle against our human nature. No one can pray for another human being and hate that person at the same time. [7]

Jesus' teaching on forgiveness was first announced during the Sermon on the Mount and later confirmed in even stronger terms when he taught us the greatest prayer

---

[6] Romans 8:35,39.

[7] See *the Gospel of Matthew,* Vol. 1, Chap. 5, of the <u>Daily Study Bible Series</u> by William Barclay. Westminster John Knox Press.

of Christianity, the *Our Father*. In this prayer, after the three petitions for the glory of God, Jesus teaches us to pray for our needs and then say: "*...Forgive us our trespasses as we forgive those who trespass against us.*" Then he added: "*If you forgive others their transgressions, our heavenly Father will forgive you; but if you do not forgive others neither will your Father forgive you.*" [8]

This is the apex of Jesus' commandment of love and forgiveness. By these words we ask the Father to forgive us *in proportion to how much* we forgive others. This means that God conditions forgiveness of our sins on our forgiving others. In other words, if we pray the *Our Father* when we are hurt by others and brood over our injuries without forgiving them, we are actually asking God *not to forgive us* and to treat us *the same way we treat our enemies*. We are actually telling God: "*Lord, **do not** forgive me as I **do not** forgive them.*"

"*Vengeance Is Mine*"
The Spirit of Non-Retaliation

There were no police and no courts of law in the days of nomadic societies, when man was roaming the earth and had no fixed abode. The first law to protect a person's right is found in the Babylonian Hammurabi Code, 2285-2242 B.C. It is the famous law of "tit for tat" -- an eye for an eye and a tooth for a tooth. This law was never intended to be applied by private individuals, but rather by the clan or the family. It satisfied the innate desire for revenge and controlled it. It was a punishment and a deterrent at the

---

[8] Matthew 6:14-15

same time. It was the best the non-Christian world could do before Jesus came.

The same law prevailed among the Jews as they meandered through the desert for forty years on the way to the promised land. Later, when they were organized as a nation, they officially appointed an "avenger of blood," who was the person in charge of executing people sentenced to death, mostly for crimes against the community. This practice continued for centuries, and the word "avenger" was even applied to God, himself.[9] The concept of an avenger is also mentioned by St. Paul when he writes that civil authority, which is derived from God's own authority, "*is God's minister, an avenger to execute wrath against him who does evil.*"[10]

This brief historical note reminds us that neither Jews nor gentiles ever had the remotest idea of loving their enemies or persecutors. This situation is still prevalent today in non-Christian countries and, unfortunately, even among many Christians, as well, in spite of Jesus' warning: "*You have heard the commandment: 'An eye for an eye, a tooth for a tooth.' But, what I say to you is offer no resistance to injury. When a person strikes you on the right cheek, turn and offer him the other... You have heard the commandment: 'You shall love your countryman, but hate your enemy.' My command to you is love your enemies; pray for your persecutors.*"[11] This is the summation of Christian moral law. For a Christian there can be no revenge; forgiveness is indispensable.

In his letter to the Romans, St. Paul outlines how a true Christian should live: "*Bless those who persecute you,*

---

[9] John L. MacKenzie, S.J., *Dictionary of the Bible.* Collier Books, Macmillan Publishing Co. New York. 1965. p.70.

[10] Romans 13:4

[11] Matthew 5:39,43-44.

bless and do not curse them. Rejoice with those who rejoice, weep with those who weep... Do not repay anyone evil for evil; be concerned for what is noble in the sight of all. If possible, on your part, live at peace with all.

"Beloved, do not look for revenge... for it is written: 'Vengeance is mine; I will repay, says the Lord.' Rather, if your enemy is hungry, feed him; if he is thirsty, give him something to drink; for by so doing you will heap burning coals on his head. Do not be conquered by evil, but conquer evil with good." [12]

William Barclay comments: "We are to keep ourselves from all thought of taking revenge. Paul gives the reasons for that. (a) Vengeance does not belong to us but to God. In the last analysis, no human being has a right to judge any other; only God can do that. (b) To treat a man with kindness rather than vengeance is the way to move him. Vengeance may break his spirit, but kindness will break his heart... (c) To stoop to vengeance is to be ourselves conquered by evil. Evil can never be conquered by evil... As Booker Washington said: 'I will not allow any man to make me lower myself by hating him.' The only real way to destroy an enemy is to make him a friend." [13]

This is the spirit of forgiveness of our enemies that Jesus wants us to strive for in spite of our natural tendencies to the contrary. The battle against nature to forgive those who have deeply wounded us is continuous, but success is guaranteed as long as we continue to pray for them and remember that we, too, need God's forgiveness for our own sins.

---

[12] Romans 12:14-21.

[13] Reproduced from *the letter to the Romans*, p. 170, in the Daily Study Bible Series by William Barclay. Used by permission of Westminster John Knox Press.

Forgiveness and Civil Authority

I cannot finish this chapter without mentioning what the Christian attitude should be towards punishment inflicted by civil authorities. As we daily read about heinous crimes, the questions that often arise are: How do we, as Christians, want convicted criminals punished by our judicial system? Can we rejoice when severe punishment, even the death penalty, is inflicted on criminals? The *New Catholic Encyclopedia* sums up the answer as follows: "Since the punishment of the wicked is a social good, the desire, even on the part of private individuals, that it should be effectively accomplished, whether in general or in particular, is reasonable and virtuous, provided that it stems from a concern for justice and not from malice, spite, or an unwillingness to forgive, or the like. This desire, however, can easily get out of hand and become sinful because of its excess, or for corruptness of its motives." [14]

Regarding to the question of capital punishment, the *Catechism* states: "Preserving the common good of society requires rendering the aggressor unable to inflict harm. For this reason the traditional teaching of the Church has acknowledged as well founded the right and duty of legitimate public authority to punish malefactors by means of penalties commensurate with the gravity of the crime, not excluding, in cases of extreme gravity, the death penalty." (Art. 2266)

The Forgiving Person

Jesus said: *"Love your enemies. Do good to those who hate you. Bless those who curse you and pray for those who*

---

[14] NCE, word *Vengeance*.

maltreat you." [15] These words throw additional light on the problem of forgiveness and love of others. The message of Jesus is clear, and the *Catechism* puts it in simple words: "Every baptized person is called to be a 'blessing' and to bless. (Cf. Gen 12:2; Lk 6:28; Rom 12:14; 1 Pet 3:9)." [16]

These words emphasize the twofold role we have to play in this life with regard to others: we must be a blessing to them, and we must bless them. We can only be a blessing to others when we do good to them and when we inspire them and serve them. We must bless them by praying for them and wishing them good. There is no room here for retaliation, and even less for vengeance. "Jesus calls us to a love that goes beyond the ordinary. It is normal to love those who love us. However, we are called to imitate Christ who died for sinners and prayed for those who crucified him." [17] It is in this spirit that Laurence Stern[18] wrote:

> *Only the brave know how to forgive,*
> *A coward never forgives; it is not in his nature.*

Personal Reflection

If I truly love Jesus, I cannot fail to forgive others, no matter how cruelly and unjustly they have hurt me. I know that Jesus has forgiven me my sins. How then can I refuse to forgive those who sin against me? After all, nobody has

---

[15] Luke 6:27-38.

[16] CCC, #1669

[17] Rev. Herbert de Launay, CRNET file, 1955.

[18] English novelist (1713-1768). Quoted from *Bartlett's Familiar Quotations*. p. 359

crucified me yet! It does not matter by whom I am hurt --
whether it be someone in a higher or lower position than
me, friend or foe -- or in what form I am insulted, or how
often. I must forgive them all.

RESOLUTIONS

The only right thing I can do when I am insulted is
to accept the insult as a test to show my spirit of forgiveness, and to bear this suffering patiently as Jesus bore the
insults of the authorities and of the crowd. I resolve never
to forget that no matter how seriously and painfully I am
insulted, my sufferings will never come even close to those
that Jesus suffered for me.

P R A Y E R

O Lord Jesus, help me to do with your grace what
my nature alone cannot do. You know how little I can
tolerate and how easily I am upset by even small adversities. I therefore beseech you to help me to keep constantly
in mind how much suffering I have caused you and how
generously you have forgiven me. I ask you to help me in
forgiving all those who hurt me. I ask you to bless them, to
give them the help they need to love you truly, and to
bestow eternal life on them as I beg you to do unto me.
Amen.

Short Prayer

My Jesus, help me to forgive others
as you have forgiven me.

25

HONESTY
"LOVE DOES NOT REJOICE IN WHAT IS WRONG,BUT REJOICES WITH THE TRUTH"

There is no limit to love's forbearance, to its trust, its hope, its power to endure." [1]

Saint Philip Neri (1515-1595) was a popular father confessor in Rome, and people from all classes of society flocked to him for advice and confession. One day a lady confessed to him that she had gossiped a lot. Fr. Philip made no comment but asked her to go home and bring back to him a pillow stuffed with feathers. When she returned with her pillow, Fr. Philip tore open the top of the pillow case and giving it back to her said: "Please, go back home and as you walk scatter all the feathers along the road, then come back and see me." So she did. And when she returned with the empty pillowcase, Fr. Philip bid her: "Now go back and retrieve all the feathers you have scattered. All of them, please, and bring them back." "But, Father," she gasped, "this is impossible. It is windy outside; I will never be able to collect even a few of them!"

"You are correct, my child," replied Fr. Philip. "And so it is with your sins of gossip. How can you ever undo the evil you have done ruining the reputation of so many people?"

The meaning of the words of St. Paul quoted above can be summarized in one word, *honesty*. But to better

---

[1] 1 Corinthians 13:6-7

understand St. Paul's precise meaning, we must analyze the verses in detail.

"Love Does Not Rejoice in What Is Wrong"
No Gossip and no Calumny

This is the negative aspect of *honesty*. It means many things. Commenting on this particular verse of St. Paul, Henry Drummond writes: "Love imputes no (wrong) motives, sees the bright side, puts the best construction on every action... It includes perhaps more strictly the self-restraint that refuses to make capital out of others' faults; the charity that delights not in exposing the weakness of others." [2]

By nature we are inclined to see the worst possible motives in the actions of others, especially of those whom we dislike. Jesus said: *"Judge not, and you shall not be judged."* [3] Yet, that is just what we do so often. We attribute to others, friends or foes, ulterior motives or selfish reasons for their actions, even though we have no foundation for our accusations. This is gossip and, sadly, it is a most common fault even among Christians.

Gossip is contrary to Jesus' central teaching about love. It is even a more serious and harmful sin when we repeat to others the gossip we heard and disclose the source of our information. This means sowing the seeds of hatred and discord among people. There are probably more friendships broken, more people embittered, more lives destroyed because of wicked gossip than there are grains of sand on the beach. Yet many people think nothing of it.

---

[2] *The Greatest Thing in the World*, pp. 35, 37.
[3] Luke 6:37

But, St. John warns: *"If anyone says 'My love is fixed in God'
yet hates his brother, he is a liar. Whoever loves God must
also love his brother."* [4]

To control our evil inclination to speak of others in
a derogatory way, we should adopt two basic rules: First,
we should never speak badly about anyone. If we have to
talk about someone, say only what we would say if that
person were present... or say nothing at all. If we find
ourselves in a group of people who are indulging in malicious gossip, we should politely let them know that we
object to such unchristian conversation. When the conversation is about criminals and their evil deeds, we must always
refer to them with compassion and understanding, even
though strongly condemning their crimes. We should never
forget that even the worst sinners and criminals are immortal human beings; they are children of God as we are. We
should also pray for them with understanding and love.
Were it not for the grace of God, we might very well be one
of them.

Secondly, we should never, never report to a person
any derogatory remark we have heard about him or her
from others. Carrying tales not only causes great pain to the
accused person, it also provokes hatred or sets in motion a
long series of vengeful actions. The fifth commandment
says: *"Thou shalt not kill."* This applies to ruining a person's
good reputation as well as to the destruction of a human
life. It is a vicious and unchristian action.

Calumny, the malicious fabrication of false accusations, is a despicable sin which cannot be forgiven without
due reparation. It is like stealing: one cannot be forgiven
unless one makes reparation and returns to the legitimate

---

[4] I John 4:20-21

owner whatever was stolen or, at least, offers due compensa-
tion. Calumny is not only a sin against love, it is a sin
against justice, as well. And justice demands that reparation
be made to the offended party. So, too, when we rob a
fellow human being of his precious reputation, we must
compensate and make reparation if we want to be forgiven
for our sin. St. Paul sums it all up with the following
advice: *"Never let evil talk pass your lips; say only the good
things men need to hear, things that will really help them. Be
kind to one another, compassionate and mutually forgiving,
just as God has forgiven you in Christ."* [5]

"Love Rejoices with the Truth"
Praising Others

There is probably nothing more controversial in this
world than writing about truth, especially about subjective
and objective truth. What did St. Paul have in mind when
he wrote to the new Christians in Corinth, *"Love rejoices with
the truth"?*[6] He meant that true Christian love rejoices in
whatever is morally good and in what is in harmony with
Jesus' teachings. Today he invites us, as he invited the
converts of his day, to rejoice in whatever good we see in
others around us.

Perhaps this is something we seldom do. By nature
we are more inclined to condemn others for what seems to
us objectionable in their behavior than to praise them for
what is good and noteworthy; we readily speak about their
faults but pass over their goodness in silence. However, if
we possess that complete love which St. Paul describes here,

---

[5] Ephesians 4:32
[6] 1 Corinthians 13:6

and if our daily life is intensely motivated by love for God, then we will see things differently. We will look at things around us in a new way and rejoice in the good we see being done. Then we will praise those who do good rather then ignoring them because of jealousy or selfishness.

Honestly praising one who does good helps a person along the path to virtue, while constant criticism only discourages and irritates. This is especially true of children and teenagers, who are most in need of love and encouragement. Even among adults, praise works miracles. We can never praise too much. It not only makes the person praised feel good, it also gives joy to the person who honestly praises. It is all part of our life of love. It costs us nothing, and it does so much good. St. Paul was right when he wrote, *"Love rejoices with the truth,"* because everything good is a reflection of God, and God is the ultimate and perfect truth.

Correcting Faults

One area of our lives in which we often lack honesty is admitting our defects and imperfections. Jesus spoke emphatically about this when he said: *"Stop judging that you may not be judged. For as you judge, so will you be judged, and the measure with which you measure will be measured out to you. Why do you notice the splinter in your brother's eye, but do not perceive the wooden beam in your own eye? How can you say to your brother, 'Let me remove that splinter from your eye' while the wooden beam is in your eye? You hypocrite, remove the wooden beam from your eye first, then you will see clearly to remove the splinter from your brother's eye."*[7]

---

[7] Matthew 7:1-5

The *Imitation of Christ* has a short chapter on this subject that is worth its weight in gold: "Learn how to be patient in enduring the faults of others, remembering that you, yourself, have many which others have to put up with. If you cannot make yourself be what you would like to be, how can you expect another to be as you would like? We wish to see perfection in others, but do not correct our own faults.

"We want to have others strictly reprimanded for their offenses, but we will not accept to be reprimanded. We are inclined to think the other person has too much liberty, but we ourselves will not put up with any restraint. There must be rules for everyone else, but we must be given free rein. It is seldom that we consider our neighbor equally with ourselves.

"God wants us to learn to bear one another's burdens. No one is without faults, no one without a cross, no one self-sufficient and no one wise enough all alone. Therefore, we must support, comfort and assist one another, instructing and admonishing one another in all charity." [8]

Lies and Lying

"Lying lips are an abomination to the Lord, but those who are truthful are his delight." [9] There is nothing in the world more glaringly opposite to rejoicing in the truth than lying. A lie is a denial of truth and love; it is "speaking a falsehood," according to St. Augustine, "with the intention of

---

[8] *Imitation of Christ*, Book 1, Chapter 16, pp. 37,39. Catholic Book Co. New York.

[9] *Book of Proverbs*, 12:22

deceiving."[10] Deception and lying are characteristics of the devil, and Jesus himself called the devil *"a liar and father of lies."*[11] Obviously, we are talking here of lies in serious matters, especially when one deceives a person who has the right to know the truth. The book of Proverbs says: *"The lying tongue is its owner's enemy."*[12]

Lying is wrong because it is an offense against truth (God is Truth), and against the fundamental relationship of love between us humans. A willful and harmful lie is always a serious offense against love for God and neighbor. St. Paul wrote to the new converts in Ephesus: *"See to it, then, that you put an end to lying; let everyone speak the truth to his neighbor, for we are members of one another."*[13]

A Summary of the Qualities of Love

Summarizing all he wrote in his letter about love, St. Paul concludes: *"There is no limit to love's forbearance, to its trust, its hope, its power to endure."*[14] Let's briefly examine these four characteristic: *forbearance, trust, hope, endurance.*

Love is forbearing. According to St. Paul, *"forbearing"* here means that true love is ready to forgive, to excuse, to cover up and ignore. It is the same idea that he expressed when he wrote: *"No creature will be able to separate us from the love of God in Christ, Jesus our Lord."*[15] Jesus has given an example of forbearance that we must endeavor to imitate. True love can bear any insult, any injury, any failure. When

---

[10] Cf. CCC #2482 quoting St. Augustine.
[11] John 8:44.
[12] Proverbs 26:28.
[13] Ephesians 4:25.
[14] 1 Corinthians 13:7.
[15] Romans 8:39

our love for others is severely tested by the wickedness or unreasonableness of other people let us ask: "Where would I be if Jesus had given up on me because of my sins and my rebellious feelings against him?"

Love is Trusting in God. True love trusts God. How can we doubt his promises? Let us remember that he has promised --

Forgiveness for our sins: *"This is my blood... to be poured out for the forgiveness of sins."* [16]

A place in heaven for all eternity: *"I am going to prepare a place for you"* [17]

Our sorrow will turn unto joy: *"Your grief will turn into joy."* [18]

He has come to bring us life, eternal life: *"I came that they might have life, and have it to the full."* [19]

Trust in Our Neighbor. Love goes a long way in increasing our confidence in others. To make a person trustworthy, there is nothing more powerful than to show trust in that person, according to his or her trustworthiness.

True Love Hopes. Hope is a Christian virtue[20] based on God's promises and his infinite love for us. According to the *Catechism*, hope addresses the desire for happiness that God has placed in the heart of every human, and it inspires our activities by directing them to honor and please God. Hope "keeps man from discouragement; it sustains him during times of abandonment; it opens up his heart in expectation of eternal beatitude. Buoyed up by hope, he is

---

[16] Matthew 26:28

[17] John 14:2

[18] John 16:20

[19] John 10:10

[20] In theology, Hope (like Faith and Charity) is called a *theological* virtue that cannot be fully practiced without God's help.

preserved from selfishness and led to the happiness that flows from charity." [21]

In our relationship with others we have to share hope with them, encouraging them, helping them to look beyond the dark clouds of earthly life to truth and immortality.

Power to Endure. Commenting on St Paul's words, William Barclay writes: "What he really describes is not the spirit which can passively bear things, but the spirit which, in bearing them, can conquer and transmute them. George Matheson, who lost his sight and who was disappointed in love, asked in one of his prayers that he might accept God's will, 'Not with dumb resignation but with holy joy; not with the absence of murmur, but with a song of praise.' Love can bear things, not merely with passive resignation, but with triumphant fortitude, because it knows that 'a father's hand will never cause his child a needless tear.' " [22]

The power to endure is indispensable in our dealings with others. For most people, the greatest difficulty in life is to get along with others. This is why Jesus taught us not only to love one another, but to place no limits on our endurance of others because God, in his infinite justice and mercy, will treat us the same as we treat others.

Personal Reflection

Now that I know what the ingredients of love are and I have a complete outline of what I should do, I must now begin to integrate this kind of Christian love into my

---

[21] CCC #1818.

[22] Reproduced from *the letters to the Corinthians*, p. 124, in the Daily Study Bible Series by William Barclay. Used by permission of Westminster John Knox Press.

life. If my love for God and my neighbor in the past has been lackadaisical, inactive and uncaring of my spiritual growth, isn't it time I change? Isn't it time to take some positive step and to make a serious effort to grow to spiritual maturity?

RESOLUTIONS

No love of God and neighbor is ever true love if it remains locked up in a vague desire and is never put into action. Act I must; and starting today I must begin to practice true love, expressing it in practical ways to God and to my neighbor, especially those I like least.

P R A Y E R
(by John Henry Cardinal Newman)

God has created me to do Him some definite service; He has committed some work to me which he has not committed to another. I have my mission. I may never know it in this life, but I shall be told in the next. I am a link in a chain, a bond of connection between persons. He has not created me for nought. I shall do good; I shall do His work; I shall be a preacher of truth in my own place, while not intending it, if I do but keep His commandments and serve Him in my calling. Therefore, my God, I will put myself without reserve into your hands. What have I in heaven, and apart from you, what do I want upon earth? My flesh and my heart fail, but God is the God of my heart, and my portion for ever.[23]

Short Prayer
O Jesus, increase my trust in you.

---

[23] *A Newman Prayer Book,* p.4

26

LIFE IS A SCHOOL OF LOVE

According to an ancient Indian story, there once was a gentleman who had a great passion for collecting diamonds; he could find no peace of mind until he possessed the most beautiful diamond in the world. After searching in vain over all of India, he traveled abroad throughout Europe and Asia looking for this most beautiful diamond. After several unsuccessful years of searching, he returned home discouraged and depressed. One day, as he was walking through his garden, he noticed a stone that had been there for as long as he could remember. It had several unusual characteristics, and he bent down to look at it more closely. To his great astonishment, he found inside the stone the largest, most beautiful diamond he had ever seen. Finally, he was happy.

The moral is that we need not go far to find happiness, for it is near us and inside us... it only takes the willingness to discover it.

Where Can We Find Happiness?

St. John, the apostle of love, solemnly proclaimed to the world: *"This is what we proclaim to you: what was from the beginning, what we have heard, what we have seen with our eyes... God is love, and **he who abides in love abides in God and God in him**... Little children, let us love in deeds and in truth and not merely talk about it."* [1]

---

[1] 1 John 1:4; 4:16; 1:18

Throughout the preceding chapters we have seen that only by abiding in God can we attain spiritual happiness and peace of mind. This means consciously sharing in God's circle of love and viewing people and material things as means of spiritual growth. We have also learned that living a life of intimate union with Jesus is a difficult task because of the evil inclinations of our nature, the strength of temptations and the work of the devil, who tempts us with many kinds of false allurements. *Falling in love with Jesus* means practicing constant self-discipline and self-restraint in a spirit of love for him and for our neighbor. This gives us mastery over evil inclinations and allows our spiritual growth.

Doing good deeds occasionally, saying some extra prayers now and then, or merely trying to be a "good guy" is not enough to truly please God or make our lives meaningful in his eyes. St. Paul writes: *"We know that God makes all things work together for the good of those who love him."* [2] Note, *for those who love him.* Love, therefore, is the way to make every day meaningful, and we must learn how.

Learning Is the Key

The key to success in our spiritual growth is **to learn** how to live a *life of union* with Jesus. *Learning* is an on-going process. From childhood through old age we are continually learning. It should come as no surprise to be told that we must *learn* how to love God and neighbor in much the same way as we have learned everything else in life. Henry Drummond writes:

---

[2] Romans 8:28

"The business of our lives is to have these things (the ingredients of Love) fitted into our characters. That is the supreme work to which we need to address ourselves in this world, *to learn love*. Opportunities abound in our daily lives for learning to love. The world is not a playground; it is a schoolroom. Life is not a holiday, but an education. And the one eternal lesson for us all is to learn *how better we can love*. What makes a man a good sportsman? Practice. What makes a man a good artist, a good sculptor, a good musician? Practice. What makes a man a good linguist, a good stenographer? Practice. What makes a man a good man? Practice. Nothing else. There is nothing capricious about religion. We do not get the soul in different ways, under different laws, from those in which we get the body and the mind. If a man does not exercise his arm he develops no biceps; and if a man does not exercise his soul, he acquires no muscle in his soul, no strength of character, no vigor of moral fiber, no beauty of spiritual growth.

"Love is not a thing of enthusiastic emotion. It is a rich, strong, manly, vigorous expression of the whole round Christian character -- Christlike nature in its fullest development. And the constituents of this great character are only to be built up by ceaseless practice.

"What was Christ doing in the carpenter's shop? Practicing. Though perfect, we read that he *learned* obedience and grew in wisdom and in favor with God. Do not quarrel, therefore, with your lot in life. Do not complain of its never ceasing cares, its petty environment, the vexations you have to stand, the small and sordid souls you have to live and work with. Above all, do not resent temptation, do not be perplexed because it seems to thicken round you more and more and ceases neither for effort nor for agony nor prayer. This is your practice. That is the practice that God appoints you; and it is having its work in making you patient, and humble, and unselfish, and kind, and courteous. Do not grudge the hand that is molding the still too-shapeless image with you. It is growing more beautiful, though you see it not, and every touch of temptation may add to its perfection. Therefore, keep in the midst of life. Do not isolate yourself. Be among men, and among things, and among troubles, and difficulties, and obstacles. Remember Goethe's words: 'Talent develops itself in solitude; Character in the stream of life.' Talent develops itself in solitude -- the talent of prayer, of faith, of meditation, of seeing the unseen; character grown in the stream of the world's life." [3]

Will you take the first step to learn how to live a life of love for God and for neighbor?

The First Step

We all know that in any undertaking the first step is the most important. During my days in China, I learned well the Confucius saying that "Even a journey of ten thousand miles begins with the first step." This truth also applies to spiritual growth. There must be a first step, and that is the moment we begin to see the light and make our decision for Christ. In spiritual language we call this moment a "conversion," that is, a *change* in the course of our lives and beliefs.

A spiritual conversion means that if our present way of life leads us away from God because of an indifference to religion or a distorted desire for the worldly possessions of riches, power, pleasures, we have to begin steering it in the opposite direction -- namely, towards God and the things of

---

[3] *The Greatest Thing in the World.* pp. 37-40.

the spirit. This does not mean a sudden change in the status of our lives or revoking legitimate commitments. It does mean changing the attitude of our hearts by entering into a relationship with Jesus that will grow and lead us to think of God more frequently through prayer and feelings of love and gratitude.

Mrs. Amy Welborn, in her column in the *Florida Catholic,* describes what a first step in the spiritual life means: "Some high school students recently discussed whether having a relationship with God was easy or difficult. A few expressed a heartfelt frustration that, for them, it was very hard to feel God's presence. If they went to church, they found it uninspiring, and they didn't really know how to pray. Their lives, too, seemed buffeted on the stormy sea of circumstances beyond their control: dysfunctional families, economic problems, the threat of random violence, and a society in which they are valued not so much as individuals but as consumers and cogs in a machine. Where was God in all of this?

"In the midst of what seemed to verge on despair, one student offered a different perspective. 'I guess from the outside, it's hard to see God,' she said. 'But I think once you've taken that first really hard step and **let God in the door of your life,** then it's easy to see God. He's everywhere you look! You can't get away from him!'

"Exactly, God is everywhere, surrounding us and speaking to us. We're the ones who don't see, and we are the ones who don't know how to listen. Why? Because for whatever reason, we have never experienced God in a personal way. Instead, we have kept him at a distance as an idea and as an abstraction, so he remains an outsider to the nitty gritty of our lives.

"Opening your heart to the living God can be a threatening prospect, because once the door is opened, the way you look at life will be transformed, and change is never easy. But is that change really any worse than the emptiness and meaninglessness of a life without God?"

The first step, therefore, is beginning to see God in you and around you, to see the features of Jesus in the face of all human beings, and to acknowledge that all you have is God's gift to you. This will enable you to begin developing a personal relationship with Jesus. The moment you begin to think of him as a living person and as the special friend who died for you, you really make a spiritual "U" turn in your life. Your heart and mind will turn to God easily, and you will begin to see things through the eyes of Jesus as a lover sees things through the eyes of the beloved.

Climbing the Ladder of Love

Turning again to Mr. Drummond to help clarify what growing in love means: "I have mentioned a few of the elements (ingredients) of love. But these are only elements. Love itself can never be defined. Love is something more than all its elements -- a palpitating, quivering, sensitive, living thing. By synthesis of all the colors, man can make whiteness, but he cannot make light. By synthesis of all the virtues, man can make virtue, but he cannot make love. How then are we to have this transcendent living whole conveyed into our souls? We brace our wills to secure it. We try to copy those who have it. We lay down rules about it. We watch. We pray. But these things alone will not bring love into our nature. Love is an *effect*. Only as we fulfill the right conditions can we have the effect produced. Shall I tell you what the cause is?

" 'We love because he first loved us,' [4] St. John writes. Look at the word because. It is the cause of which I have spoken: 'Because he first loved us.' The effect follows that: we love; we love him; we love all men. We cannot help it. Because he loved us, we love. We love everybody. Our heart is slowly changed. Contemplate the love of Christ, and you will love." [5]

The words of St. John above, **"We love because he loved us first,"** sum up everything concerned with our growth in love. We may love God because of the reward he promises, or we may love him because we are afraid of hell; but both reasons are self-centered and unable to bring us the fullness of love. Loving God because he loves us means understanding God's circle of love and what brings our souls to the fullness of love, thus helping us to develop a real communion of love with Jesus.

This is why life is a "school of love." We begin to see Jesus in everything, to do everything for his love, and to sacrifice our self-love for his sake. Joy or pain, pleasant or unpleasant events, the drudgery of routine work or the excitement of adventure, old things or new in every waking moment -- all these will help us practice love, and practice will help our love grow.

This is the extraordinary simplicity of God's circle of love: we need not do anything extraordinary to achieve the heights of love, but simply to try to do everything extraordinarily well, to the best of our ability, to please God and show him our love in return for his love. This is what Mary, his mother, did for him. With the exception of the virgin birth, she lived a very ordinary life as a woman, wife, mother, and

---

[4] 1 John 4:19
[5] The Greatest Thing in the World. pp. 40-41.

widow. All she did was to perform her duty and to love him as his mother and disciple.

This is also what countless souls did -- simple, loving souls who went through life just doing their duty from day to day and taking advantage of any circumstance to offer God their love. St. Paul's words, *"everything works together for the good,"* were fulfilled in their lives. Today, we venerate such souls as saints, people who practiced Christian virtues almost to perfection. We can apply to them the words of D. James Kennedy, "In the midst of heartache, disappointment, and pain, God can do the unimaginable, he can... TURN IT TO GOLD." [6]

What a consolation and a relief to know that whatever we do for the love of God... whatever happens to us and is borne with love... whatever comes to pass in our daily lives, even the most repetitive of tasks... can be changed into acts of love to please him who *loved us first.* While the days and years of our lives go by, we know that nothing goes to waste. Every action, every thought, every feeling -- *everything* we do or endure -- is stored in the heart of God to whom we will return through the death of our body. We will then be immersed in that boundless love from which we came, thus completing God's circle of love.

This is the real meaning of Jesus' description of the Last Judgement: *"Come, you have my Father's blessing. Inherit the kingdom prepared for you from the creation of the world. For I was hungry,... thirsty,... a stranger,... naked,... ill,... in prison. I assure you, as often as you did it for one of my least brothers, you did it for me."* [7] Mr. Drummond comments: "The test of a man is not 'How have I believed?' but 'How have I loved?' The test of religion, the final test of

---

[6] *Turn It to Gold.* Servant Publications. Ann Arbor, Michigan.
[7] Matthew 25:31-46

religion at the great Day is not religiousness, but Love -- by what we have *not* done, by our sins of *omission* are we judged.[8]

The End of the Quest

We began this book by writing about *The Way to Happiness,* and we asked the question: *Where can we turn to find true, lasting happiness?*

We have now reached the end of our quest. True and lasting happiness can ultimately be found only in love for God. Because we come from him, and *because he loved us first,* we in return love him and all his creatures. Here on earth our love for him is a *sacrificial love* that has to be tested by temptation and suffering, just as his love for us was tested; but even in our darkest hours his help, his comfort, his companionship will never fail us. And when the test is over, our souls and bodies will return to him completing his circle of love, and to share his everlasting happiness.

This vision of life with its happiness and suffering, death and eternity, light and darkness is not make-believe. It has been fully revealed to us by God, himself, through the Old and New Testaments. Though all the mysteries contained within the Bible cannot be completely explained (because mysteries are beyond the limits of human intelligence), the Bible does offer us an acceptable explanation that satisfies the needs of the heart and mind, of faith and reason.

The rest is up to us. In his love, God has made us free to accept him or reject him. A conscious refusal to accept him as he has made himself known to us can only

---

[8] Drummond, pg.57.

lead us to a very dark future and misery on earth. However, if we acknowledge and accept his love, if we endeavor to give him the place he deserves in the lives of our souls, minds and bodies, and if we accept the tests he demands of us, then we will have found *the way* to a spiritually meaningful life on earth -- and an eternity of love and happiness in *God's Circle of Love.*

PRAYER - ACTION - SACRIFICE
The way to grow in Love

"*Spiritual growth,*" growth in love for God and neighbor, is the goal of the life of every adult Christian searching for true happiness. Jesus, who revealed God's plan of love for us, invites us to share in his great *Circle of Love* through our personal growth in love.

Even though *spiritual growth* has been described at length in this book, some readers may still wonder **how can we really do it?** How can we let our souls govern us in our daily living instead of allowing our passions to lead us astray and away from God? There are three steps that are indispensable if we are to grow in love and attain spiritual happiness: PRAYER - ACTION - SACRIFICE. They are the means to spiritual growth and happiness.

P R A Y E R -- the First Step

When two people are attracted to each other, they first want to spend time and communicate with each other. In the same way, if we are attracted to Jesus, the God-made Man, and to his love for us, we will be eager to spend time and communicate with him; and this is done through prayer.

PRAYER is a heart-to-heart *conversation* with the person who loves us more than any other in the world, Jesus. What can we *talk* about with Jesus? Four major topics of conversation express our love:

ADORATION -- to spiritually prostrate ourselves before him and adore him in all his power and majesty because he is our ALL.

THANKSGIVING -- thanking him because he gave himself to us along with all the spiritual and temporal blessings we have.

REPARATION -- begging for forgiveness and offering him our own sufferings to be united to his on the Cross in reparation for our personal sins and those of the world.

PETITION -- appealing to him to help us grow in love for him,[9] and then asking him to console us in all our worries and concerns, to assist us in solving our problems, and above all, to enable us to see and love him in *all* people, friends and foes. Never forget that Jesus *wants us* to ask him for favors and help: *"Ask and you shall receive. Seek and you will find. Knock and it will be opened to you."* [10]

The beauty of prayer is that we can pray anywhere, anytime, under whatever circumstances because prayer is a conversation between two spirits: Jesus and our soul. There is no need to even formulate words. The saintly pastor of the village of Ars in France, St. John Vianney (1786-1839), noted that a poor, illiterate peasant was daily spending hours in the Church staring at the Tabernacle. One day he asked him, "What do you say to the Lord?" The illiterate peasant answered, "Nothing Father. I just look at him, and he looks at me." This is love. This is prayer.

---

[9] *"Seek first the Kingdom of God, and all the rest shall be added unto you." Matthew 6:33.*

[10] Matthew 7,7.

To alternate personal conversation with occasional reading of ready-made prayers, especially the Liturgical prayers of the Mass,[11] is a recommended approach to one's prayer life. The reading of books about religion enlightens our mind, increases our knowledge of Jesus, and makes our conversation with him easier.

A C T I O N -- *Step Two*

"*Why do you call me, 'Lord, Lord', but not do what I command?*"[12] Love without deeds is no love at all. It is hypocrisy, a desecration of love. In our growth in love, deeds are the real yardstick we have to measure our progress in love; the more we love, the more good deeds we will do. And there are deeds of different kinds.

There are deeds done directly for Jesus, such as attending church services, not only on Sundays but daily Mass and Communion as well, as often as we possibly can; a daily meditation lasting, perhaps, ten to fifteen minutes; frequent mental prayer at home, in church, while driving or doing chores; reading the New Testament or other good books on religion. These are all *active* deeds of expressing love directly for Jesus.

There are deeds done for our neighbor, also, such as visiting and assisting the sick, shut-ins, those who need comfort and assistance -- *actively* helping others physically or

---

[11] We are currently going through a renewed interest in prayer, and numerous books on this subject are continually being published. Please assure yourself that they are genuine Christian books, and do not come from unorthodox theologians or the New Age Religion.

[12] Luke 6:46.

spiritually as described by Jesus at the Last Judgment in Matthew 25:31-46, and the practicing the Christian virtues described in chapters 15 to 25.

Jesus spent all his time on earth doing kind things for others; so we, too, should at all times endeavor to do as much good for others as we can. We must resist, however, the temptation to reduce our prayer time (for other than exceptional circumstances) in order to do more good deeds. God wants us *to be* good before *we do* good to others. Actually, no spiritual good can be done to others unless it is accompanied by prayer and sacrifice.

S A C R I F I C E -- *Step Three*

Self-discipline and the patient acceptance of our sufferings are integral and indispensable elements of growth in love, even though they may require much sacrifice. William Barclay writes that the penalty of being human "is to have a split personality. In human nature the beast and the angel are strangely intermingled. Man's trouble has always been that he is haunted both by sin and by goodness. The coming of Jesus unites that disintegrated personality into one. He finds victory over his warring self by being conquered by Jesus." [13]

True love for Jesus requires self-discipline, even the renouncing of many licit pleasures, but in the end it frees us from the slavery of our passions and gives us control of self and peace of mind. This is our preparation for the joys of heaven. Love can make sacrifice sweet; and when accompa-

---

[13] Reproduced from *the Gospel of Mark*, p. 25, in the Daily Study Bible Series by William Barclay. Used by permission of Westminster John Knox Press.

nied by trust and confidence in Jesus, Jesus will make our crosses more bearable -- he will help us carry them. When suffering, it is better to be on the side of the "good thief," than on the side of the unrepentant "bad thief".

PRAYER-ACTION-SACRIFICE   --   a slogan that summarizes what we must do to live a life of love and share in *God's Circle of Love*. It really is a program of Christian living, and my wish to you is that you may keep it always in mind as the way to grow in love. These three words point the way to the heart of Jesus, to a most meaningful and constructive life, and to that spiritual happiness that is the ultimate quest of every human being.

Appendix A

A Word About PIME

The Spirit and Work of PIME

PIME is an international organization of Catholic priests and brothers (also called "lay associates") exclusively dedicated to working in the foreign missions of the Catholic Church to bring the message of Christ to non-Christian nations.

PIME is an acronym of the initials of its Italian title, which in English is translated Pontifical Institute for Foreign Missions. The spirit and work of PIME are well expressed the following mission statement:

"We, the PIME missionaries of the United States Region, are an expression of the missionary nature of the Church in the United States and of the international character of PIME. We are a family of apostles committed to the ongoing discovery, witness and proclamation of the Kingdom of God through evangelization, particularly of non-Christians in other parts of the world.

"We live in community, offering one another mutual support. We work as a team, while respecting and encouraging individual initiative and creativity. We embrace a simple and hospitable lifestyle."

The Beginning and Growth of PIME

On July 31, 1850, after years of diligent preparation by the bishop and diocesan priests of Milan, PIME was formally established and dedicated exclusively to bringing the message of Christ to non-Christian lands. Two years later the first missionaries went to work for Christ in Papua New Guinea, Oceania. Blessed John Mazzucconi suffered martyrdom there in September 1855. In 1858, the society sent missionaries to Hong Kong, and later to China, India, and Burma.

Today there are close to 700 members of PIME and over 1,000 Sisters of the Immaculate Conception, a religious society of women founded by PIME. In addition to serving in Italy and the

United States, PIME missionaries work in Japan, Bangladesh, Hong Kong, Taiwan, Myanmar (Burma), Thailand, the Philippines, India, Papua New Guinea, Guinea-Bissau, the Ivory Coast, Cameroon, and in six provinces of Brazil -- Amapa, Amazona, Mato Grosso, Sao Paulo, Parana, S. Caterina.

PIME in the USA

The presence of PIME in the United States began in 1948 when Cardinal John Mooney of Detroit invited his old personal friend, Fr. G. Margutti, PIME, from Bangladesh, to establish a residence in Detroit to help the PIME missions devastated by World War II.

In 1951, Fr. Nicholas Maestrini was assigned to assume Fr. Margutti's work when Fr. Margutti returned to Italy for health reasons. In 1952 PIME became international and established its first branch outside Italy in the States, extending PIME's work in the States to recruiting, preparing, sending and supporting PIME missionaries in the foreign missions.

The Work of PIME in the World Today

The work of PIME missionaries involves much more than bringing the knowledge of Christianity to non-Christians and administering the sacraments. It involves helping the poor by raising their standard of living through education, and alleviating the suffering of millions of underprivileged people, orphans, leprosy victims, the aged and ill by providing food, clothing, and medicine for them.

The vast array of PIME's work includes: nine seminaries in mission countries for the training of local clergy; over 1,000 schools educating over 300,000 students; orphanages caring for 8,000 poor children; approximately 2,400 churches and mission stations; leper hospitals and anti-leprosy program, mission hospitals and outpatient clinics treating millions every year.

PIME's international headquarters are in Rome, and the Very Rev. Franco Cagnasso is the superior general. In the United States, the regional headquarters is located at 17330 Quincy Ave., Detroit, MI 48221-2765.

INDEX of MAJOR SUBJECTS